AN Awesome RIDE

AN
Awesome
RIDE

CAMERON MILLER
& ANDREW CLARKE

EBURY
PRESS

EBURY PRESS

UK | USA | Canada | Ireland | Australia
India | New Zealand | South Africa | China

Penguin
Random House
Australia

Ebury Press is part of the Penguin Random House group of companies whose
addresses can be found at global.penguinrandomhouse.com.

First published by Ebury Press, an imprint of
Penguin Random House Australia Pty Ltd, 2019

Cover photography by Nick Williams
Cover design by James Rendall © Penguin Random House Australia Pty Ltd
Typeset in 12/17.5 pt Adobe Garamond Pro by Midland Typesetters, Australia
Printed and bound in Australia by Griffin Press, part of Ovato, an accredited
ISO AS/NZS 14001 Environmental Management Systems printer

A catalogue record for this
book is available from the
National Library of Australia

NATIONAL
LIBRARY
OF AUSTRALIA

ISBN 978 0 14378 813 3

penguin.com.au

MIX
Paper from
responsible sources
FSC® C009448

This book is dedicated to
all who have lost their battle
and to those who fight the battle every day
and the families that fight with them.

INTRODUCTION

No PARENT SHOULD have to bury a child. Sadly, I did. I knew almost immediately after Shaun was born that it was just a matter of time.

There were many occasions I thought it was *the* time, but in the seventeen years I had with Shaun I got to spend my life with the most amazing and uplifting person I have ever met . . . and am ever likely to meet.

Shaun was born with a death sentence called CHD – congenital heart disease. Life threw him a curve ball, and he batted it away with an amazing spirit. It was, in his words, an awesome ride and I'm pleased I was on the ride with him.

This book is as much about my journey as it is his, and that means it is two books in one. There is Shaun's part of this book, the original *An Awesome Ride*, which was first published in 2012 in the months after his passing. Then there is mine, which took me more than five years to get down on paper. We've included both stories here because it's impossible to separate them.

Who knew that Shaun would become a hero to CHD kids and an inspirational teen around the world, assisting in thousands of teenage suicide preventions, with his positive words and courageous outlook on this journey we all share.

My life has never been easy. I have faced many challenges, but thanks to Shaun I know they have all made me a better person. As he would say, live life to the fullest, and that is now what I'm trying to do.

Cameron Miller
August 2019

SHAUN

1

'HI GUYS. I have some bad news I want to tell you all. I have chronic heart rejection and I won't be here for as long as I thought. But I want to say this has been an awesome ride.' That's what I said in my YouTube video that started this whole thing.

Two minutes fifty-four seconds was all it took. I put the iPhone down the end of the bed and just let it rip. Wish I'd remembered to put a shirt on . . . I can't believe I didn't think of that. People are saying all kinds of stuff – that I look about ten years old – and am I for real and things. To be honest I wasn't thinking all that clearly. I had this idea of doing a video to say my final goodbye to my friends and family when I was lying in that damned hospital bed. I never thought it'd go viral.

It's funny what people find interesting. So much of my life has been spent surrounded by doctors and nurses. Don't get me wrong, they're great – they're the reason I'm still here – but like a lot of sick people all I ever dream about is never having to see the inside of a hospital again.

My name is Shaun Miller and I live in a house in the Melbourne suburb of Mill Park with my father, Cameron. I'm seventeen years old and proud of two things – my dad and my football team, the mighty Essendon Bombers. Make no mistake, I can tell you now it's going to be a battle to get to eighteen, but boy am I going to give it my best shot. You see, I've had not one but two heart transplants and was doing okay until around the beginning of 2012 when things started sliding for me.

I had to go into the Royal Children's Hospital for a biopsy, which is one of those procedures where they take a tiny piece of you and whack it under a microscope. It wasn't good news. I knew just from the way none of the doctors and nurses would look at me. One of the specialists asked to see Dad. They didn't want me to know about the results. They asked Dad not to tell me. They just wanted me to get on happily with life as if everything was normal, but Dad disagreed.

'You know what?' he said. 'I've always been open and honest with Shaun. I want you guys to tell him.' That's when they came into my room and told me the news that my body was rejecting my transplanted heart. Chronic heart rejection. There was nothing they could do for me.

'How long has he got?' I heard Dad ask.

The surgeon thought about it and then said, 'Between one and twelve months, I guess.' This was 16 April 2012. Straightaway I worked out that my eighteenth birthday on 23 January 2013 was nine months away. Would I make it?

Suddenly I heard this huge thud and realised that Dad was on the floor, out cold. Poor old Dad had fainted – which later on we had a good laugh over – but I guess my doctor was wondering if he'd had a heart attack. There was a bit of a commotion with nurses rushing in and stuff.

I felt sorry for Dad. Because I've cheated death many times I kind of knew it was going to come to this, so I'm just going to roll with it. I'm not sure how Dad's going to cope. One day soon afterwards, he was looking sad. I could see the news was getting to him.

'Come here, Dad,' I said, and he was probably thinking I was going to give him a hug. Instead, I slapped him on the face. *Whack!* It had never happened before so he was real shocked. I was just telling him to pull his shit together.

Being told by the doctors that I'm going to die soon and there's nothing more that they can do to help me is by far the hardest pill I've ever had to swallow. And believe me, I've had my fair share of pills. I don't really know how to explain it. It's not like I didn't know I was living on borrowed time all my life, but I guess that's how it is for all of us. It's not like we can hang around forever. We all know it's going to end – we just kid ourselves or something.

That's when I had the idea, lying in that hospital bed, that somehow I had to tell all my friends what was going down – and in the months I've got left maybe we could do some crazy stuff. I wanted to say a proper goodbye to all my friends, but some of them live far away – the other side of the country; even the other side of the world, like my friend Sondra from Alabama.

At first I was going to type out a message on Facebook but I don't really like writing all that much. Yeah, I know, so the guy's writing a book – work that one out. But I prefer talking because I find I can express myself better that way.

So when I told Dad I wanted to do a video and upload it on my Facebook page, he was dead against it. 'Don't do it, Shaun!' he kept saying. I think he was worried I might say something embarrassing or freak people out, but I explained that even though the doctor said I might have up to a year, I might only last a week.

It was important to me that I could say goodbye to my friends and family and tell them what was happening, without having to explain it over and over and answer a billion questions about how I'm feeling. I wasn't after sympathy. That's why I said, 'Please don't cry for me. I'll be okay.' And I wanted to tell everyone about my girlfriend, Maddy.

None of this made any difference to Dad – he still reckoned it was a dumb idea. Too bad. One thing about living on death row, so to speak, is that you can take no notice of your parents and just do what you like. And that's when I went to my bedroom with my iPhone and said goodbye.

It's not a very long message, but I said everything I wanted to say: that I had no regrets, that we should all live life to the fullest, because you never know what's going to happen, and I asked my family and friends to make sure my dad will be okay after I'm gone. Done.

When I talk about living life to the fullest, I don't mean all this YOLO stuff – You Only Live Once – partying and acting cray cray 24/7. It's not an excuse to just let loose and do whatever. It's about expressing your love to the people around you every single day. If you love someone and you haven't told them, then do it, because life is short. Living life to the fullest is about never giving up, and carrying on even if you're sick. It's about giving everything your best shot and not holding back, because there might not be a tomorrow. Live life how you want.

When I finished recording the video, I logged onto Facebook and pressed the 'upload video' option. Waiting, waiting, waiting. The status bar popped up but it never budged from 0 per cent. It was taking so long! I tried closing it and starting over again, but in the end nothing I did could get the video to upload. As you know I'm on seriously borrowed time now, so I was getting a little impatient.

That's when I thought of YouTube, because watching videos is what people really use the site for. I didn't have a YouTube account, so I signed up for one. It didn't take long. I just chose a user name and password and was able to upload the video within five minutes. I thought I did it right – it seemed pretty simple – but I wasn't quite sure because I'd never used YouTube before. I went to sleep hoping I'd uploaded it successfully and that my friends were able to see it.

The next morning I woke up to find more than thirty missed calls and messages on my phone. This got me worried that something horrible had happened. Had someone I know been involved in some accident? But the first text mentioned my goodbye video. I jumped straight onto my computer to check if my video had uploaded. I couldn't believe it. It had gone viral with over 30,000 hits. Within a week it was nudging one million views.

With all this happening, me and Dad got to talking about what we were going to do – meaning, of course, what did I want to do with the time I had left. 'Okay, three things,' I told him. 'Number three: let's you and me go to Disneyland in America. What do you say?'

'No problem,' he said. But I saw a familiar frown on his face.

'Can we afford that?' I wanted to know.

'Well, we'll think of something,' he replied.

'So, the second thing I want is to have a mega kick-arse party somewhere. We'll invite all my friends and have the time of our lives. Yeah?'

'Sure. That's easy.'

And my last wish, my number one thing, was to write this book, to tell you all the story of my short life to date. It's like, you know, ordinary on the outside, but so many special things have happened to me which can't be just coincidence, and some pretty amazing people have popped up on my radar. I hope when you read my words they bring a smile to your face and somehow maybe I'll leave behind a footprint in your heart.

CAMERON

2

I WAS BORN on 14 May 1971, and my earliest memories are just of struggling to breathe. I spent a lot of my childhood in and out of hospital with asthma, and that's what made Shaun's journey even harder for me. I knew what he was going through in terms of a disjointed life, of a battle to get continuity at school and the ability to form those all-important friendships that make childhood so much fun. I knew what he was missing out on, because I'd missed out too.

Asthma is a horrible respiratory condition which is usually connected with an allergy or some other form of hypersensitivity. If you don't know what's causing it, you can't do much about it. And then sometimes, even when you do know, you're stuck because the allergen is just in the air at certain times. Back in the 1970s, the science of dealing with asthma was not what it is now, and it placed a huge burden on my parents, Dorothy and John, and cost me many days at school and of being outside having fun.

I grew up in Lalor in Melbourne's north, which was very much a working-class suburb then, as it is now. Dad grew up in Northcote and played footy for the local club, and Lalor wasn't far from there. He was a hard worker and he spent most of his working life with what was known as the Melbourne & Metropolitan Tramways Board. He started as an apprentice electrician at fifteen years of age and, because he was a good worker, he was able to climb his way up the tree, so to speak. Through most of my childhood he was a power control operator and he did a lot of shift work, which helped with the pay.

Dad worked hard so we could have a good life, although I'm sure being a shift worker with a sick child wouldn't have been easy. Perhaps I was lucky that Mum had worked as a nurse – she was good at reading the signs and dealing with me.

Mum left school at fifteen and was still a teenager when she got married for the first time. However, that marriage didn't last and she was abandoned by her first husband, who left her saddled with debts. She had no education, which meant that in those early years she could only get shit jobs, and it was a real struggle to pick up the pieces and start over again. She never forgot those struggles, so education was a big thing for her with her own children. This is why she often had a hard time with my health problems and its impact on my schooling.

Mum eventually managed to get some training and then worked as a nurse until she got hepatitis C. That ruined her career because she had to give up her nursing work. She was then employed at ACI Glass. The building was situated near the West Gate Bridge and she was there when the bridge collapsed in 1970. Thirty-five workers died that day and she saw it all. As you could imagine, it was an event that left a big impression on her.

Mum grew up in Portland in western Victoria and her father – James Peter 'Roy' Potter – was a big figure in the RSL down there when she was young. He was eventually given a Medal of the Order of Australia in 1987 for his 'service to the welfare of ex-service men and women'. We're pretty proud of my grandfather, but as you can imagine he was a strict man and Mum grew up with those values. She has softened a bit now, mind you, but she was a strict mother – which I think is a good thing.

Mum and Dad met at a dance and, as they say, the rest is history. They were both good parents, which was really important given my health. Most of my childhood was spent on an asthma pump. Until I was about ten, asthma was a constant, major problem, and I figured it was going to be that way for the rest of my life. I couldn't see any light at the end of the tunnel.

My sister, Susanne, was born when I was three (13 January 1975 to be exact) and luckily she escaped any health issues. Years later, she told me she hated how much attention I got, but she knew, as I did, that I couldn't help it. We fought like cats and dogs and one day she was giving me the shits so much that I grabbed some scissors and cut all her hair off. I got into a fair bit of trouble when Mum walked into the room to see all of Susanne's curls lying on the floor.

We are very different people today. She's a scientist who has been to university and has PhDs and the like, and she married another scientist too. Shaun always thought it was pretty cool having two smart people who could keep an eye on what was being put into his body. I am proud of her too.

I went to Lalor North Primary, which I really enjoyed. To get to school, all I had to do was jump the back fence and run through an empty block of land. It took maybe forty seconds, but sometimes it felt like kilometres. I had some good friends there, which was handy given that the asthma pump I needed looked like something out of an old science-fiction movie. It was a pretty memorable thing for a young kid to be carrying around. Just the other day, a family friend commented on the big green asthma pump I needed to use before going to bed every night.

Fortunately, today it's not as tough. The pumps are smaller and simpler to use and don't make you look like a freak.

My schooling was messed up a lot because I was in and out of hospital. I failed Grade 4 – they had no choice because I was hardly there. I repeated that year, but, other than that, the school just kept putting me up to the next grade even though I was rarely ready for it. It put a dampener on my education which I pay for now.

For me, though, it wasn't just the lost days of school. It was things like how hard it was to play footy. Most of the time I couldn't walk to the letterbox without becoming short of breath or getting asthma, so playing footy was just a pipe dream. I'd walk out the front door and I'd feel my lungs tightening up. I knew that soon I'd barely be able to breathe and I'd be on the pump for a good hour just to try to pull myself out of it.

All those chemicals in the body stunted my growth too, so while I was never going to be a ruckman I could have been a lot taller than I ended up. My size made me a bit of a target when I went to secondary school. That was my life until I enrolled at technical college and the bullying began to ease up, after I'd started doing weights, swimming etc to get fitter.

During those years at school, I missed out on a lot of things. I never got to go on a school camp, for instance. I did, however, do karate, which was interesting in itself. My instructor was a priest named Father Michael Glennon, and he was a god of sorts to the students. However, very early in my time, I started seeing that something wasn't right about him.

He'd pull a student away from a class and into a corridor and he'd get behind him and rub his chest. That kind of thing. I remember telling him that it wasn't right to touch us like that, and he told me he didn't know what I was talking about. I also remember saying once to a teacher, 'I know he's a priest, but there's something not right about Sensei Glennon (as we called him).'

It turns out I was spot on, and perhaps my radar – and my asthma – protected me from what he was doing to so many other children at the time. For instance, I was meant to go to his 'Peaceful Hand Youth Foundation' camp because I'd just won a karate tournament, but my asthma prevented me from going. Apparently, it was at these camps that Glennon molested many of his victims. His list of crimes is quite staggering. Even after he'd been sent to jail in 1978, after he was released seven months later the Catholic Church still let him operate as a priest – although it didn't give him a new parish – and line up more children. He wasn't laicised until 1998.

The frightening thing is that I remember that he really liked me, so I'm sure I was in line for abuse as well. Glennon used to say to my parents, 'He's gonna go far. Don't worry about the asthma. He's very talented. He's a very good boy.' Blah, blah, blah.

He was found guilty of sexually abusing fifteen children in a series of court cases, the last of which was in 2003. In all, Glennon was sentenced to a minimum of twenty-six and a half years in jail. He died in prison in 2014. I do wish the teacher at my school had listened to me a little more, and I'm sure he does too, now that everything has come out.

I'm very glad it never happened to me. I had enough to contend with.

While it wasn't quite a cure, surfing did start me on the path to a normal life with regard to asthma. Mum and Dad built a little shack in Apollo Bay, on the Great Ocean Road, when I was about two. When I was ten we started going there more regularly. It was a place filled with both good and bad memories.

The surfing didn't start for a while, so I had to endure a few scares in the early days down there. As I've said, asthma treatment and management was pretty crude back in the 1970s. When I had an asthma attack in Apollo Bay, we could either try the local hospital or head back on the four-hour drive to Melbourne.

There was a tent in the local hospital and the staff would heat it up, zip me into it and pour water on me like it was raining. I'd be in there for eight hours while they tried to settle down the attack. It was a lonely experience, because while I was in there no-one could talk to me. I felt like a freak. I was like the bubble boy out of *Seinfeld*.

It was horrible, so we tried to avoid that and risk the drive back to Melbourne instead, where it was a little more pleasant for me.

When I was about eight some of the mates I'd made down there started teaching me how to surf. It was life changing. I'm not sure whether it was the salt water or something else, but it worked for me. I could literally sense my lungs opening up and it was the most amazing feeling.

From there, for me, it was weights and exercise and it all began to come good. No-one had ever recommended this sort of activity, but as I got fitter and stronger my asthma subsided – and it had all started to turn with the surfing.

SHAUN

3

WITH THE YOUTUBE video getting massive hits I've done television interviews, spoken to them at the *Herald Sun*, and one day the phone rings and Dad says to me, 'Neil Mitchell from 3AW wants to talk to you.'

I couldn't believe it. 'Me?'

'Yeah, he's saying lots of listeners who've seen your video say they're blown away by your positive attitude, considering, well, you know.'

Neil Mitchell reckons there've been plenty of teenagers before me who reached out to the world through song, but none like me who just spoke to them. While I'm talking to Neil a woman rings up and offers to pay for Dad and me to fly to Disneyland, all expenses paid. Just incredible stuff.

Dad's says he's working on my Kick-Arse Party and he's found this guy who's going to help me write my book. We talk about it and this writer's given me stuff to do – kind of like homework, I suppose. He says I need to sit down with just me and Dad and ask him about what happened with him and Mum and stuff in the beginning. See, from the earliest I could remember I didn't have a real dad at all. I always wondered what happened there, but no-one ever talked about it much in our family.

Let me tell you about my grandparents. There's Nanna and Poppy John. Nanna's bossy and always telling me I don't eat enough and keeps trying to feed me. Annoying, I know, but it's because she loves me. She was a nurse when she was younger so maybe that's where it comes from. Makes a sensational toasted sandwich, though.

She met Poppy John at a dance. Poppy John was employed by the Tramways all his life. Same job, same shit, every single day. He's quiet and gentle and my dad, Cameron, was born in 1971; then, about three years later Dad's younger sister, Susanne, was born. Susanne is one of my favourite people in the whole wide world. She's real smart and always there when I need her, but she's bossy too. Must be a girl thing.

The Millers were big on education. That was the way to get freedom and independence, according to Nanna, so she really encouraged her kids to study hard to get into university. Susanne blitzed it and went to university where she did Science. After that, there was no stopping her. After picking up her degree, Susanne did her PhD. I have to admit I don't really know what that means, except that you need lots of brains to do it, and it takes years. When she finished we were allowed to call her 'Dr Miller', even though she wasn't that sort of doctor. That still wasn't enough so she did a business degree. All in all, she was pretty handy when it came to homework.

Susanne worked at this laboratory analysing the metal they dug up in mines in Western Australia, and then she was part of a team researching malaria. While doing this and her PhD she met her husband, Ken, who was a physicist with the same company, but now he works on legal stuff.

I love my Uncle Ken. He's a good guy and he's a whiz with computer stuff. His mum is Japanese and his dad is English, which makes him the polar opposite of the rest of our family. Ken's pretty quiet and reserved. He's a very calming presence, especially when dealing with all the drama my family goes through. The great thing about having these scientists around is that it helps when trying to make heads or tails about what's happening to me with drugs, side effects and medical stuff. Because they're scientists, they just tell it like it is. I like that.

The other Miller, my dad, was nothing like that at all. In fact, the complete opposite. He couldn't wait to leave school, and never went to uni. Dad doesn't like talking about school. I think there was stuff going down there. Anyway, because he didn't have much education, his first job after leaving school was an apprentice glazier, and at one point he worked part-time at the Carlton Football Club. They gave him stuff to do like cleaning the mud off their boots and carrying their junk. From that he started giving the players rubdowns and massages, which he happened to be really good at, so he did a massage course.

He says he used to run with the players. No offence, Dad, but you're a bit fat now, so I can't really imagine that – LOL. Dad became a qualified masseur and started his own mobile massage business. When it wasn't making any money he did other bits and pieces here and there and started getting involved in the entertainment industry. He's no Adam Sandler, but he did lots of little odd acting jobs. Over time he switched from being in front of the cameras to working behind the scenes on his own projects.

I didn't have a dad in the beginning, except for maybe sometimes. I lived with my mum, and this guy used to come round every now and then, and it wasn't until I was a bit older that I figured out he was my dad. He met Mum at a party when she was nineteen. She was just out of high school and working in a nursing home or something. Dad was twenty and they were attracted to one another and started hanging out and stuff. When I ask him what Mum was like back in the day, he goes, 'She was heaps of fun.'

It was one of those relationships which was always a bit rocky. Over the years they were always breaking up and then getting back together. I saw a photo of them at my dad's twenty-first. They both looked so young and happy. I've heard the stories about when they were together, but I can't really imagine that because for as long as I can remember, they've hated each other's guts. Dad says it was all a bit of a shambles. He was young, mega-immature and clueless, really.

All this was happening and then Mum took a home pregnancy test and it came out positive. When she broke the news to him, Dad didn't take it all that well. He thought they were way too young to start a family and their relationship was too rocky to give it a go. I know there was chat about getting rid of the baby, which is kind of weird to be talking about, because had that happened, of course, there would have been no me. No heart transplants, no drama . . . nothing. In the end, it was Mum's call, and I was welcomed to the world on 23 January 1995 at the Royal Women's Hospital in Melbourne.

Right from the get-go, there were huge problems. I was transferred to the Royal Children's Hospital (which was where over the next few years I had operation after operation) and I had my first operation there. It saved my life for sure, but it was only the beginning of my battle to stay alive.

I'd been born with congenital heart disease, which is the most common major birth defect. What it means is that the blood vessels around my heart weren't formed properly. My heart was never going to function like any little kid's normal heart and I'd have to take lots of drugs every day for the rest of my life.

When I look at the way my parents carry on, even today, it sometimes makes me wonder when they're going to grow up. All I can imagine is that they were a lot more immature when I arrived on the scene and really began to make their lives hell. It took everything they had to look after me, which meant there was no time for being young and having fun.

Things were already shaky and then this happened, so the pressure piled up. Mum and Dad tried to stay together and behave like a proper family for my sake. They rented a unit in the hope that they could make it work, but it just didn't. Living together was increasingly difficult. Dad no longer looked forward to coming home from work and the pair of them fought like cats and dogs.

In the end Dad cracked first. He was miserable living with Mum and their relationship had started to become quite destructive. One day, when I was about one, Dad collected up his things and went back home to his parents, and Mum went home to her family. So I lived with Mum and Gran and Pa. They did a great job of looking after me when I was little because I was really sick.

The thing is that life didn't really get any better for anyone. Even though Dad was 'free', his life was a mess because he felt guilty for not being there. Mum and her family started hating him for leaving, so she and Dad decided to give it another go. Dad was thinking, 'After all, I am Shaun's father. The mature thing to do would be to look after my son. Maybe we can make it work and it could be really good.'

Things were fine, for a few days or weeks, and then it was all over, again – only this time for good.

My mother ended up with full custody, and sometimes I got to see Dad on weekends. That's just how it was. It's true that Dad wasn't there very often in the early days. Given how unhappy he was, it was probably for the best, and I had Mum and Gran, my pa, and aunts and uncles.

While Mum said terrible things about Dad – she called him a girl when he was crying and stuff – she was mostly a good mother. No issues there. It's a fact that he abandoned me – not because he didn't love me, but because he had to leave to save himself. Dad knew that I would be all right, no matter what. When things were at their lowest, when it really mattered, he was there for me.

Seriously, my dad is amazing. I suppose all kids say that, but he's got it all happening.

CAMERON

4

WHEN I STARTED at secondary school at Keon Park Tech, while my asthma was still a big thing for me it was easing up. Not that it made schooling any easier, because bullying had taken over as my curse. Those first few years, when I had to endure both asthma and bullying, were pretty tough. Then there was the fact that, with the educational issues that I've mentioned – missing school because of asthma – I was struggling to get anywhere with my studies. All in all, being at a new school with no mates, the sick, small, dumb kid in the corner was just a plum target.

Year Seven was the most horrific time in my entire life. From the minute I walked in there at Keon Park Tech, I wasn't at all confident and the bullying started pretty quickly. I was harassed and bullied from day dot. It started with a group of about ten kids picking on me and a mate of mine, Paul Walpole. Verbally at first, and then it progressed. It began each day on the train in the morning, went right through the school day and then onto the train station after school. Maybe if I hadn't let it get to me so much the first day it may not have been so bad, but they saw weakness and they went for it.

Once I was locked inside a music locker – which was a lot bigger than a normal locker since they had to hold instruments – for about four hours. It was worse than the tent at the Apollo Bay hospital. That was scary, but it wasn't the worst of it. That was when I was thrown off a moving train.

If you remember, those old 'red rattler' trains had doors you could open. One day on the way home from school, they just opened the door and *boom*, threw me out. It wasn't going too fast at the time, but even stationary that isn't a nice fall. I scored a few injuries from that and broke a tooth.

I was constantly telling my parents about the bullying, but they didn't seem to believe it was as bad as it was. The teachers did nothing in class either. I'd get punched in the back of the head and they'd say, 'Stop mucking around.' I'd have blood on the side of my face – is that mucking around? I was thinking, 'Where is the justice here?' That school was something else. I complained a few times, but it fell on deaf ears.

Because of the bullying my studies suffered – even worse than missing days with asthma – which was the last thing I needed. One thing I learned from bullying, and people don't realise or talk about it much – especially the bullies – is that it can destroy someone's education, as well as all the other damage that's being done.

When you're bullied every single day and there's no way out, eventually it gets too much. It was being ignored at home, as well as by the teachers, and as it escalated, so did my inner rage. These kids were ruining my life and it took a good three months before I exploded. Some people in those situations end up committing suicide. For me I just lost control.

This kid wasn't one of the really bad bullies, but he was the straw that broke the camel's back. We were in the textiles room one day and he threw me to the floor. I landed face first on a beam and broke another tooth, and that was it. I could feel it building like an asthma attack. When it came, I just couldn't stop. I'd never really used my karate skills before, and I suppose Father Glennon was right – I was pretty good.

After I hit this kid a couple of times, he said, 'Let's go on the oval,' and we did. He copped it. I ended up breaking both his eye sockets, as well as giving him a few other bruises to remember me by. I really hurt him, and I didn't mean to – as I said, I was out of control.

Because of the fight, I got into a lot of trouble. I was pulled up by the principal with my parents and I nearly got expelled for it. 'I was just defending myself – I'm the victim,' I told them.

In the immediate aftermath of the fight, while the adrenalin was still pumping, it had felt good. There'd been a crowd out there on the oval and I actually got a lot of respect after that. I felt like it was my championship round, my way of saying, 'There you go, bullies, I do stand up for myself.'

I got the nickname 'Psycho' out of that. Then people wanted to start fighting Psycho to prove they were better than me and that made it worse. That's when I started bailing out of school. I was meant to be learning and these people were ruining it for me.

Anyway, after that year was done I was allowed to move to Lalor Tech, where most of my mates were. It was still a tough school, but it immediately felt more comfortable. I had upped the ante with my martial arts as a result of the bullying I copped at Keon Park, and I was doing Zen Do Kai, an advanced form of karate for self-defence. I knew how to handle myself now, but unfortunately it didn't stop me from getting into trouble – not that I ever went looking for it.

I got a new nickname there: 'Aggro'. I didn't want it, but it was better than Psycho at least. That stuck until I left school. Even some of the teachers would call me Aggro instead of Cameron.

My early teenage years were good. I was about fourteen and had control of my anger, thanks to the therapy sessions the old school made me attend. Now I also felt like I was getting on top of the asthma. Whether I was just growing out of it, as some do, or whether it was the surfing and other fitness things, I don't know. And nor did I care.

It felt like an ever-present threat though, albeit a fading one. I was still struggling at school, but I was beginning to find things that interested me. I was really ramping up the fitness – doing weights and other things in the gym – and as I got fitter, I kept getting better with the asthma and more capable with life. I started reading about fitness too, which is where an interest in massage came from. On the back of that, I did a trainer's course where I learned things like strapping.

Mum organised a meeting for me at the Carlton Football Club through someone she knew there. Once I got my nose in, there was no way it wasn't going to happen. It was a pretty exciting time in my life, even more so as a fifteen-year-old schoolkid, and, remember, this was when the Blues were at the top of the pile, not struggling like today. I think I was the youngest trainer they'd ever had.

I had some great experiences there – I even got roasted by club president John Elliott once. I was a Collingwood supporter then – my whole family was – and Carlton was playing the Pies at the

MCG. I was sitting on the bench and found myself cheering for Collingwood. Elliott tapped me on the shoulder and said, 'What do you think you're doing, young man?'

I said 'Oh, I'm just . . .'

He didn't let me finish. 'Because you're at Carlton, you're Carlton and that is it. No barracking for the other side.'

'All right, okay.'

Once I came to grips with that, I really enjoyed my time with the Blues. Finally, I felt like I could say I didn't have any asthma. It felt good, and it felt like the rest of my life could begin.

I soldiered on at school until Year 11. Despite my interest in massage and the other aspects of being a trainer, I wasn't going to earn a living from it, given most of those positions at the time were voluntary. So I started thinking about what I was going to do with the rest of my life.

I got a glazing apprenticeship at O'Brien's Glass in Collingwood, which was pretty demanding. Glazing is a hard job and because it's so dangerous you have to be on the ball. After O'Brien's I went to another glazing company and it was like I was back at school. The bullying started all over again.

Here I was at this new business and a lot of them were on speed or other drugs. I'm not into drugs, I never have been, and I didn't like them in the workplace, so I made my feelings known. I didn't want to have to rely on a bloke who was high on whatever. But as I made my feelings known, they turned on me – the whole lot of them. 'Yeah, great. It's happening again.'

I went through some pretty dark times in my youth and early adulthood. I had fleeting thoughts of suicide, but nothing serious, not like it was after Shaun passed away. I reckon I've suffered from some form of depression most of my life, with either asthma or bullying as its trigger. But we didn't talk about depression back then. We weren't very enlightened.

I had no idea where my life was headed, but I was pretty sure this wasn't where I wanted it to go. I wished I'd got the marks at school to do something like physiotherapy. I would have liked that, but it wasn't going to happen.

When I met Olivia, my reputation as Aggro, or Psycho, was well behind me and I was a young man trying to make my way in the world. I was eighteen when we met at a party in Epping. She told me that when she was young she'd choked on a chicken bone or something, and it had caused massive problems for her. For instance, she had to learn how to walk again after all the problems that developed from being in a coma. I'm a very empathetic person, and this story touched me. We talked a lot and eventually the relationship started to turn into a normal boyfriend and girlfriend thing.

Olivia liked me for who I was, not because of some reputation or because of anything I'd done. I'd like to think it was because I was stunningly beautiful and funny, but neither was the case, so I guess she was just into the real Cameron and not some persona I was putting on to impress her. Like me, she'd grown up in the northern suburbs of Melbourne, and after the chicken-bone incident she struggled with her schooling as well. So we'd both done it tough at school. We just clicked.

I was doing a few things for work now, like being a lifeguard and a swimming teacher at Reservoir, and that was a far less toxic environment than the glazing business, so I was enjoying it more. Everything was pretty good with us for quite a while. We were both still living at home when we found out she was pregnant with Shaun.

That was a pretty scary time, I can tell you. I was twenty years of age and really pretty naïve about the world. We decided we'd have a go at doing it right, so we got a flat together in Mackey Street, Lalor, not far from home. It's fair to say that this is where we learned we were just not that compatible.

Although Olivia was pregnant, she was still smoking and drinking, and I wanted her to stop. We had some arguments over that, but I never won. So when we had that first scan and they told us something was wrong, I blamed her.

It was the first ultrasound and they checked the heartbeat and said that the baby had a murmur in his heart. 'What the hell's a murmur?' I asked. 'Give it to me in layman's terms.'

They tried to explain it as best they could. After a lot of discussions, they prepared us for the worst. 'There's a possibility the baby might not survive at all, and in all likelihood if it does survive, it won't make it to eight years of age.'

If I'd listened a little bit better, and maybe had a better education, I might have reacted differently. I didn't understand what was going on, because I didn't hear it all. I was trying to ask questions but I was too stunned to listen to all of the answers. Not a lot was known about congenital heart disease, so even when they told us it was a common birth defect I still blamed Olivia's behaviour.

They spoke openly about the prognosis, and I knew then that my son was in for a tough life – however long it was. There was talk of transplants and other operations, but none of it was going to be easy.

'Why is this happening to me?' I was thinking. 'I went through enough myself, going in and out of hospital, and now my son's going to have to go through this as well?' And why did it happen? No-one could tell me, so I drew my own conclusions.

Olivia didn't cope well either, but I was so angry with her that it didn't matter to me. I couldn't look her in the eyes. As far as I was concerned, Shaun's birth defect was all her fault.

I had to get out of the house to try and clear my head. I got in my car and I just drove. Then I cried and cried – I couldn't stop. Finally I returned home and she said with venom, 'Glad to see you back.'

Our relationship was clearly going downhill fast. I didn't handle it well at all – I simply wasn't mature enough. All I wanted was a healthy baby, and they were telling me he may not live at all, and that if he did he'd need an operation within three weeks and then who knew how many more from there?

The rest of the pregnancy was a blur. Olivia and I tried to make living together work, but I couldn't do it. I was always upset and I was struggling with the idea of what life was going to be like for my yet-to-be-born son. I don't think I was the best person to be around. I'd started thinking about why I'd bother to live at all when something that should be great, being a father, was now going to be a nightmare. So I went back around the corner to live with Mum and Dad, and Olivia moved home as well. For the next few months I went into a bit of a shell and I didn't come out.

Mum and Dad were shattered too. They knew what I'd been through with the asthma and they knew what this was doing to me. They never spoke about it in depth, but I could tell they were upset for me that I was once again going to have to go through hell with health issues. Only this time not mine, but my son's.

They tried to help as much as they could, but I wasn't listening. I'd just go to my room and shut the world out – including them. A lot of my friends tried to get me to go out, and that didn't work much either. Most of the time I'd just get in my car and drive. I didn't want to know anybody.

It didn't help that the one time I got the courage to go out, I saw Olivia at the Epping Pub at 2 am, drinking and smoking. That made me so angry because I'd decided that her drinking and smoking was the reason I was going through all this in the first place. I just lost it. I had a really good go at her. I said, 'What are you doing to your unborn baby? You heard how bad things are going to be. You're four months away from giving birth to our son, and you're drinking and smoking? How dare you do this!'

Obviously I now know that her behaviour might not have contributed to Shaun's problems. I might have been right, though – the research is not definitive yet and smoking is listed as a possible contributor. I wanted Olivia to start looking after herself and Shaun. I wanted her to stop smoking and drinking, and she never did.

She basically told me to get fucked. We had a bit of an argument before a bouncer tapped me on the shoulder and said, 'I think it's time for you to go, young man. You've made a bit of a spectacle of yourself.' I tried to explain, but he wouldn't listen and he kicked me out.

From that point on, it got even harder for us and we hardly spoke. However, we did find some common ground; after all, we did have a baby coming into the world. I ended up going to all the appointments and stuff to do with the birth and the baby, but that was it until Shaun was born.

When we got the news about Shaun's birth defects, we were given the option to abort or continue. In my mind, we needed to look at that option and work out what was best. We'd been told how much pain he might have to go through and how many operations he was likely to have. I only thought about it long enough to say the words – about ten seconds really.

I'm not sure how long Olivia thought about a termination, since we weren't really talking, but she did spend the first eight years of Shaun's life telling him I'd wanted to kill him. And that my family had wanted to as well. She'd tell him directly, 'The Miller family wanted to kill you, Shaun.'

Naturally, that idea filled his head for many years. When I picked Shaun up for my weekends when he was about four or five, it would take him a long time to relax and start talking. I could never work it out, until he began to explain what Olivia had been saying about me. I told him that it wasn't true, but I was worried that every time this young kid, my son, looked at me, he was thinking I'd wanted to abort him. That must have been so scary for him.

I still don't understand why Olivia wanted to do and say those things. I really wish we could have just moved on without the shit in our lives, but we couldn't. At times we were as bad as each other – at least until Shaun was born, and then all I could do was think about him. It did more than just hurt me, it hurt Shaun too – probably more than me. Anyway, while I was at the appointment in which Olivia and I had been told about Shaun's birth defects, after those ten seconds I'd said to myself, 'I can't do that. It's not my right to do it. I just have to deal with what's going to come.'

I didn't realise how much was to come, but that's okay. In my eyes, Olivia and I didn't have the right to terminate the pregnancy. That would just happen, or not happen, and God would look after what he was looking after. What if they fixed the problems and my child grew up to be an amazing person? Ten seconds, that's all it took for me to let it go.

In hindsight, I wouldn't change anything, and despite all his medical problems Shaun was in fact that amazing person. Imagine if a decision Olivia and I made that day had robbed the world of his presence.

The call came at 8 pm on 23 January 1995. I was up in Mernda in the northern suburbs with Gibbo, one of the clients in my mobile massage business, which was doing quite well. I dropped everything and drove straight to the Royal Women's Hospital.

The birth itself was freaky – or what happened immediately after it was. In terms of birthing, from what I understand it was fairly straightforward, but once he was out of Olivia it all started. He was blue and, as expected, he was in big trouble. The doctors went to work on him. We had no idea if he'd survive.

I was in shock. I was watching as if I was in another room and this was just on TV. In hindsight the doctors and nurses did a great job on the prep for what we could and should expect, but no words really prepare you for that.

Thankfully, Shaun survived and a few days later, after he was stable, they moved him to the Royal Children's Hospital just up the road. That's when things between me and Olivia got even worse. She didn't want to see me and she didn't want me to see Shaun. It got to the point where I had to say to the nurses, 'I am the father. You can't stop me.'

I'll never forget going into the 7 West Ward at the hospital – that was the cardiac and renal unit – and seeing him in a steel cot.

He always had a smile on his face, which was amazing, but he was in big trouble because only half of his heart was working. This was when the operations started.

Shaun was born with double outlet right ventricle (DORV), ventricle septal defects (VSD), an atrial septal defect (ASD) and pulmonary stenosis, and he struggled to pump enough oxygen engorged blood around his body.

Lumped together it was known as congenital heart disease, which was really just a way of talking about all the heart defects with which someone can be born. Some CHD is relatively minor, while in other cases, like Shaun's, it can be much more severe. Some babies don't even survive those first few days, if any at all.

I was on a steep learning curve, as I had been since Shaun's initial diagnosis. Essentially the heart has four chambers – two atriums and two ventricles. The atrium is the receiving chamber for blood coming in. A valve then opens and lets it pass to the ventricles, and from there it's either pumped around the body for oxygenated blood from the left side, or to the lungs for the blood returning to the heart from the right side.

In Shaun's case, he had holes between both atriums and both ventricles, meaning the oxygenated blood was mixing with the blood that was low in oxygen. In effect, this meant that the oxygen levels in the blood being pumped around his body were lower than they needed to be. You can hear these defects with a murmur – which is essentially any sound that happens between the beats – when you listen in.

There are obviously degrees for each of these, and more often than not surgery is required to fix one of them. So it was almost certain that Shaun, with two or more defects, would need surgery a few times early in his life, since it was unlikely his struggling body could repair itself. Fixing the two major problems, they said, was not going to be easy.

Olivia wanted to take Shaun home, which anyone could see was the wrong thing to do. His oxygen saturation levels were low, and if he left the hospital he wouldn't have survived long at all. We were both struggling to cope, and sadly we couldn't even rely on each other for support. We were just at each other's throats.

As expected, Shaun was three weeks old when he had his first heart operation. In essence they were trying to connect one piece of the heart to the other, which was a pretty complex operation on anyone, let alone a three-week-old baby. When Shaun was born we were told that his heart was the size of a walnut, so I was trying to work that out. How could they do that sort of operation on something so small? It was way over my head.

Afterwards, the surgeon came out and said it had been touch and go – that they'd nearly lost him on the table. I was shattered and in utter despair. It was as if I'd given this surgeon my son to look after and he'd nearly killed him. It was irrational, but it was how I felt. Then he explained that this was just the first of many operations, but that at least Shaun would be able to go home.

By this stage, both our families were at war. Looking back now, the behaviour by everyone – me included – was quite disgusting. Poor Shaun was lying in hospital with this big cut down his front from where they'd operated. They'd had to break his sternum to do the operation and his little chest was basically just taped up and sewed together.

I walked into his room one day at the hospital before we took him home, and as he opened his eyes he looked up at me and grabbed my finger. It was an amazing moment. It's something I'll remember forever, and it touched me deeply. I knew something had to change with the way we were behaving. I knew I had to find a better way of fighting for him. So I sucked it up and tried to put my feelings for Olivia and her family aside – and let me tell you that at that stage it wasn't easy. I was really worried about Shaun going home with Olivia, but I had no power to stop it, so I just had to make it work.

Not that he was home for long, because two weeks later they operated again. I couldn't understand why they wanted to cut him open when the last cut hadn't even healed. They started explaining it to me, but all I heard was 'blah, blah, blah'.

That year was a really tough time for me. My mind would race off in all sorts of other directions and my depression was kicking in even harder. I couldn't see any light at the end of the tunnel for Shaun, and I was at my lowest ebb.

I reckon they opened him up twenty times before he was twelve months old. Every time they went in, they found something new. That meant they either stopped the operation so they could think and plan, or they simply did what they were there to do – and then scheduled another one.

To top it off, Shaun was in a ward with other kids with serious heart problems and some of them were passing away. It was a real eye-opener and the reality started to hit home that he was going to have a hard life.

It was just not fair.

Olivia's and my relationship was downright toxic and was poisoning everyone around us, except Shaun thankfully. We tried living together after Shaun was born, and that lasted about six months but was never easy for either of us. In hindsight, we should have just accepted it was never going to work, and for Shaun's sake we should have agreed to live apart but work for him.

I remember one night when Shaun was just a little baby, Olivia and I had an argument about me getting a better job. I'd had enough, so I grabbed Shaun and I put him in the baby seat of my green V8 Commodore and started the car. She must have heard the engine when I started it and came running out of the unit, banging on the window. I ignored her and drove off into the night, talking to Shaun about how I wanted to be a better father.

The next day, we broke up and I moved back in with Mum and Dad. Then I started to have access issues with Shaun, even though what I had done was best for all of us. I'd been working hard on it from my end, though, which really meant I had to suck it up all the time, just to see my own son.

Shaun was consuming my whole life, and I was giving him everything I had. That feeling grew stronger every day. I remember one time I took him into the hospital to get some blood tests done and we went into a room with Santa Claus. It was a really good set-up with snow and everything, and as he sat there playing and smiling at me, the desire in me to fight for him grew another leg. Shaun means 'gift from God' in Irish, and although Olivia came up with the name I felt it was perfect for him.

Olivia had custody, and after a year the courts gave me every second weekend with Shaun, which was about all a bloke could expect back then. I struggled to work out where I was placed in his life. In the eyes of the judicial system, I was just the father and that meant nothing to them.

Olivia knew how I felt and she used it against me. It was little things that became big things. We'd be down at Apollo Bay with my parents and she'd call up, changing the time Shaun had to return to her place. She'd threaten me, 'You better have Shaun back in the next so many hours, otherwise I'm calling the police.'

And I'd say to Mum, 'What do I do?' I didn't want to rock the boat and I didn't want to take any risks.

Mum was calmer than me, and she'd say we just had to drive him back. For her that was how we avoided any extra drama. But we had a court-mandated handover time and eventually I told Olivia just to ring the police – then she started to back off. I wish I'd done that earlier.

And there was another complication. I'm not sure how Olivia had the time or the inkling, but she ended up seeing this bloke I really didn't like. She went through a succession of boyfriends but settled for a bloke named Fletch. He just reminded me of the bullies at school. The first time I met him, he called me over with 'Hey you, Knackers', which wasn't a good way to start.

He was short, shorter even than me, and had tattoos all over him, which back then wasn't cool in the same way some people think they are today. Then as he got in closer with Olivia, they ended up living together and he began to push his way into our business with Shaun.

Part of the problem was walking into her house and seeing my son with a man I didn't even know. It was like 'Who the hell are you?' That meant he started from behind the eight ball in my eyes anyway. She was obviously happier to give him rights over my son than me, and that pissed me off even more.

Personally, I wasn't ready for a relationship and I couldn't see how Olivia was either. I was single all the way through my twenties and well into my thirties. I wasn't ready, and Shaun wasn't ready, to have another person in his life in that way.

The problem wasn't just Fletch. The other people Olivia was hanging around with didn't help either. Now I'm nothing special in terms of growing up in a working-class area and the like, but her friends were taking things to a new low level. The swearing was constant, and they were always smoking, whether Shaun was near or not. Given that he was struggling for oxygen at the best of times, I didn't like it one bit.

Part of me felt like a failure. Because of the illness and because of the people Olivia was inviting into her life, I hadn't been able to keep Shaun safe. I kept thinking, 'I've failed him.' You could see he was unwell. He always had blue lips, always had blue fingers, always had blue toes – and I was powerless.

I think in some ways my life was a bigger struggle at the time than Shaun's, and his was bloody tough. I mean, we knew what was up with him and that he was suffering immeasurably at times, and I worried he was in a lot of pain, but we had to go through the series of tests and operations and hope each one made him better. Meanwhile I was spiralling downwards with my depression and that was affecting everything around me. I couldn't even talk to my mates about it. Looking back, it would've been great to have a very good friend grab me and say, 'Let's talk about this.' But blokes didn't do that sort of thing in the 1990s, and maybe still don't.

Olivia was struggling too with what I believe was some form of post-natal depression. She'd get angry with me for no reason and start yelling. In fact, every time I went to pick him up she'd yell at me, probably just because I was there.

So we were as good as each other at the time. We were both suffering from depression and both putting our heads in the sand. It wasn't helping anyone.

I've said it before and I'll say it again – I could have handled things with Olivia better. But when you're twenty-one, you're not meant to go through this sort of stuff. Being told that your baby boy might die, how do you handle things?

From that first operation until he was eight years old, Shaun was at the Royal Children's Hospital every week. He was taking a drug called Warfarin, which is a blood thinner, and he had to have his levels checked during those visits for blood clots, a possible side effect. You also had to be careful with Warfarin because if you get cut you can bleed a lot; too much in fact, which was dangerous.

It was like a revolving door – we should have had our own permanent room.

So much of those early years felt like Groundhog Day. A lot of this care was thrown at me, so even though I wasn't with Shaun every day, I was taking him to his visits. It wasn't ideal father–son time, but it was time and I really didn't mind too much. But as time went on, Olivia got harder to manage. One day she'd want to take him for his hospital visits, and the next day she had no interest, so I was really just trying to juggle all that and make sure Shaun was getting what he needed.

Aside from his physical problems, he was developing like a normal child. He started talking at the right age, for instance, so there was no mental impairment or anything, which was amazing considering the issues he had getting oxygen around his body. His brain was developing faster than his body, and I think he learnt to rely more on his thinking than anything else. Shaun was confident from a very young age and he never lost that.

SHAUN

5

THERE'S BEEN A bit of a hiccup. I was feeling pretty exhausted and Dad didn't like the look of things and took me back to the hospital. The doctors are saying I've picked up a slight chest infection, which doesn't sound serious, except that when you have a heart like mine anything and everything that happens to you is serious. When you're dosed to the max on immuno-suppressant drugs, it makes sense that your immune system doesn't work and can't kick in when you get a cold or whatever.

They've whacked this PICC line into my arm, which drip-feeds antibiotics into my chest to target the infection. Just a huge drag really. This means I can't have a shower properly and it's going to be almost impossible to get a good night's sleep. Because of the PICC line I can't even roll over. And my family's worried I'm being worn out from all these media interviews and stuff, but it's something positive to keep me going. Anyway, I keep meaning to tell you about my girlfriend, Maddy, who's fantastic, but I'll come back to her.

When Mum and Dad broke up for the final time the deal was that I'd get to see him on the weekend. He was supposed to pick me up every Friday night and take me to Nanna and Poppy's, but this didn't always happen. Mum was sometimes unpredictable towards Dad. And Mum's family were just like her. If they were around when Dad came to pick me up, they'd answer the door and tell Dad what they thought of him. It was usually stuff like he wasn't a man for not sticking by Mum and me.

I was only a kid, but I had to watch this and never knew what to think. Every now and then they'd refuse to hand me over to Dad and slam the door in his face. Eventually, Dad felt too uncomfortable coming to pick me up so Mum said she'd drop me off – only that arrangement didn't last long.

See, Mum's side of the family never forgave Dad's side for bringing up the idea of terminating me as a baby. No-one was allowed to forget this. And they especially didn't want me to forget this. On my sixth birthday I asked Mum if I could invite Dad, Nanna and Poppy John to my party.

'Why would you even want to see these people, Shaun?' she asked me. 'They wanted to kill you when you were in my tummy.'

This confused me. Didn't the Miller family love me? They were always really nice to me whenever I saw them. Why did they want to kill me as a baby? Years and years later, these accusations are still going around. Whenever there's a dispute someone yells, 'You just wanted to kill Shaun anyway!'

It's all point-scoring, tit for tat – 'he says, she says' – except it's just pointless stuff. I mean, it's not as if Mum ever wanted or hoped that Dad would come back and live with us.

And where was Dad in all this? He couldn't handle it. Now that I'm seventeen I can see how he was caught in the middle, under pressure from Mum and her family. They were saying, 'You're hopeless,' 'You're not a man,' 'Pathetic,' 'Disgusting,' and worse. Meanwhile Dad's family were saying much the same thing. You know, 'You're his father – be a father,' 'Don't listen to them,' 'Don't put up with that crap – you have rights,' and so on.

Poor Dad. He was a mess. No matter what he did, no matter where he went, he was disappointing everyone. Arriving at Mum's house was like parachuting into a war zone. Without fail he'd stand there not knowing what to expect, and then someone would abuse the daylights out of him. This would be repeated when he dropped me off.

In the beginning, Dad argued back and when Mum yelled at him, he yelled back, but she was too strong for him. You could see he didn't have the stomach for this kind of thing. Then, he started skipping weeks and didn't bother to come and take me at all. Sometimes, Nanna – Dad's mum – would pick me up. Then she'd get a blast for getting involved and was told that her son wasn't a man, *blah blah blah*.

Mum was caring and I know she loved me, yet sometimes it felt like her hatred for Dad dictated what she did. My whole life I've needed medication and had to take heaps of pills a day to keep me alive. If I became sick, I had to take more. Mum worried about my health, and one of the reasons she refused to let me stay with Dad or my grandparents was because she didn't think they'd take care of me properly. She claimed they didn't give me the right medication, but Dad's family said she didn't provide enough information about what pills and what dosage.

So you see, the war between Mum and Dad started to be not just about me, but my health. And the crazy thing was they only lived ten minutes apart, so it didn't need to be that hard – except that the aggro seemed to get in the way.

One time at the hospital a nurse said to Dad, 'You really need to pay more attention to Shaun. He doesn't always take certain medications when he stays with you.' This was really upsetting for Dad, because he hadn't been told that I was on that particular drug. When he asked for details, the nurses were reluctant to give them to him because Mum was my primary guardian. When Dad complained that Mum hadn't told him what was happening, the hospital said, 'You need to sort this out between your families because this is a sick kid we're talking about.'

At Nanna's house one weekend I started to get a cold. She was worried and took me to a doctor who prescribed antibiotics. When I went back home, Mum rang Nanna straightaway, saying those antibiotics could have interfered with my other medication. For that, Mum didn't let me see Dad, Nanna or Poppy for three whole months. They were devastated because they'd only been trying to look after me.

Father's Day when I was seven was when it all blew up. Mum said I could spend the day with Dad. It'd been a long time since we'd seen each other and I was looking forward to it. When he knocked on the door, though, Mum laughed at him and said, 'You're not having him,' and shut the door in his face. For Dad and his family, that was the last straw. Sick and tired of all this nonsense, they hired a lawyer and fronted up to the Family Court.

What they asked for was guaranteed weekend access, plus a dosette box, which stored my drugs in the right doses, and an exercise book kept that recorded when I took my medications.

The judge gave the Miller family every second weekend, half of my school holidays, plus Father's Day and Boxing Day. They were happy with that because it meant they could now play a much bigger role in my life. Unfortunately, the verdict caused the rift between Mum and Dad to widen. The Family Court said they had to have mediation with a counsellor, but their sessions ended up being pretty horrible and didn't improve things much.

SHAUN

6

'VIOLET' IS WHAT the kids at Epping Primary School called me, after the girl from *Charlie and the Chocolate Factory*. Violet chewed the gum even though Willy Wonka told her not to, and she turned all fat and blue, like a big blueberry. One thing I never was was fat, and I didn't look like a girl either. I guess they came up with the nickname because I used to get blue everywhere – especially in the fingers and toes and lips. 'Hey, Violet, how you doin'?' they'd go.

The truth was that I was pretty miserable because I was always sick and weak – too weak to run around the playground. At lunch-time I'd watch the boys playing football and wish I could join in too, but just walking from one classroom to the next was exhausting. Not being able to play made it difficult for me to make friends, plus I was always having to go back to hospital. All I wanted was to be just like the other kids.

I have a name for the heart I was born with: 'The One with the Lot'. There were so many complications with it that I can't even remember most of them. The doctors say I was born with a Double

Outlet Right Ventricle (DORV) with non-committed Ventricle Septal Defects (VSD), transposition of the Great Arteries (TGA), and Pulmonary Stenosis. Big words, huh?

It's easier to say complex congenital heart disease. Basically, it didn't work very well.

All this meant that I was never getting a sufficient supply of oxygen pumped around my body. It sure was a bit of a car wreck, my heart. I had heaps of operations as I grew up to try to repair it, and when I was eight years old my dodgy, faulty heart began to fail completely. It all happened one afternoon. Dad picked me up from school and we were grabbing something to eat at Maccas. I love Maccas. Who doesn't? Especially when you're going to hospital with nothing to look forward to.

Anyway, we were sitting at our table when all of a sudden I vomited. I threw up all over my tray, drenching my Happy Meal and the free toy with blood. Only it didn't look anything like blood. At first, people around me in the McDonald's thought I'd just vomited up stuff like chocolate milk or something, but it was blood – and brown blood. You don't need to be a rocket scientist to know that's not good.

The look on Dad's face was bad. One look at that brown slime and he knew something terrible was going down. When he tried to help me I noticed I couldn't move my legs all that well and when I stood I could barely walk. Something definitely wasn't right with me and I was pretty scared. Not being able to control your body is always frightening.

Dad rushed me to the 7 West Ward. At first the nurses didn't react like it was urgent or anything and he started yelling, 'He's really sick!' When they checked my oxygen saturation levels I didn't even make the minimum reading. The norm is between ninety-five and 100 – which was more than double where I was at. That certainly made them take notice.

I was going into heart failure. My kidneys were shutting down and all my other organs would soon follow. They wouldn't let me drink water because it would mean extra work for my heart, pushing the fluids round my body, and the last thing it needed was more pressure. The nurses fed me little ice chips which melted slowly in my mouth and they kept rechecking me, hoping to see some signs of improvement. But nothing was changing – except it was getting worse. I was feeling pretty crap, but I didn't know how bad it was.

After a few hours the doctors asked to speak to Dad privately in the hospital corridor. As he walked off, he turned and threw me one of his 'it's all good' smiles, which, of course, was a lie.

While I was lying there in the bed, alone with my thoughts, the most incredible thing happened. I know you'll all think I'm crazy, but I'm going to tell you anyway. It felt like there was another presence there in the room with me. I remember feeling tired and weak, in a lot of pain, and life seemed to be leaving my body, like a tide going out and never coming back.

This voice spoke to me, which was weird because I could hear the words, but not the sound. 'Your time is not up, Shaun. You have great things to do and you need to do them. Make me proud.'

To me this was like speaking to God or something. Not that our family was religious. We didn't go to church and never really talked about that stuff. It was an epiphany. Big word. Later, when I was on a HeartKids camp – a camp for children with heart disease – a counsellor told me that's what it was. An epiphany – when a person receives a message and experiences a life-changing realisation.

Meanwhile, Dad was out in the corridor where the doctors told him I probably wouldn't make it through the night and if I did, I wouldn't survive for long without a new heart. 'You need to prepare yourself,' they said. As he was standing there listening to the doctors, he looked through the glass and started freaking out. My arms were raised and reaching out to the middle of the room. He reckoned later that it looked like I was trying to hold onto a ray of sunlight streaming through the window, even though it was night-time. And he could see my lips moving like I was talking to someone.

Dad raced back inside and of course there was no-one there – just me on the bed and the sounds of the monitors beeping and all that. He remembers that I had this smile plastered on my face. I was smiling because of that epiphany.

For so long I'd been unhappy about my life and carried it with me wherever I went. There was so much negativity in me. I was bitter because I wished that I could kick a football around, or just run crazily outside like the other kids. I hated that I had to take horrible-tasting pills every day, go to doctor's appointments all the time and somehow always end up back in hospital. But as I lay in that hospital bed with nothing but death to look forward to, I suddenly had the revelation that things were going to change. 'Hey, Dad,' I whispered, 'it's going to be okay.' He was crying and just patted my arm and held my hand.

Both families stayed by my side day and night. They took turns – Mum did the days and Dad the nights. There were lots of tests and stuff and then, in the middle of the night, Dr Rob arrived at the foot of my bed and said, 'Beautiful boy, we have a miracle. We've got a heart for you – we're going to save your life.'

They'd found me a new heart. I went into surgery straight-away and was in the operating room for the next fifteen hours. The doctors had warned my family there was a pretty big chance I wouldn't survive the surgery. All the family sat outside anxiously waiting to see what happened. Finally, one of the surgical team appeared in the waiting-room and announced the good news.

CAMERON

7

SHAUN JUST KEPT on doing what he was doing. No matter what shit was thrown at him, either by us or his body, he just kept rolling along with a smile.

Going to primary school was hard for him. Because of the blue lips and fingertips, which a lot of the kids didn't understand, they called him 'Violet'. Shaun hated it. I know they were only kids, but it hurt me to see him upset.

Most of the time back then, he couldn't walk twenty metres without getting tired, but he still went to school as often as he could. A two-week spell was a pretty good run for him. The teachers put Shaun's locker close to his classroom so he didn't have to walk very far, which he appreciated, but he still had yearnings to just be a normal kid. At lunchtime Shaun used to watch the other kids kicking the football and dream it could be him playing. As Shaun said, 'Dreaming doesn't need energy.'

He enjoyed school when he was there, but it was hard and he had limited education. In between hospital appointments, other medical appointments and the heart clinic, there wasn't much time for continuity. The teachers loved him, though, and were pretty good with him.

Shaun stayed positive all the way. He was always smiling, and he was the one who'd pick people up when they were feeling down. He was an old soul too. Some of the things he'd say astonished me. You were often left wondering where he could have heard the expressions he used.

Over time I'd learned how to cope with Olivia, but I never learned how to cope with Fletch. He suffered from short-man syndrome and he was an angry little ant – I can say that because I'm short too. He was so destructive and he was in Shaun's life for way too long. He started throwing his weight around, and it just built from there.

As if Shaun didn't have enough to deal with. As if I didn't have enough to deal with.

For many years, my life with Shaun was fairly simple. Every second weekend he'd come around and we'd just watch movies. He didn't really have the energy for much more than that. His favourite movie was *The Sandlot*, which is about kids growing up in the 1960s in America and playing baseball, which I imagine was as much about Shaun dreaming of his future as it was anything else.

Unfortunately, when Shaun was eight Fletch was really starting to be a thorn in my side, and sticking his nose into things he didn't have any right to get involved in. I don't know why it mattered to him, but he began to act like he was Shaun's father or that he owned him. I think for him it was about having power over someone. In this instance it was two people – me and Shaun.

One night around then I was running late getting Shaun back, and Fletch arrived at my place with a mate. He was drinking Jim Beam cans on our front lawn before he came to the front door and started having a go at me. He was always trying to provoke me because he knew if I got in a fight with him, I'd lose Shaun. I knew not to touch him – *ever*. It wasn't easy, so I guess my anger-management classes when I was younger were worth it after all.

Another day, when Shaun was about seven, Fletch turned up and greeted my mum with 'Where's that bastard Cameron?' When I got to the door he started getting stuck into me. Shaun had been asleep, but he heard the commotion and came to the door. When he saw me arguing with Fletch, he fainted. Straight back – *womp*.

I could see Shaun out of the corner of my eye. His eyes rolled back in his head and he just went down. This was pretty heavy stuff and it really hit me later that night. This was a real changing point for me in terms of what I needed to do to protect Shaun.

Of course, my first thoughts were not about what Fletch meant to Shaun – it was really just that his heart had given in. We had a defibrillator nearby – we'd all done the training – and I was getting ready to use it when he opened his eyes. As soon as he was capable of talking he said, 'I don't want to go home.'

That was when I knew something was up. Even though Shaun was awake we called an ambulance, and the police turned up as well, because Mum used the word 'violence' when she rang 000. They were powerless. 'Look, Cameron, we understand where you're coming from, but legally you were over an hour late on your court orders.'

I couldn't believe it. I told them, 'Shaun has just seen his step-father and fainted. That's how scared he is, and you're telling me that I'm late on my orders?' I was late because Shaun had been sleeping, which was more important to me than Olivia and Fletch's timetable.

I'd rung to tell them. That's when he'd turned up. Not Olivia, but Fletch.

Shaun fainting was a trigger for me to start finding out what his home life was really like. I was shocked as he started telling me the stories. But as it turned out no-one with any authority gave a damn. We spoke to DHS – the Department of Human Services. They said it was just sour grapes and to go and annoy someone else.

But it was more than that. The system was so wrong back then – I had fewer rights than Fletch because he was living with Olivia. I really hope the system is better now.

Fletch seemed to love the fact that he had this power over me. Let me tell you about the time I got Shaun's hair cut. We'd gone to a hairdressers – it wasn't like I'd pulled out scissors and clippers and gone to work on his head. When I dropped Shaun home that day, Fletch was in the garage.

'So, Knackers, what makes you think that you can get Shaun's hair cut?'

'Because I'm his father?'

'I don't care. You have to ask my permission when you get his hair cut.'

This was not about what was good for Shaun, it was just about how this bully could serve it to me to make himself feel better. I'd love to know if there was ever any more to it than that, but I doubt it. I'd seen Fletch's type many times before.

He was continually poking and prodding and looking for a reaction, but that day I just walked away, with an even greater resolve to do something about him. It was never easy with him around, so I began to talk to lawyers, even if they weren't much help to start with.

CAMERON

8

IN JUNE 2004, Olivia and I sat with the surgeon, Professor Christian Brizard, at the Royal Children's Hospital as he told us he wanted to do a Fontan procedure on Shaun's heart. Professor Brizard, who was the head of the cardiac unit, explained it as an operation for kids who only have one fully functioning ventricle. Aside from the lack of efficiency, one part of Shaun's heart was working too hard to keep the blood moving. So, with only one ventricle and plenty of leakage, he was never getting enough oxygen. Professor Brizard thought the procedure would help.

I knew this was a big operation. Professor Brizard said that Shaun had to reach a certain age before the body could tolerate it. Ideally, it would have happened when he was born, but apparently the procedure would most likely have killed him. So the doctors had had to sit there and hope Shaun actually reached an age where they could do the operation. Now they felt he was strong enough to cope.

Theoretically, it would be a permanent fix. I was really hopeful this was it.

Professor Brizard was from Paris, so when he was explaining the whole operation I was struggling to understand him. 'We're going to do the Fontan and do it this way and do it that way and we're going to connect this and connect that.' It sounded as if he was talking about connecting a motor, which in some ways he was – with a strong French accent.

It was scary. Professor Brizard warned us we could lose Shaun on the operating table, but he believed the risk was worth it. He obviously felt that this operation was crucial, and he was very strong in his recommendations. Olivia and I agreed.

The operation itself went for fifteen hours, which is a long time to be sitting in a hospital waiting-room, just as it is for a child or anyone to be on an operating table. We'd sat outside a few times already while Shaun had operations, but this was a big one and the wait was freaking me out a bit. When the doctors came out smiling, it was such a huge relief.

They told us the procedure had gone really well. 'Okay, there were a few complications in surgery,' said Professor Brizard, 'but I think Shaun's going to be fine.'

I was ready to chuck balloons in the air and I even almost hugged Olivia. I now know the Fontan usually does fix the problem to a certain degree. Doctors can't correct the CHD, but they can make the heart work well enough for a normal life.

In those fleeting minutes and days following, I thought, 'Shaun's made it to eight' – the number they'd given us before he was born – and now he was fixed. It was all working and he was going to be fine.

A few days after Shaun had been discharged, I picked him up early from school because he wasn't feeling well and headed into the hospital for a scheduled check-up. We got there early, so we went to the McDonald's at the hospital. We sat down to eat when Shaun told me he wasn't feeling too well. Then all of a sudden, he threw up everywhere. Blood. There was a big pool of it on the floor – I'm sure *that* McDonald's has seen worse – and he said, 'I'm sick, Dad, I'm sick.'

It was terrifying. I picked him up and rushed up the stairs – I didn't worry about the elevator. I flew up the seven flights like I was going for a walk in the park. 'I need some help here!' I called out to anyone who would listen. 'I really need some help!'

I didn't think they were moving fast enough so I was yelling and screaming, and eventually they paid attention. They put Shaun on what's called a SATs machine and started to measure how much oxygen was in his blood. Usually you're hoping for somewhere up near the 100 mark. Most healthy people would be in the nineties, something in the eighties is room for concern, and Shaun was normally in the seventies. Today he was below the level they could read on the machine! Less than fifty.

His heart was so damaged and bruised from all his operations that even the Fontan procedure hadn't been enough. He couldn't eat or drink now because of the energy required to push the fluid and food around his body, so all the nutrients he needed were going in intravenously. We had ice chips to feed him so his mouth didn't get too dry. But Shaun was getting worse and this was the most confronting his illness had ever been.

The doctor – Dr Rob, as Shaun called him – asked if he could speak with me privately in the corridor. As I walked out I turned to Shaun and gave him a smile, but he knew something major was up. Dr Robert Weintraub, who'd worked with Professor Brizard, said that Shaun was going through massive heart failure. 'We're going to need to call your wife in,' he said. I told him I wasn't married. Strangely, even at that time I didn't want anyone to think that I was.

Once Olivia had arrived, we sat in Dr Rob's office where he very bluntly told us that Shaun needed a heart transplant within forty-eight hours or he was going to die. I was numb, and some of what was being said just didn't register. I did hear that there'd only been three transplants done that year. It was hard to get donors, and even harder to get a good enough match. In Shaun's case it would have to be a child who died to donate the heart. He was preparing us for the worst.

A few days earlier, I'd thought that Shaun was fixed and I'd been looking forward to the rest of our lives together. Now, I was preparing myself to not have him with me at all, if things didn't go well in the forty-eight-hour timeline.

It was moments like this I wished Olivia and I had a better relationship, but we handled the situation on our own and separately. I walked in to Shaun and said, 'I'm sorry, mate, I feel like I've failed you in your life.' I was crying and he just looked at me and said, 'It's okay, Dad, don't worry.'

The chances of finding a heart were slim, and Shaun could hear all the talk. He was putting it all together and he asked me if he was going to be okay. How do you reply to a question like that when you honestly don't know the answer? So I just said, 'Mate, you're going to be fine.'

But Shaun knew how serious it was. 'There's something not right in my heart, Dad, I know it. I've never felt this bad before. I'm only eight – I don't want to die.'

Where were we going to get a heart from? Someone with the same size heart cavity and with the same blood type had to die, and then we had to get the heart to him quickly enough. It just wasn't very likely. I was bracing myself for the worst.

We were told to bring in anyone who needed to say goodbye to Shaun. Olivia made that hard, though, especially with that guard dog Fletch barking at anyone who came near. She didn't want any of my family to come in. I stood toe to toe with Fletch and told him never to tell me what to do again. I'd had enough of him. From that day on, it was going to stop. My family were going to see Shaun and I didn't care what he thought.

The next day was pretty tough as people came in to say goodbye. I'd barely left the hospital or Shaun's side, apart from the odd toilet break and to get some food. But around midnight at the end of that first day, I did head outdoors for some fresh air. It was pelting down with rain and when I was outside I just dropped to my knees. It was starting to get to me. I was praying at the top of my voice, crying for help. 'If you are there and you can hear me, please, please help my boy!'

Shaun talks about having an epiphany, which I walked in on when I returned to his bedside. I'll tell you what I saw. He was on no medication, except a saline drip to help his fluids and the ice chips I was allowed to give him because his kidneys were shutting down. It was after midnight now. He was holding my hand, and I could see from the monitors that his vital signs were very low. The clock was ticking – he was now down to only twenty hours to live if he didn't get a heart. I was so scared just watching the life slowly leave his body.

Then incredibly Shaun looked up at the ceiling like he was staring at something. He raised his hand to shield his eyes like you would if a bright light was shining directly at you. I looked up and there was nothing there. We were in darkness except for the monitor, which gave enough light for me to see him clearly.

Then he started to talk, although it was all very quiet. I listened but I couldn't make out a word and even put my ear up against his lips, but I still couldn't hear him. Although his lips were moving like he was talking, it was total silence. I tried to get his attention. I was too scared to shake him but I said, 'Shaun, are you okay?' There was no response. He was in some sort of deep trance, and it went on for about fifteen minutes. He just kept talking, with no sound, into thin air.

It was half an hour after midnight when he came out of it.

'Dad, something amazing has just happened.' I was trying to talk to him quietly, because there were other kids in the ward and I didn't want to wake anyone, but Shaun was just booming it out. 'I was looking up to the sky and all of a sudden a big light opened up from behind a sliding door. I got asked to go towards this light by an old man.'

'What happened next?'

Shaun wouldn't go into full detail, but he said the old man told him not to come through the door. 'I've been told to go away and be positive – I've got work to do. And I've got really good news. I'm getting a new heart.'

I played it straight with Shaun. I told him how slim the chances were of getting a new heart, but he was having none of it. The old man he identified as God had told him he was okay.

Not more than five minutes later, a nurse walked in and said, 'Mr Miller, there's a phone call for you.'

I left the room to take the call. After the person on the phone checked who I was, they said they had a heart for Shaun. Did I want it?

Wow.

'Of course!' I said. I was thinking, 'What a strange question,' but over the years I've learned that these places all have their processes.

A few minutes later, and before I'd had the chance to talk to Shaun, Dr Rob came into the ward, grabbed Shaun's hand and said, 'Beautiful boy, we have a miracle . . .'

Now there was a rush of activity. I had to leave the ward and answer some routine questions I thought they should already have had the answers to. Like Shaun's height and weight and whether I thought he was okay for surgery. To me, it was strange and frustrating – all I wanted was for it to happen. Anyway, once I answered everything, the work really started.

Dr Rob explained the situation. 'We need to prep Shaun early,' he said. 'Because he's had so many operations on his heart, he's got a lot of scar tissue. It's like cutting through concrete. So we need to go in two hours before and cut him open – to get through the wall and get to the heart.'

We were braced for the fact that Shaun might not survive. But he wasn't going to survive anyway, so some chance was better than none.

The heart was coming from somewhere a plane flight away. It was from a little girl who'd died in a car crash. As it turns out, one of my cousins and a good friend of Shaun was the pilot of the plane that brought it over. It's strange how clinical you get over things like this. Normally I'd get sad if I heard the story of a child dying like that, but this time I didn't have that feeling. I still can't really explain the feelings in any way that makes sense.

As they were getting ready to take him away, Shaun had the biggest smile on his face. I'll never forget that look. Family members had started to arrive at the hospital, and as he left on the gurney he waved like it was nothing. His last words were, 'Don't worry, I'll see you all soon. Don't worry. Much love. I'll see you soon.'

He went through those doors and didn't come out for another fifteen hours.

It was as tough a time as any I can remember. Both our families were in the waiting-room, and the tension was so thick you could cut it with a knife. Fletch didn't help things. I wished he was elsewhere – but I was stuck with him there in that little room. Every time I looked at the clock it didn't seem to have moved, and those fifteen hours felt like 150. And I had to sit quietly, not wanting to get into a fight with Fletch . . . or Olivia . . . or her family.

All the time, my biggest thoughts were for Shaun. That's what I wanted to focus on. After the Fontan operation we'd had a couple of really good days and we thought he was going to be fine. Now he was in the middle of another big operation and was getting a new heart, and we were all feeling positive but uncertain. I knew Shaun had a big fight in front of him, but I also knew he was up for that fight, and that he'd do it with a smile on his face.

Finally, the surgeons appeared. They said the operation had been a complete success, but the first few days were critical because so many things could still go wrong. Tissue rejection was the biggest problem, as well as a host of other issues. It was going to be a very scary time. Yes, all the signs were good, but remember it was only a few days earlier that we'd thought things were okay after the Fontan operation.

Shaun was in a special room and we had to be all dressed up like a surgeon to go in and see him. As soon as I saw him, I was at ease. There were tubes everywhere coming out of his body, which was pretty confronting, but his colour was good. He was getting so much oxygen to all parts of his body.

He couldn't talk because of the tubes, and he was in and out of consciousness anyway, but he did grab my hand to reassure me because he could see the tears in my eyes. It was great to feel his touch.

But there were little issues. One day, when I was in there with Dad, the nurses said Shaun was carrying too much fluid. They returned in a couple of minutes with a tube and bucket.

'What are you going to do with that?' I asked.

'We need to push it into his rib cage to drain the fluid.'

They started to work on it while Shaun was a bit drowsy, but fully conscious. I asked about painkillers and they said they couldn't give him any. So they just pushed the tube through Shaun's rib cage and water poured into the bucket. Within seconds it was half-full.

For three days he had tubes out of each side of his body and neck. It was worrying. However, after that they decided Shaun was doing so well they took them all out and sent him into a normal room. Then they started to get him out of bed and had him walking up and down the hallway. This was amazing. I was so relieved.

Sometimes it was hard to work out how Shaun was. His spirit was so uplifting that you never got time to wallow when you were with him. It was only when you weren't with him that you wallowed.

When he and I had a chat in the days after the transplant, he said some things I'll never forget.

'Dad, I don't want to freak you out or anything.'

'All right, Shaun, what are you going to tell me now?'

'I left my body and I watched the transplant.'

'How did it feel?' I asked, wondering what an eight-year-old would have made of it.

'It felt unbelievable, Dad.'

Yes, we'd all been amazed by his spirit, but things like this started to happen more regularly now. I was beginning to realise there was much more to Shaun than just a sick boy.

SHAUN

9

EVEN THOUGH I spent most of the next few weeks lying in a hospital bed with all these draining tubes hanging out of me, I felt amazing. I was so happy to be alive and my body felt like it was hooked up to a jet engine. I swear I could feel the pumping power of my new heart surging through my system.

There were two things I kept thinking about – my epiphany with 'God', and where my new heart came from. Heart-transplant recipients aren't supposed to know anything about their organ donor, but someone accidentally let slip that one of the medical team flew all the way to Adelaide to get my heart. Just like they do on TV, surgeons there put the heart in an esky, and this person picked it up and flew back to Melbourne. Cool, huh?

Obviously, being a child, I had to have a child-sized heart, so we'd already guessed it was from another kid. There'd been some concerns that the heart might be unsuitable for me because it was a smaller size – the chest cavity determines the size of the heart you transplant. It was okay, though, and in the end this heart fitted me perfectly.

Later, one of my relatives put some of the pieces of the jigsaw together. Friends living in Adelaide at the time read in the newspaper about a tragic accident with a young girl. She was going to dancing classes when she was in a car accident and was killed. The newspaper said the little girl's family decided to donate her organs. Of course, we never found out for certain whose heart it was, but there weren't many organ donors back then, and all this guesswork made me think it must be that little girl's. It's sad that she died, but what a miracle it is that she gave me life. And I know we're not supposed to know all this stuff, but it helped me to think of her and her family.

I always wanted to thank her family for making that decision. If only they could hear from me that their daughter's heart was an awesome gift. Without them, I would have died in that hospital that night when I was only eight years old. There was so much yet to do.

I know there's a reason why you don't know who your organ donors are, and vice versa, but I was determined to make them proud of me, even though they didn't know me. I know this doesn't make sense. See, I kept thinking about my chat with 'God', who had looked after me. From now on, I was going to make it my business to help other people, including my dad, whose life was still a mess. I felt like I had a mission.

After the operation I stayed in hospital for weeks and weeks. I was put in my own isolated room in the Intensive Care Unit. Now that I was on immunosuppressant drugs, I had to be kept away from all the other patients, as the doctors didn't want me exposed to bugs and things. I found it quite difficult to move anyway. I could only walk down to the end of the corridor, but I had to do it really slowly and I had to stay connected to the drips and tubes and everything.

Susanne was working close by, so she visited me on her lunch breaks. She told me about posters she'd seen around the hospital advertising the telecast of a wrestling match on TV. The hospital had set up a 'wrestling ring' in the Starlight Room where kids could hang out and watch it. There was nothing I loved more than watching the wrestling, but because I was too sick to leave the ward the nurses agreed I could wander down the corridor for an hour or so to watch. I was really excited.

For two weeks I waited for this to happen. Every day leading up to it I'd ask Sus, 'Is it today?' Finally the big day arrived and the nurses helped me out of bed and walked me down the corridor. Even though they'd put up posters and stuff, there was hardly anyone there – just a lady and her two toddlers. Unbelievable. I guess wrestling wasn't that popular with the other kids in the hospital.

The TV wasn't set to the right channel so Sus picked up the remote and flicked it to the wrestling. 'Excuse me,' the woman complained, 'my children are watching *Teletubbies*.' I could see Sus tensing up and about to give her a blast, and tell her how I'd been in intensive care and isolation and waiting and waiting and waiting for this one day.

I squeezed Susanne's hand. 'Don't worry, Sus,' I said. 'It's okay. Let the kids watch *Teletubbies*.' Sure, I was disappointed for me, but no more feeling negative and sorry for myself. Hey, I'm lucky to be alive. Right?

And none of that matters when you're lying in bed in hospital and in walks the amazing Matthew Lloyd. At first – because he was in a white gown and stuff – I almost didn't recognise him. My hero, the best player the Bombers ever had, was right there in front of me. And he was so tall he moved to one side and whacked his head on the overhead telly. He was rubbing his head and I asked, 'Are you okay?'

'I really need to go to the toilet,' he said.

I pointed to the bathroom and said, 'Take a leak in mine.' That broke the ice and after he came back we chatted heaps about Essendon and stuff. I told Matthew about my life before my transplant and that I was super-excited that I'd be able to play footy now. Mum had arranged Matthew Lloyd's visit for me, so that was really nice.

Even though I was pretty lonely at times, in the two months after the transplant it was so good feeling that new heart beat inside of me. I felt like I could do anything. My cheeks, fingers and lips were no longer blue – they were a healthy pink! To pass the time the nurses started bringing games to play into my room and I did lots of physiotherapy exercises. Schoolwork went down the drain, but I figured I'd sort that out later.

So imagine what a blast it was when I was finally allowed home, and went back to school. I could run around the oval and kick a footy around like any normal kid. One of the greatest moments of my life happened when I played my first game of football. All my family were there and there was plenty of crying going on.

Me? I was so thrilled that this was happening. There's a photo of me at my first game. Because I was smaller than the rest they couldn't find a footy jumper anything like my size, so I was wearing this jumper which was so large it was almost to my knees. It was the smallest they had, but it looked like a dress.

Sadly, my football career didn't last long. Everyone decided that it was probably a bit rough for me. I was half the size of the other kids and a whack to the chest could have been a waste of a ripper new heart. I'd waited all my life for that moment and bang! – it was all over. After that I was into ten-pin bowling, but not for long. You don't get too many sports that have less body contact than bowling. Maybe just cards or knitting. No thanks. I'll just play Xbox.

That first heart transplant seems like a lifetime ago. Sometimes it feels like I'm back where I started, and, without trying to sound too over the top, it's like I've been given a death sentence, but the guys in the firing squad can't find their guns or something. When people find out about me they often seem surprised I'm so cool about it. Positive is the word that comes up most.

'But you seem so positive,' they say. Friends like Sondra from Alabama and the boxer, Garth Wood, reckon I'm the one giving out these positive vibes. All I'm doing, though, is listening to the big hitters in my corner – the Millers, my girlfriend Maddy and the amazing Zane Dirani – a martial arts expert and the most incredible guy I ever met, but I'll tell you more about him later. They inspire me to go the distance.

Kids with heart problems, and other things like kidney failure, end up at the 7 West Ward of the Royal Children's Hospital in Melbourne. I've spent so much time there over the years, it's become my second home. The staff there have looked after me all my life, and I like to think of them as my extended family. They weren't just good, they were fantastic.

7 West is like a little world where these great doctors and nurses look after a lot of kids who have huge problems to deal with. It can't be easy dealing with all our ups and downs, the heartbreak and the stress. But they do an amazing job.

One nurse in particular who is unforgettable is Nurse Anne, one of the transplant coordinators. She's a hard-arse – deadset – but fantastic at her job. The way I see it, Anne practically runs the hospital. All the doctors and nurses are petrified of her. She breaks everyone's balls, especially mine. Always hassling me about my medication, telling me off if I'm on my phone at night instead of sleeping. She's tough, but deep down I know Anne's a real softie. One of these days I'm going to thank her for what she's done to keep me alive.

Taking medication doesn't guarantee you won't get heart rejection – it just puts it off for the time being. When you have an organ transplant, your body tries to get rid of this foreign object. It's like, 'Who the hell are you? Get out of my body!' And it never gets used to it – it goes on for the rest of your life.

Most of the drugs I take are designed to suppress my immune system so that my body won't attack the new heart. With a suppressed immune system I get sick very easily. This is a constant problem – trying to get the balance right, so I can have enough of an immune system to beat off the flu, but not one that will reject my heart.

Life after a transplant is funny. I felt kind of strange and it's hard to explain. These new drugs I had to take were making me super hairy, especially on my back and arms. I swear I looked so different. It was weird being this li'l hairy kid. Only adults are hairy. Even some of my friends didn't recognise me, and I was like, 'Hello! It's me, Shaun!'

For a while I was worried I was turning into a werewolf or something – hence the nickname I gave myself, 'Teen Wolf'. They say it happens to girls and boys on those drugs, but it's only temporary, thank God.

I remember asking Nurse Anne if there was anything I could do to take the hair off. She told us about some cream which you rub on and rub off with a wet towel. Dad did this on my back and OMG – he had hairy palms. We both couldn't stop laughing.

I said to Dad, 'Stop that or you'll go blind.' LOL. It's okay if you don't get it – boy joke.

Up until my transplant I attended Epping Primary School from Prep. It was all stop/start stuff for me. Some years I'd be okay and other times I was so sick that I hardly went to school at all. It seemed like I was always repeating this grade and that, because I missed so much. Not that it mattered to me. What I learned at school wasn't all that interesting really.

I know my teachers won't like reading this, but I mainly liked being able to go to school so I could make new friends. The other kids in primary school were pretty friendly. And they'd let me play with them in the sandpit and on the monkey bars. After my heart transplant I could do things without getting puffed out and spent recess playing football and cricket. That was so much fun.

One of my really good friends from primary school was Jake. My mum and his mum actually knew each other; they met in the hospital when they were pregnant with us. Jake was born a few days before me and we lay next to each other in the cribs as babies. We ended up going to the same primary school. It's a small world. When I had more and more time off school, Jake and I sort of drifted apart, then he went to a different school anyway. We try to catch up regularly, and when we do it's as though we haven't been apart at all.

One day I told Jake that I was positive our Grade 4 teacher, Miss Hurley, was a witch. We'd been reading Roald Dahl's *The Witches* – he was one of my favourite authors. I thought I was an expert in recognising witches. According to the book, witches are actually bald and hideous creatures who try to hide it by dressing like normal women and wearing masks, gloves and wigs. They often get wig-rash so they try to reach under their wigs discreetly to scratch their bald heads. I swear I saw Miss Hurley move her head and scratch her scalp just like how the witches in the book do. In horror I pointed at her and yelled, 'You're a witch!'

She sent me to the principal's office. He didn't believe my claims that Miss Hurley was a witch, despite all the evidence. While he was shaking his head I said, 'You have to admit she's pretty scary looking.' The principal seemed to be trying to stop himself laughing. He then went on about how this was not a nice thing and that I had to go back to the classroom and apologise to her. So I did. But every day that I sat in her classroom, the more convinced I was that she really was a witch. Then one day at home my head was itchy so I started to scratch it. I remembered Roald Dahl's book again and began to think that maybe I was a witch too. I thought I could do magical spells and stuff. I had a crazy mind back then.

See, even though I'm now seventeen, I look like a thirteen-year-old. If I'd been born with no heart problems, I probably wouldn't have ever been a big kid, because both my parents weren't tall. But having so much less oxygen in my blood because of my heart meant that my ability to grow was affected. That, plus when you can't run around and do stuff you don't develop muscle.

As well as taking heaps of tablets I had steroid injections to help me grow bigger and taller to catch up on all the growing I missed out on. Dad has to give them to me. It's not nice for either of us. Nowadays, when I stand next to my friends, I'm almost up to their noses. Sure I'm still short, but not as short as I might have been.

CAMERON

10

SHAUN'S NEW HEART had a massive impact. Firstly it gave him life, but it also had other changes. We know the heart was from a girl who was killed in a car crash while heading to her dance classes, and thankfully her parents donated her organs. They gave my son a second chance at life, and for that I'm forever grateful.

But there were other changes the hospital just didn't want us to talk about, nor did they want us to talk to the donor's family. I didn't understand why at the time, but I do now.

Shaun suddenly started playing with dolls. He'd never done it before, but now, with the heart of a girl, he was. Realising that could either be a really positive or a completely destructive thing for her parents to know, I kept quiet for many years. But I think enough time has passed for me to talk about it.

'Don't you find it odd that he's had a heart transplant from a girl and now he's playing with Barbie dolls?'

They told me not to worry about it. They said they didn't want to talk about it – and never to bring it up again.

They were very conscious that hearts are very hard to get, especially for children, and they didn't want anything to impact that. They were uneasy with the questions, probably because they didn't have any answers, or more importantly maybe didn't want the answers. But really they didn't want people thinking that just because their child's heart was inside another person, perhaps their child was still alive in some way.

It is funny, though. After a week Shaun stopped with dolls and never picked them up again. Maybe that was just the transition?

It was hard to believe Shaun's transformation after receiving this new heart. The blood was pumping, the oxygen was hitting his muscles and organs, and all of a sudden he had all this energy – and that meant lost time to make up. His confidence rose, he played sport, and, for the first time in his life, he did all the other things that other kids did. He was all about having fun.

He was even enjoying his time in the spotlight. Having a heart transplant at the age of eight generates a bit of media attention, and the hospital and others were happy to use Shaun as a good-news story and to keep the focus on organ donation. Shaun was very world-wise, and he was becoming even more so now that he felt so healthy. He was a good talker and he was being rolled out for all sorts of media, including TV.

We were all glad to play our part in that. I mean, if those parents hadn't agreed to a donation, we wouldn't have had Shaun. How many others were missing out?

He played golf with the Nine Network's Melbourne news-reader, Peter Hitchener, up at Sanctuary Lakes and they got on like best mates. His natural charm was winning people over. This new Shaun was a great kid having a blast.

But for me it wasn't all roses. Shaun was given a Starlight Wish and was heading off to Queensland to visit the theme parks. It was great for him, but it really cut me deep when he told me.

'Dad, I've got a Starlight Wish. Me, Mum and Fletch are going but you can't come.'

That was a real kick in the guts. He wanted me to go, and I wanted to, but I couldn't. That was a pretty tough thing to absorb. However, all I really cared about was that his life was becoming a positive journey for him.

Everything in his life, except for Fletch, was good. Shaun said the heart was like a jet engine. You could hear it beating without putting your ear up to him – *boom, boom, boom*. His colour was normal and his energy levels amazing.

Much to everyone's dismay, when he was young Shaun had decided to barrack for Essendon. He did it because of the colours – he liked red and black more than the black and white of Collingwood. In his eyes, red was for the blood that ran through his body and black was for the horrible stuff that was in his arteries. He ended up loving the Bombers with a deep passion, and eventually he converted me as well.

We developed a very good relationship with the club over time too. It started just after the first heart transplant, when Shaun was still in isolation to protect him from infection. One day, the nurses began to gather around outside his room and they were all talking amongst each other. Something was happening. I just didn't know what.

Then Matthew Lloyd, the superstar full forward for Essendon, popped his head in the window and said, 'Hi Shaun, I heard you're not feeling well.'

Shaun sprung to life. Matthew Lloyd was in his room!

Matthew walked in and immediately bumped his head against the television above Shaun's bed, almost knocking himself out. He recovered from that but still looked uncomfortable, so Shaun asked him what was wrong. He was all dressed up in his gown and he was pretty awkward and nervous. 'I really need to take a leak,' was his reply. Shaun pointed him to the toilet and a much more relaxed Matthew Lloyd returned.

Matthew began to joke around with Shaun and it was just a great time. He came in a bundle of nerves, but he gradually relaxed. Shaun asked lots of questions – 'Can you kick this amount of goals? Can you try to kick ten?' Matthew was good with the banter and would return it to him. It was a side of Matthew Lloyd I'd never seen, and I think he really enjoyed himself that day.

I think Shaun just eased him into it. Yes, the full bladder was an issue to start with, but Shaun had this way with people. After talking to him, Matthew's nerves disappeared. It was amazing to see.

From there, things just kept growing with the Bombers. They were fantastic with Shaun, better than they needed to be. A lot of his friends wanted to come and see him while he was in isolation, and they couldn't. It was great the hospital let Matthew come in. I guess it was the power of footy in Melbourne, but he still had to be prepped for the visit and jump through hoops just to give Shaun someone new to talk to, rather than just his close family.

*

In some ways talking about a new heart feels like talking about a replacement battery, but nothing could be further from the truth. The body has systems in place to protect itself from outside invaders, and for most people that is generally viruses and bacteria, or maybe the odd splinter. Rarely does a bit from one human being go inside another person, but when it does the body treats it as an invader. It has no idea the new heart, kidney or whatever is there to save it.

Shaun's body knew this new heart was not his, and it did its best to get rid of it. The first step in protecting Shaun was the anti-rejection drugs. They look like horse pills, and Shaun had to take a mountain of them. He always did it with milk because he said it was easier than with water, which sounded strange to me – but whatever made it possible made me happy.

He also had to have regular biopsies to test for rejection. He had a couple in the first month – then it went monthly and then bimonthly as it stretched out. This was as simple a procedure as Shaun had to put up with, and it was done as an outpatient. The biopsy is performed through a vein located either in the right side of the neck or in the groin, using a bioptome, a long thin tube with a tiny cutting edge.

For each of these biopsies Shaun would need to be in Royal Children's Hospital very early, around 6 am, and he'd have to fast, which is called 'nil by mouth'. I had a deal with Shaun that I'd fast with him and I wouldn't eat until he could.

The anaesthesia team used to let me sit with Shaun as long as possible – as long as I put on a gown, a cap and special protective covers that slipped over my shoes to keep the outside world out of the operating theatre. I used to hold his hand as they anaesthetised him. They'd rub some cream on his other hand to numb it, then they'd insert the anaesthetic needle under the skin and ask him to count to ten. He'd usually be asleep by five.

Normally a biopsy would take around two hours. Dr Geoffrey Lane did all Shaun's biopsies with Dr Rob sitting in on them. The ones in the neck were pretty tough, but the groin was the one that would knock him for six.

The results were pretty quick since it was all about looking at the pieces of heart muscle they'd removed under an electron microscope. When we got bad news I'd hold it all together until I was on my own, and then I'd fall apart. I never wanted Shaun to see me cry.

I hated waiting for the results.

But as I found out, a negative result wasn't always that bad. It happened to Shaun four times with this first heart. They'd play around with the medication and throw him onto a steroid drip and then he was all okay again. Good as gold – well nearly.

It didn't take long after heading home from hospital that Shaun was bursting with life and energy. So now he turned his attention to footy. He'd always wanted to play football and he made no secret of this fact during some of the media that came with being an eight-year-old boy having a heart transplant. Before he even left the hospital, the Mernda Football Club – from just up the road from home – came and spoke to us about giving him a run.

Unlike me, Shaun could actually play football. He could kick a footy and take marks too. Shaun was undersized for his age, but although the size difference was scary for me as a father, it didn't worry him at all.

I remember asking him once, 'Are you sure about going to play in the Diamond Valley? It's pretty rough out there, mate.'

His response was typically simple. 'Yeah, absolutely.'

So when he got out of hospital, he had to do all his physio and what they call 'blowing bubbles'. This was to test that he was getting enough oxygen and that everything was okay with the lungs. Often after a heart transplant there can be a build-up of fluids around the lungs, and with this simple process with a bottle and a tube, Shaun would blow bubbles, which would help with the fluids in his system.

Once he got the all-clear, we headed down to the footy club. His jumper went down past his knees – it was like a dress but he was over the moon. He had to wear a chest protector and it was nervous times – for me, anyway.

'Shaun, maybe just take it easy,' I told him. 'Don't go in too hard.'

My God! The ball bounced and he immediately tackled the biggest bloke on the field and put him to the ground. Then he grabbed the ball and kicked it down to the forward line. He was so hard at it, it blew me away. He got hurt during the third quarter with a big hip and shoulder from some giant. I knew I wasn't allowed to, but fearing the worst, I ran onto the field. Fortunately, he was only winded. That absolutely freaked me out, though.

Even with that scare, he kept wanting to play, which he did for a while. But it was just getting too hard. CHD really ruins lives in more ways than one. In Shaun's case it ripped him away from the sport he loved.

SHAUN

11

I WENT TO my first Heart Camp when I was ten years old. Each year the Royal Children's Hospital – through the Heart Throb Auxiliary – raises money to pay for this camp for kids with heart problems. It's four days and three nights over a weekend, usually in November, and each year it's held somewhere different. Kids come from all over the place. Even though it's called a 'camp' we're not sleeping in tents and stuff, but cabins. And we don't go hiking or make fires. It's stuff like archery, going to the aquarium, zooming over a river on a flying fox, or swinging out over it on a giant swing.

The nurses were the ones who convinced me to go. Nurse Anne told me camp was fun and I'd be meeting other heart kids. I'd never even been on a school camp before, because teachers don't want to know you when you have a heart condition and something might go wrong. I can't blame them, but on Heart Camp there are doctors around and the organisers know what everyone can and can't do.

Plenty of nurses and doctors from the 7 West Ward are there so it's as safe as being at the hospital. And everyone has a set nurse – about five kids to one – and the older kids always look after the younger ones. The other good thing is that you're meeting kids with similar problems and limitations who often feel a bit lonely, so it's great to be around others in the same boat.

Dad had asked the hospital if he could come with me on my first camp and they very definitely said 'No'. Parents are banned and for good reason too. The whole idea of the camp is to provide a place where sick kids can talk to each other. But that won't happen if we're shy and quiet beside our parents. It's hard like that to break out of our shells and let loose.

On the bus I found a seat next to the window and watched as the other kids boarded. They were just regular kids – like me. If you walked past them on a street you'd never know there was something wrong with them. Some of the kids already knew each other from previous camps, but I sat by myself.

As I was walking down the steps of the bus when we arrived at our camp, I heard this amazing laugh. It was beautiful – really fresh and full of fun. The laughter was coming from a young girl, about my age, with long brown hair. She seemed to notice that I was looking at her, so I said, 'Oh hi, I'm Shaun.'

The girl smiled. She was real pretty. 'Hi, I'm Maddy.'

I may as well fess up now and tell you that I had a crush on Maddy from that moment. Not that it made any difference. After our first meeting I was the invisible man, more or less, for a long time. I reckon that she hadn't a clue who I was, even though I'd introduced myself. She became one of the main reasons I kept going to Heart Camp.

Her real name is Madeleine and this is her story. She's the oldest kid in her family and has two younger brothers and a younger sister and they all live in Melbourne with their mum and dad. Maddy was born with Mitral Stenosis and she's had five open-heart surgeries. When she was a baby she seemed fine, but when the doctors listened to her heart with a stethoscope, they could hear a murmur.

She was six months old when she had her first surgery. Since then she's had two repairs and two replacements on the mitral valve. With her condition, she can't get piercings or tattoos either, because if they become infected, her mitral valve will be damaged. And she's on blood-thinning medication so any type of bleeding is not good for her. Even though the operations were successful, repairs and replacements eventually wear out. However, apart from replacing the valve every once in a while, the doctors say she can have a normal life.

As I was saying, Maddy never noticed me and I can prove it. After I'd been going to camps for a couple of years there was a fun night when we played the old game of Spin the Bottle. A bunch of us were sitting in a circle, and when it was my turn I spun it and it slowed to a stop and pointed right at Maddy. The rules are that we had to kiss. I jumped up and blurted out, 'I've been waiting for this!'

Maddy had this puzzled look on her face. 'Who are you?'

'Shaun. I'm Shaun.'

'Hi, I'm Maddy.'

It was a bit of a blow to the ego, but at least I had the opportunity of kissing her, which was definitely worth the wait. I thought Maddy might realise then that I had a crush on her, but it never happened. However, the great thing was that after our Spin the Bottle kiss we started to click and became close friends.

We laugh over stupid things that no-one else gets. On the last night of camp every year there's a talent show. One time Maddy convinced me to dress up as a girl. Why I agreed I have no idea – I mustn't have had a brain then. I wore one of Maddy's skirts and tops, a headpiece, and a whole heap of make-up – blush, eyeliner and mascara. Embarrassing stuff now that I think back on it. The trouble is that Maddy refuses to delete the photos from her phone. She'll whip them out occasionally and start giggling and I'm thinking, 'Oh God, why'd I do that?'

Of course we often get up to mischief at camp. The girls sneak into the boys' cabins and the boys sneak into the girls'.

Another thing I liked about camp was helping other kids. I remember this kid who was seven years old talking to me because he had surgery coming up and was real worried. I told him all he had to do was stay positive.

I said something like, 'Okay so you have to fast before going in to the surgery, but think about it like this. You're just going to fall asleep. Then when you wake up you can eat some nuggets.'

Dumb stuff, but this kid goes, 'Oh wow, okay!'

It was always good times at camp. And I made heaps of new friends who go through what I go through: Ash, Tommy, Aaron, Bee, Matt, Luke, Paige, Sophie, Courtney, Jayden, and of course Maddy. They get me. They've experienced it themselves. We're in an exclusive club called the Zipper Club, because our scars look like a zipper and each time the doctors need to go inside your chest again they open up the zipper. Maddy has a zipper and I think she's beautiful.

What's great about having a group of friends like this is whenever I'm sick or in hospital, I can talk to someone who understands me. We all go through much the same thing and chat all the time on Facebook. We've tried to meet up face to face but it's hard because everyone lives all over Australia. So our main catch-up is at camp.

On one of my first ever Heart Camps I met this great guy, Christian Williams. Some people say about me that I never give up, but I'm nothing compared to my friend Christian. His dream was the London 2012 Olympics. He was into lacrosse, one of those weird games the American Indians played, and he captained the Australian U19s squad, then the U21s and went off to the Institute of Sport in Canberra.

One day Christian noticed that he couldn't run a single lap around an oval without feeling like he was going to pass out. Sometimes, he'd black out during training, or literally wake up on the side of the road after doing sprints, covered in his own vomit, and not have a clue where he was or how long he'd been there. He knew there was something wrong, but because he was so young and so fit the doctors didn't listen to him. Once he said to a doctor, 'I think I just had a heart attack.' They'd say, 'No way. That's impossible.'

As an athlete his instinct was to keep pushing and it was about two years before he finally got some serious help. He walked into the Alfred Hospital in Melbourne and said, 'Listen. This is ridiculous. I know my body and I know when something isn't right. I'm not on drugs, and I'm sure as hell not faking it. Can someone please help me!'

They did all these tests and scans and stuff, and sure enough he had a heart condition called Atrial Tachycardia. That second word is real hard to say. It's a rhythm problem which causes the heart to beat too fast. At rest, his heart rate was 150–160, which is double the normal rate. Christian's heart would race out of control then stop completely. He was gutted when he was given the news about his condition. That's when he became involved with HeartKids – which is how I met him.

One of the hardest things for Christian was that the diagnosis came as a complete surprise. I've been battling with my heart problems all my life and still find it hard to accept. There's no history of it in his family, and he's otherwise really fit and healthy. 'There are others way worse off,' he'd say, 'although I'd rather have a dodgy hamstring.' He's good for a laugh.

Because of his condition, Christian was told that if he continued playing lacrosse it'd kill him. He wasn't ready to give up sport just yet – he loved it too much. Next he started hammer throwing, as it was less strenuous on the heart, and he became a top hammer thrower for Victoria. But then his doctors said he had to give that up as well, so Christian got into luge instead. Luge is a Winter Olympics sport where these guys all jump into this rollercoaster thing flying down this tube.

When the doctors found out, they went berserk. 'Christian, you've got to be kidding. Are you trying to get yourself killed!?'

No matter what sport he tried, it turned out that his heart couldn't handle it. He was at high risk of sudden death during exercise.

'What about ping pong?' I asked him.

'Nah, only the Chinese are good at ping pong,' he said.

'Okay then,' I said, 'what about lawn bowls?'

'What?! I'm not that old!'

Since then, Christian has gone into archery, which is the sport he reckons is the least likely to kill him.

I'll never forget how much Christian helped me at Heart Camp. All us kids were sitting in a circle with a psychologist. I used to be very quiet around other kids. I didn't know how to act. I was self-conscious about my height and hated being such a midget. That day, the psychologist encouraged us to shout out anything that came to mind. It could be something that made us angry, something that we were scared of – whatever.

I ended up saying some things about my stepfather which wasn't too crash hot. I was a bit hesitant to share that stuff, but the response from Christian and the others in that circle surprised me. It made me realise that I was valued for who I was and that the other kids actually liked me. At that camp I felt better about myself. Now if I see someone who's feeling the same way I say, 'It's all right. I'm short as well.'

Somehow, over the years, I really thrived at Heart Camp and came out of my shell a bit. Once I was able to express what I felt about things, I could get on with being a kid and not worry about what people were thinking of me and all that stuff. At the end of the day, kids with heart problems are just kids! Sometimes people forget that. A lot of people I meet instantly paint this picture in their heads of how horrible life must be for me, whereas I just see myself as a normal kid who loves to play Xbox.

SHAUN

12

AFTER DAD WAS out of the picture, Mum was still young, so of course she started seeing other guys. Over the years a few came and went, and then she began dating a guy named Fletch. I have to be careful what I say about him, because my opinion is obviously affected by what happened down the track. So maybe I'll just try and stick to the facts. Fletch is a skinny kind of guy, with a beard and a few tatts.

Unfortunately, when Dad used to come to the house to pick me up, Fletch joined in on the 'game' of causing trouble between Mum and Dad. I mean, he could have been smart and said to her, 'Shaun's not my kid and this is none of my business.' Instead, he had to put in his two cents' worth. And he was far worse than Mum.

Although she was always horrible to Dad, at least she wasn't threatening. Almost every time Dad came over to pick me up, Fletch would be standing there leering at him. He kept trying to rile Dad up, trying to make him snap so he had an excuse to fight him. I was proud of Dad. He ignored Fletch and did everything to avoid trouble.

I thought Fletch was mean to my mum as well. Sometimes he bossed her around, and I loved Mum so this was hard to watch. Her health was not so good either. She developed viral meningitis even though she was in her late thirties and it's more common in children.

Some weekends I'd be at Dad's, crying and begging him not to take me back – not because of Mum, but because of Fletch. It was terrible for Dad. Because of the legal system there was nothing he could do. Mum would threaten to call the police if I wasn't home by exactly four o'clock on a Sunday afternoon. I think she knew I wanted to live with Dad, but it hurt her to think of losing me because she'd been there all the way for me.

One weekend I was having a normal visit with Dad. We were having lunch with Nanna and Poppy when there was a knock at the door, and when Dad answered it, he closed the door and stepped outside. I opened it and standing there on the front step was Fletch and one of his mates. I knew straightaway they'd been drinking. 'Oh my God, what are they doing here?' I thought. 'This is my safe place. What do they want?'

I was so terrified I actually passed out. Poppy John slammed the door on them and called the police and the ambulance. The police arrived and told them to clear out. They were just being bullies, but they didn't stop to think about how it all affected me. The ambulance guys were great and made sure I was okay.

Around 2006 Mum and Fletch announced their engagement. The wedding was in September and on the big day Mum seemed very happy so I was happy for her. My stepsister and I were in the bridal party. We had to look sharp. Even Fletch was in pretty good spirits that day.

My relationship with Fletch was at odds from the start. I think he saw me as a smaller version of my father who he – for no real reason at all – hated big time. Maybe I was a constant reminder of the man he despised. For me things were at their best when Fletch ignored me. I hated being left in the house alone with him and often stayed in my room when Mum was out. And if Fletch wasn't an easy man to get along with when sober, things went to a whole new level after he'd had a few drinks. He was angrier, louder and more horrible.

One thing he did was turn me off drinking for good. Now when I see people drinking I feel uncomfortable – even if it's at a barbeque and everyone's having a good time. Seeing someone pick up a can of beer instantly reminds me of Fletch. He made me feel like crap. I was miserable wherever I went and became quiet and introverted. It was blatantly obvious to anyone that I didn't enjoy living with Mum and him.

During this period, my health was not so good and being so stressed out and living in that house didn't help. The biggest problem was that the new heart I received when I was eight was failing.

Transplant organs are not a cure for life. They say a new heart can give you anything from ten to fifteen years, but that wasn't the case for me. I was only thirteen, and for the second time in my life I was put on the waiting list for a new heart. My doctors discovered that my arteries were narrowing and becoming blocked. I had chest pains due to a lack of oxygen-rich blood flowing to my heart. I had coronary artery disease – exactly the same as I have now.

It's one of those things that sometimes happens to transplant patients. Eventually, due to the lack of blood, the heart will stop, so I needed another heart. As you can imagine these were unhappy and scary days for me and both my families.

I'd already had one miracle. And miracles don't come along very often, so how on earth could I get another? The funny thing was that I remember Dad started going to church – let's just say this was new for him. He figured that getting a little closer to God might bump me up on the miracle priority list.

One night I was minding my own business watching TV. Then my little stepsister came in and changed the channel. 'Hey! I was watching that.'

'My show's on, so too bad.'

'Please switch it back,' I asked. 'You can watch it on the other television.'

'No, because it doesn't have Foxtel and mine's on Foxtel.'

I suggested that she wait half an hour for my program to finish, but she wouldn't budge. Furious that she wouldn't even let me flick to my program in the ad breaks I lashed out, 'I'll bloody kill you, you little brat.' Big mistake.

Fletch obviously heard this from the kitchen. 'Oi,' he said threateningly, 'come 'ere.'

I walked into the kitchen and stood there crapping myself. He was sitting in a chair and slowly stood up real close to me. 'What'd you just say?' When I hung my head and said nothing, he repeated it, this time louder. 'What'd you just say?'

'Nothing. I didn't say anything.'

'You're a little liar,' he said. Then he shouted, 'What did you say? Answer me, you bastard! What did you say?'

I was shaking and mumbled, 'I said I wanted to kill her.'

Fletch grabbed me, put his hands around my neck, and slammed me up against the sink. I was pinned and unable to move. He was very strong and the pressure was hurting me. I tried to scream but nothing came out. He probably said things to me, but it wasn't really registering because I was just concentrating on trying to breathe.

Who knows how long he had me like that? It seemed like forever. Finally, he let me go. I struggled to get my breath back and went to my room like some piece of garbage. He probably thought it was no big deal, like this was his idea of discipline and stuff, but I was terrified.

Sometime later Mum came in and sat on the bed. When she asked why I was crying I told her, 'He hurt me. He tried to choke me, Mum!'

She stood up and from the doorway said disappointedly, 'You mustn't tell lies, Shaun.'

I cried myself to sleep that night and it wasn't the first time.

The downside for bullies is that there's one thing they can't control – nature: that prolonged pressure applied to skin results in bruising. Next day at school I made very little effort to talk to the other kids. Usually I was very into class discussions, but I was completely out of it. My teacher noticed something was up and took me out of the classroom for a talk.

She asked what was wrong. 'Just family stuff,' I said.

'You can tell me anything, because I'll help you any way I can.'

'It's nothing really.'

She was watching my face real intensely, trying to understand my reactions, I guess. And then she noticed something. 'What's that?' she asked, pointing to my chin. I had no idea what she was talking about. 'Oh my God, it's a bruise.' When Fletch grabbed me he must have left his thumbprint on my face.

With those words the system which protects the welfare of children sprang into life. My teacher took me to the principal who alerted the Department of Human Services and they came and interviewed me at school. Then we drove to Mum and Fletch's house. The DHS case manager and her assistant knocked on the door and spoke to Mum and him.

I told the DHS people I wanted to go and live with my dad and they agreed that was best. 'What about your things?' one of the DHS people asked. Mum then disappeared for a few minutes. She walked into my room and closed the door behind her. When she came out she had in her hand a bag packed full of my stuff.

Instead of handing it to me, she chucked the bag onto the front yard. And because she hadn't zipped it properly, my clothes and stuff ended up scattered all across the lawn. 'Just get out, Shaun!' she yelled. I was heartbroken and devastated. All I'd done was tell the truth.

DHS drove me to my grandparents' place. Dad met me with a big hug and a lovely smile. 'You're safe now,' he told me. Everyone was so relieved that I was safe.

This was the beginning of a special period in my life, but something told me that we hadn't heard the last of Fletch.

The next day I was interviewed by the police at Fawkner Police Station. The detectives there said, 'Shaun, we're going to talk to you one on one and videotape you. Okay?'

'That's cool.'

Basically I told the detectives what went down a couple of nights earlier and they recorded it all on video. After that, they took photos of my bruises. The cops said the next step was to interview my mum.

Around a week later the police rang Dad. They said that when they spoke to Mum she denied everything that I had claimed happened, and told them Fletch would never do a thing like that. So they tried to interview Fletch, but he refused to say anything.

Because of all this, there wasn't enough evidence to charge him. 'Even though we have Shaun's evidence, which is very good,' the detective said, 'it has to be beyond a reasonable doubt to get a conviction.'

What hurt the most, though, was that Mum had chosen Fletch over me.

Since leaving Mum's place, I'd grown more distant from her side of the family and that really hurt, so because of this I dropped the hyphenated surname and started calling myself Shaun Miller. It was a pity because I really missed seeing them. I hoped they knew that I love them heaps and didn't stop thinking about them. For the next few years I had very little contact with any of that side of the family.

Apparently, after I left, Fletch cut my face out of all the photos of me in the house, including the ones of me at their wedding. After what happened I didn't really want anything to do with my mother again. Not because I'm carrying a grudge – I'm not like that – it's just painful to think that she chose him over my safety.

When I started thinking about writing this book, I wanted to tell the real story about my life. This did happen. Fletch was a bully and bullies shouldn't be protected – ever. If me telling my story helps just one kid speak up, then it'll be worth it.

Although I was safe now that I'd moved in with Dad, I was still frightened of Fletch. He terrified me. Even being removed from the house by DHS didn't stop my fears. I remember being so distressed after that day that I barely spoke to anybody for a week. Then I kept having terrible nightmares which lasted over a year.

Dad started receiving anonymous abusive text messages and then phone calls where the person would hang up the moment he answered. The police told him to get a restraining order against Fletch.

The whole process of getting the restraining order took almost a year. When Dad and I walked out of the courthouse, we were stoked.

CAMERON

13

THE GAMES WITH Olivia and Fletch had started pretty much as soon as things settled down from the first transplant, and for three or four years they progressively got worse. Heart transplants aren't a be-all and end-all – they're often nothing more than a bandaid solution. Stupidly, Olivia and Fletch couldn't see that. They thought he was fixed forever, so they turned their attention back to me and, even though I didn't know it at the time, Shaun.

I'd started working with lawyers to try to get more time with Shaun, but the courts back then rarely gave more than every second weekend to fathers. I did get extra time each week on a Wednesday night, which I was happy about, even though I thought I deserved more.

My lawyers were pretty shocked to hear about some of the behaviour towards me and my family. I wish I'd got legal advice earlier, if only to give me enough confidence to pursue what I knew was right.

As it turns out, that Wednesday night was such a great thing for us. Shaun and I started to bond even more and I loved that.

I was still living with my parents at that stage, and Shaun had his own room there. Because I needed a steady income, I was back in glazing working for my mate Pat in his business, Quick Glaze, and also had my massage business on the side for the days I didn't have Shaun.

From the age of eight until Shaun was thirteen, it was like Groundhog Day. It was just the same thing: pick Shaun up, take him home and, if I dropped him back to Olivia, have the door slammed in my face. That was on the days she wasn't in a bad mood and would let me take him. It was a nightmare.

Olivia and Fletch got married when Shaun was nine, I think. They made some moves to have Fletch appointed as Shaun's legal guardian, but I blocked that pretty quickly.

Fletch had stopped his shit with Shaun for a while and was being super-nice. It made Shaun uneasy. He told Shaun he was there now and that I'd be gone soon enough. Shaun was really open with me now, although he was still holding some stuff back. But one day he started to tell me about the other stuff, about the abuse when Fletch had drunk a bit. It wasn't just to Shaun either – Olivia always had bruises. Shaun told me Fletch had pushed her face into a cake one day when he was angry.

Shaun wanted out of there now. I've still got the emails he was sending me. He was meeting regularly with a psychologist at the hospital and I think he was talking to them about what was going on at Olivia's house. I did call DHS a few times, but they were having none of it and told me I was paranoid. I wasn't. I knew I had to do something.

At one stage, the hospital called Olivia in and the psych had a discussion with her about how she felt Shaun would be better off living at my place, because he'd be a lot happier. She disagreed and had a go at the psychologist – which kind of proved the point.

Then Olivia started to get worse at home. It was all over the place because Shaun was rejecting Fletch's 'niceness', so Olivia would say to me, 'Just take him.' And the next day she'd be the other way.

So we started work on getting custody. I was still regularly being threatened by Fletch. I got anonymous phone calls too: 'Let go of that court shit right now or you are going to get it.' I couldn't understand why it mattered to him. When I heard how Fletch was treating Shaun, it wasn't like he appeared to have any concern for him. Then one day he grabbed Shaun by the throat and pushed him up against the wall. That was it.

Shaun was now petrified of Fletch. Even the day before he died he said he didn't want Fletch near him or his grave.

What Fletch didn't understand when he put his hands around Shaun's throat that day is that because Shaun was on Warfarin, he could bleed easily. It meant he bruised easily as well, and the mark of Fletch's hands was so visible the police acted straightaway.

Some of Shaun's emails to me showed a distinct pattern and his mother knew what was going on. He said she'd put make-up on him to cover up some of the bruises that Fletch left when he hit him. But Shaun's emails hadn't been enough for DHS. They'd just fobbed me off again.

These bruises were finally what we needed. Because I wasn't allowed to see Shaun all the time, I had no real idea how bad it was, but after this incident I got a call from the school. Shaun had told the school principal everything. When the principal saw all the bruises around his throat, she called in DHS, and now they finally cared.

After the DHS, the police got involved and then the Sexual Offences and Child Abuse Investigation Team (SOCIT), to make sure there wasn't anything more sinister going on, which thankfully there wasn't. I wasn't allowed to go to the school yet, but the principal told me not to worry. She said that because of Shaun's allegations she had to handle the situation according to very specific guidelines, but that it would be okay and Shaun was being well looked after.

But I was worried.

However, DHS did handle it – finally. They immediately told me they'd be taking Shaun away from Olivia and Fletch and that I'd need to be his full-time carer, at least for the short term.

At about six o'clock that night the DHS people looking after Shaun went to Olivia and Fletch's house. They told them they knew what was going on, that Shaun had told them everything, and that they were taking him out of their care because they believed he was physically and emotionally in danger. I wasn't allowed to be present, so I was sitting and waiting at home. I was going to do this by the books, but I wanted to know what was going on, so my sister and her boyfriend sat in a car nearby and watched it all. They said there was a lot of shouting, and Shaun confirmed later there was lots of arguing.

At one stage, the police had to restrain Fletch. It took a long time to get Shaun out the door with some of his stuff, which was the whole point of the visit. It was pouring with rain, and when Olivia came out of the front door with the rest of his stuff, she just threw it onto the lawn. Shaun was devastated.

They brought Shaun to my house in Lalor and went over everything with me. Shaun was so happy to see me, but he wasn't talking. He didn't say a word. As you'd expect, this had all shaken him a lot.

The detectives came over the next day. These big beasts from Fawkner SOCIT walked through the door – one guy was so huge he nearly hit the top of the doorframe with his head. They asked Shaun what he wanted to happen.

'I really want Fletch to go to jail for what he's done to me. He really hurt me. He strangled me and I couldn't breathe, and I thought I was gonna die.' To my mind, this was staggering, given that Shaun was now waiting for his second heart transplant – we're getting ahead of ourselves, but we'll talk about that soon. 'I want him to feel pain like I felt.'

One of these giants then said, 'We'll make sure of it.'

A couple of days later Shaun had to go down to the police station to make a formal report. Before the officers started the recording, they asked him if he knew the difference between lying and telling the truth. Shaun said, 'Yes, I wouldn't perjure myself.'

It was quite funny. They turned to me and said, 'Where did he get that from?'

'I don't know,' I said, 'but that's Shaun.'

They took him in and they did a full video. I wasn't allowed to be in there so I don't know what was said. Afterwards they told me they had to investigate some more. A week later, they came back and told me Olivia wouldn't support what Shaun was saying.

They said, 'We've sat down with Fletch and Shaun's mum, and the mum swears on a pack of Bibles that physical abuse never happened at any time. We have to have what's called "beyond reasonable doubt" to make charges stick, so we can't really do anything else. But although we can't charge Fletch, we think you need to get a restraining order against him.'

Shaun was devastated that his mother lied for Fletch. In the car on the way home he turned to me and said, 'I've got no mother, Dad. From this day on, I've got no mother.'

I didn't know what to say. I was speechless. I was beyond tears myself.

If Olivia had told the truth and supported her son, they would have charged Fletch and he would have been locked up. It might have helped her too, given she was being hit as well. Instead she was happy to cause more harm to her son.

The police were upset that they couldn't help Shaun the way they wanted. We went out to Essendon Airport one day and they took him up in the police helicopter. It was a great gesture and Shaun really appreciated it.

Then we started on the restraining order. Fletch decided to fight it, which meant he came to court. We were getting two restraining orders – one to cover me and one to cover Shaun, so we both had to be there. We were all sitting in a room together and there was a big Kiwi security guard there for our protection. Fletch eyeballed me and Shaun.

The security guard saw all of this, and Shaun told him that the looks were making him uncomfortable. The guard said, 'Is that right?' He walked over to Fletch and spoke to him for about five minutes. He came back and said to Shaun, 'I think he's got small man disease. He won't bother you again.'

Since the burden of proof was different to criminal matters, we didn't have any trouble getting the restraining order, and Fletch was out of our lives for two years. And because Olivia was supporting Fletch that was it for her too, because she could only see Shaun without Fletch. Shaun and I were so relieved. So were all of my family.

Not that it was all over. I found out I had to go back to the county court for a DHS hearing as well. That was about three or four months later and, fortunately, I was able to do that without

Shaun. Both Olivia and Fletch were there and they weren't happy. They were just giving me evil looks whenever they could. In the end the part in front of the judge for me was maybe two minutes, and it was over.

Then the judge turned around to Olivia and Fletch and said, 'I understand that you abused this child, who has been waiting for a heart transplant, a second heart transplant. He has been through more than enough in his life. What have you got to say for yourself?'

They said they didn't physically abuse him, but they didn't deny abusing him in a way that I rated as mental abuse, even if they didn't see it the same way.

The judge just kept going at them and in the end he awarded me full custody of Shaun. That was pretty much it for Shaun with his mother, so in 2008 at the age of thirteen he wiped her out of his life. He didn't want anything to do with her, and for a few years she didn't seem to want anything to do with him.

She did eventually reach out to Shaun. After a lot of stalling, he allowed her to see him with what we called McDonald's visits. With the restraining order in place, I couldn't take him to his mother's house while Fletch was there. I was too scared anyway, so it was McDonald's for her.

We did get a second Apprehended Violence Order when the first one ran out, but we were always disappointed that Fletch didn't have to face court for his actions. He should have gone to jail, but at least we got him out of our lives.

SHAUN

14

ALTHOUGH I WAS feeling great, every now and then I'd find myself back in 7 West with Nurse Anne and the rest of them. At the hospital they're always checking that we're taking the right medication at the right time. The pills I take mean the difference between life and death and yet I hate them. Hate pills with a passion.

After that first heart transplant, I had to take a stack of tablets every morning and every night. I'm supposed to take them at the exact same time, but sometimes I don't want to and my family get really upset with me. Like they get frustrated and start crying and stuff, because they know the consequences. Don't worry, so do I. I'm not stupid. But they taste yuck and you lose your appetite. And you can't wash them down with water because they leave a horrible taste in your mouth, so I use milk. I hate it when the pills fizzle in my mouth, and I take so many that I'm really fussy about my brand of milk. I like Pauls milk, and it needs to be super cold. These small things make a big difference.

Nothing I eat afterwards tastes any good. My family are always telling me I don't eat enough. Although they keep me alive, the side effects of my pills are that they increase the risk of skin cancer and my chances of getting infections. Plus, they rot my teeth. Once I had mouth ulcers so bad I was hospitalised for three weeks. Dr Rob says medication and teenagers are a battle, and he's right. I know about this firsthand.

Most teenagers battle with stuff like pimples and school marks, so my battles are different. Kids my age shouldn't have to worry about this stuff because we just want to be out kicking the footy around and kissing girls.

I've made good friends with other kids at the hospital. One is Zavier, a kidney transplant patient. He was in the same room as me for a few days in 2007, so we got to know each other. We played computer games together and all that and we've been friends ever since. Zavier's had a tough family life. Now he lives with his nanna and grandad. He's twenty-one now and his nanna still helps look after him. She's an amazing lady. Zav gets me because he takes tablets and has had stacks of operations too. He lives in the country; otherwise we'd hang out all the time.

Another great mate is Nick, who is also a kidney transplant patient. Nick was born with kidney failure, so he's currently on dialysis every night for up to twelve hours. On the day I met him, Nick was scheduled for surgery and was lying in the bed opposite me. I noticed that he looked quite glum.

'Don't worry, buddy. I've been through a lot. You can handle this!' I said to him encouragingly.

I don't think he realised how miserable he looked until then. I cheered him up a bit and then it was time for his operation.

When he came back a few hours later he looked much happier. 'Told you, mate. It wasn't that hard!'

He grinned and said, 'Thanks for the advice.'

We've been great friends ever since. I'm only a year older than Nick, who's sixteen. We live in different areas so we don't go to the same school. He lives right near the hospital which always makes me a bit jealous, because I hated the early morning heart clinics and my trip was so long. It meant we'd have to get up so early to avoid the traffic and Dad would get mega-stressed if we were running late – which was always.

When Nick and I got to know each other better we started to hang out every couple of weeks and we still do. If it's a weekend I'll go over to his house or he'll come over to my place. Like me, Nick loves playing Xbox and watching WWE or AFL. We've been to a few footy games with both our dads, who are now friends as well. Like me, Nick just lives with his dad, so that's something else we have in common.

Let me tell you about my friend, Michael. This guy has it all. Seriously. He's not a heart or kidney patient – he's as healthy as can be. We're the same age, but he's heaps taller than me because he's got a regular heart. Michael used to stay over and Dad would take us to Maccas. Michael would eat like a horse and freak Dad out. He used to joke about my appetite. I was cheap to feed – LOL.

Michael was an awesome tennis player. You've no idea how hard I had to work to get around that tennis court when versing him. Michael has these long arms and legs and he's just got it. He's also smart because he hasn't missed lots of school like me, Zav and Nick. Like I said, he's got it all – smart, tall, fit and athletic.

But you know what – he takes it all for granted, and last I saw of him he was getting mixed up in some crazy shit, hanging out with some bad eggs, missing school and getting into trouble. Dad had a chat to him to try to make him see that he was going off the rails. I'm not sure whether that made a difference or not. But, Michael, if you read my book I want to tell you that you're pretty awesome and you've got a lot going for you. I want you to try for me. Do all the things that I can't. Okay?

And every year I continued to go to Heart Camps. It was great catching up with the friends I knew there, especially Maddy. The thing I love about her is that she isn't afraid of anything. Like me, she's small, and yet despite all those operations and all the danger she faces she's so strong as a person.

She's in Year 11 and studies Health and Human Development, PE, English, Maths and Business Management. I used to miss a lot of school, but Maddy only misses a day or two a week. As well as heart problems, she has a weak immune system so she catches the flu easily. She also gets chest pains from one of the wires from surgery sticking out and rubbing against her sternum walls. When she's sick, the school sends her work to do at home and if she's in the hospital, they only send her the work that's compulsory.

Her dream is to go on to study at university and become a paediatric nurse. She'd be a great nurse because she has a beautiful smile and she's really smart, so I know she can get there.

Because she takes blood thinners to reduce the risk of a heart attack or stroke, Maddy can't really play sport. We both love watching sport on TV, though, especially football. We're massive Essendon Bombers supporters; nearly everyone I know is. I like watching my WWE as well but Maddy's not that into wrestling. She says she doesn't really like watching people knock each other out.

Maddy's probably the world's biggest Eminem fan. She'll listen to him on repeat for a whole day and could probably go a whole week. We bought tickets to see his concert when he toured Melbourne, but she got sick and ended up in hospital that night. She also likes Lady Gaga and her wacky costumes. Personally, I prefer Shannon Noll songs. My favourite one is 'Lift'.

Neither of us read books much but we are huge Facebook-a-holics. Facebook is our reading. Back in the day, we used to only see and talk to each other once a year at the Heart Camp, because we weren't great friends yet. But then Facebook came along and changed all that when we were around thirteen. We could chat online and catch up whenever. It was because of that and Heart Camps that we became close friends.

Because I always had these feelings for Maddy I'm a bit embarrassed to admit that I hated it when other boys liked her too. A few years ago, when Maddy was about fifteen, she had this boyfriend who treated her like crap. He was a massive jerk. Always bagging her out and borrowing money from her. It was as though he was ashamed of her. All Maddy's friends disapproved of him, especially me. 'You have to dump him,' I told her.

'You need to back off. This is my business,' Maddy shot back angrily. Even though he was such a loser she was always trying to defend him. I tried to stand by her anyway. She was one of my closest friends. I don't know why she wanted to stay with him, but I wanted to still be there for her. I figured she'd work it out eventually.

Maddy and this guy ended up having a massive argument one day. Somehow her parents and his mates got involved. It didn't turn out good, because she was so stressed out she was rushed to hospital. Then this jerk told her it was her own fault that she ended up there. He didn't even bother visiting her. He just never understood how sick she was. I went to see her in hospital. I'd just sit by her bed and be there for her. After that I think it dawned on her that she didn't need this guy in her life. Secretly, I was hoping she needed me instead.

CAMERON

15

In 2007, Shaun had started secondary school at Craigieburn High. On an excursion to Werribee Zoo, he had some issues that landed him back in hospital. Luckily it was just heatstroke, but there were signs that his second heart was beginning to struggle.

His biopsies were routine: into the hospital at 6 am and wait with Shaun until they were ready for him. The anaesthetist put the needle in his arm, they counted back from ten to one, and he was away, as ever, before the anaesthetist even got to five. I always kissed Shaun goodbye because you didn't know what was going to happen. Things could go wrong – including a stroke – whether they went through the neck with the catheter wire – the easier one for both the patient and the doctors – or the groin, which sometimes they had to do to get access to different arteries.

Sometimes the results came back with nothing; other times the doctors needed to tweak his medicine a bit. In January 2008, they told us that Shaun's body was finally succeeding in rejecting the heart and that his arteries were thinning. He was going to need another heart – thankfully it wasn't as urgent as when they'd told us last time. It didn't matter, though, it hit me like a tonne of bricks. I was more broken than Shaun.

When I walked in to see him, and he hadn't been told at this stage, I just broke down. I really couldn't believe it was happening again.

Later that year, in June, during one of Shaun's stays at the Royal Children's they wanted him to have a stent put in at the Alfred Hospital, ten kilometres away but on the other side of the city. His energy levels were really starting to drop, and they hoped that by putting the stent in and opening up the heart he could get back some of that lost verve. However, they couldn't do it at the Royal Children's.

We were in the back of the transport ambulance on our way across Melbourne. It was one of those ambulances that wasn't really fully set up for emergencies. Shaun was getting some chest pains, so the paramedics began to put these little patches on him for angina, which is a really bad chest pain caused by a reduction of blood flowing to the heart, and he soon had about four all over this side. By this stage angina was something we were used to. Shaun had had maybe twenty angina attacks since they'd told us about the heart rejection, so I thought this was just another one of those.

It was pouring rain and we were just sitting in a Punt Road traffic jam – which is an event most Melburnians will well understand – when this angina attack turned into something else entirely. It was massive. I could see Shaun's chest thumping, *smack, smack, smack*, and he was sweating and screaming out, 'I'm dying.' Both he and I were freaking out.

The driver was calling 'Code blue, code blue,' as he tried to get the ambulance moving. I was freaking out, watching as they scrambled to get out of the traffic and to find the equipment they needed. The guy in the back was going nuts. I don't know whether he was new or something, but he was freaking as well. He was screaming 'Code blue, code blue' down the radio, pouring with sweat, because he thought he was going to lose Shaun in the back of the ambulance.

We made it to Emergency at the Alfred, and thankfully the angina calmed down. It had been horrible. I don't want to see someone with an angina attack ever again. Shaun said the pain was just incredible, and I could see it in his face and body.

The problem was that his arteries were collapsing and they needed to put a stent in there, which they did next day. They put one in his heart as well, which made him the first person at the Alfred ever to get that procedure. They gave him a pretty solid anaesthetic and he was out for hours after the operation, which is always a worry as a parent. It was really no drama at all, though – he just slept longer.

From that point on, until he got the new heart, Shaun needed to carry a defibrillator with him all the time. He was good with nicknames, like when he called his heart 'The One with the Lot'. He called his defibrillator 'R2D2', which was his way of dealing with something outside the norm. It wasn't an easy thing for a young kid to cope with all that was going on in his life, but he took it in his stride.

Other than the defibrillator he was good. The stent had worked and he had his energy back. Shaun was at school again and being just a normal kid – albeit one with R2D2 in tow.

CAMERON

16

IN 2005, MY friend Phil was getting married and the wedding was going to be in Fiji. At this stage he was in the army, but we were mates from even before our primary school days together. He asked me to be his best man, which I was more than happy to do. The second part of the deal was that I had to pick up the bridesmaid, Penny, from the airport. I was still a pretty shy person, but I agreed, and it turned out to be a very good decision.

I hadn't been looking for a relationship, but Penny just burst into my life and I was falling for her even before we left Fiji. But although our little holiday romance continued when we got home, we were leading two different lives. I was over in Lalor and she lived in Dandenong, about fifty kilometres away, and was a manager at the Burvale Hotel in Burwood. That meant we really only saw each other on the weekends – but I was still head over heels.

Our relationship was really good, but because of the distance and the timing of things, she didn't get much time with Shaun. But as we got closer we began to find ways to spend more time with each other, and in the early part of 2008 that also meant time for Penny with Shaun, so she started to bond with him. When I had to go to Hollywood for a week, Shaun stayed with her.

After the DHS hearing that granted me custody, I had some big decisions to make. Mum and Dad were selling the house in Lalor where I was living with them, which meant we had to find somewhere new to live. It blew me away when Penny said, 'Cameron, I'd like to give Shaun a life. It's not about you or me. It's about Shaun now.'

'What would you like to do?'

'I'd like you both to come and live with me in Dandenong.'

'Really? You'd do that for us?'

'Both of you can come and live with me in Dandenong while we're waiting for the second heart transplant.'

It was amazing. I think Penny fell in love with Shaun more than me, but after we moved in, it was as happy as I could ever remember being. Her dad was a builder and they fixed up a room for Shaun. He started going to Carwatha College in Noble Park, which was nearby, and he enjoyed it, even though he had to carry R2D2 with him everywhere.

The principal at Carwatha was amazing. We gave the school a copy of the restraining order and they put photos of Fletch up in the staff areas so that Shaun was protected. He also had a social worker there named Soozie Pinder – I'm still friends with her today. When she was looking through Shaun's file she couldn't believe how much he'd been through. So she also made sure his life was as safe and easy as possible.

It was always in the back of my mind that Shaun might collapse at any point and that he'd need the defibrillator to keep him alive.

It happened at school a couple of times, and he had to be rushed to hospital three or four times while waiting for the third heart.

Shaun was also suffering night terrors, which was jarring with his happiness at everything else. He'd dream that Fletch was burying him alive. We had appointments with a psychologist at the Children's Hospital to help with the night terrors, and we both felt that even though we had the restraining orders, it wasn't enough.

It's funny – they call them night terrors, but apparently they occur more when you sleep during the day, which was something Shaun always needed to do. From the very first day at Penny's they were happening. He would only be asleep a few minutes when all of a sudden, *boom*, he was screaming.

It was the same dream over and over again. We started seeing the psychologist every day at around 4 pm, for about eight weeks, which is a big effort from Dandenong – depending on the time of day it could take ninety minutes or more. All this was happening while we were waiting for the second heart transplant. Thankfully, Penny was there with me.

CAMERON

17

FROM THE MIDDLE of June, we waited for the phone call. With Shaun's first heart transplant, we were already in the hospital, so all I had to do was leave the room and answer a few questions and everything just happened. This time we were hoping not to be in hospital when they got a heart, so we were well versed in what we needed to do when the call came.

It was 6 pm on 29 August when the phone rang. 'Cameron, we've got a heart for Shaun. Quickly, come in.'

Boom, straight in, only to be confronted with the elephant in the room – Olivia.

Doctor Rob took me aside and said I needed to let her know. 'You've made the decision and we understand about the problem with the two families, but you need to ring her.' Great. I didn't like talking to Olivia at any time, so I wasn't looking forward to that phone call.

'This is going to be interesting,' I thought, 'the two families coming together for the first time in quite a while.' As it turns out, they were fine. At least at first.

Because of the number of operations Shaun had already had on his chest, the transplant posed even more challenges than usual for the doctors. They started the prep really early, which meant we had to say goodbye to him well before the operation. In a strange way, I think Shaun was looking forward to it. I know he wasn't a fan of being operated on, but he also knew that each one helped him.

As they wheeled him away, he said, 'Goodbye, everyone,' and then noticed who was in the room. 'Hello,' he said, because he hadn't seen Olivia and her family for a while, 'goodbye, goodbye, I'll be fine, see you in fifteen hours.' And there he was, blowing kisses like it was some sort of parade. It was quite funny really.

Like last time, this one was a long wait. By the time Shaun got prepped it was about midnight, and it was well into the next day when they came out to tell us about it all. After midday, I think. Both families were there in the Intensive Care Unit (ICU) with him, and it had started out great. For a couple of hours everyone was nice to each other and I remember thinking, 'Wow, this is not bad.'

But then after a little while, they started niggling again and I thought, 'When are these people going to grow up?' Shaun could have died, and all they wanted to do was argue.

'We want to see Shaun first,' said Olivia's family although because Olivia was sick, she couldn't go in.

I just thought, 'Whatever – you go see him first.' I knew it was the last thing Shaun wanted but it wasn't worth the fight. Only a certain number of people are allowed in ICU, so I thought, 'If I'm there after them, I can stay a lot longer.' So I did that.

He was only in ICU for two days, which I still find amazing given the magnitude of what he'd been through. A few days later he was home. It's remarkable how the new heart worked and Shaun got the energy and life he'd been missing. He was able to go and do things – within reason – he couldn't do only days before; something as simple as walking to the letterbox without needing to rest.

Obviously the routine from here was the same: plenty of rejection medicine and regular tests to make sure all was going well. In Shaun's case, the issue was always rejection. We'd waited six months for this heart, and then we had to wait and see how well it worked.

It is different for everyone. Shaun's mate Aaron, who was a little bit older, had a transplant around the same time as this one. Last time I saw him he was still going well – he's out fishing and playing footy and the like. But for Shaun it was a battle. His body didn't like this foreign invader and worked to get rid of it.

So his life went back to normal. He didn't want to be the sick kid, and he spoke about that often. 'The biggest problem about these (other heart) kids,' he'd say, 'is when they're sick, they play on being sick, when they should be at school socialising with other kids. Because these kids are in hospital, they can't even socialise.'

That's where I'm proud of Shaun. He never found excuses not to go to school. He loved being with people. Some of his best friends were hospital kids, though. He was in so much contact with them that was inevitable, but he didn't want that to define his life and his friendships. He tried to get them out and about – he was like a mentor to them, only he was the same age or younger. He was always a leader.

After this transplant, his sport of choice was tennis. He joined a club in Dandenong and started playing, and he could bloody well play that too. I wished I had his talent and drive at sport, but I didn't. I did, however, love watching him play any sport. He played for Dandenong Tennis Club right up until we moved back to Mill Park, and then he joined the Lalor Tennis Club.

He had his goals at that stage and he was just living a normal life.

CAMERON

18

By now, I was working in the movie business. It was a long way from the glazing and the massage, but I'd always been passionate about that world. When I was younger I'd done some acting in local theatres such as The Catchment Players out of Reservoir, just near my home. I wasn't the greatest actor, but I did love it and my involvement grew. I had ideas for movies, which started me thinking and dreaming about what was possible. I'd begun to move on those dreams in 2005 after Shaun was doing okay.

As Shaun says, during my acting career I was no Adam Sandler. I'd got an agent, though, and did some acting courses. My first role was in a play called *Oliver* – I'll never forget that one. It was opening night, and I was playing a copper and had to do a dance. We had these solid wooden bats that we had to swing around, but you needed to watch what you were doing because everyone had to swing at the same time.

Some idiot to my left swung too hard and whacked me in the head. Knocked me out. They pulled me off the stage by my feet and

I wound up in the doctor's surgery with a huge lump on my head, rosy cheeks, lipstick – full make-up – and all in a cop uniform. I wasn't in Emergency or anything like that – it was just a doctor's surgery. I got some weird looks in the waiting-room, let me tell you.

I then got some work as an extra. My first role was in a TV ad for 'Stand Up Against Sexual Abuse', then another ad with Ansett Airlines. I started getting a series of little roles in TV series too – including *The Man from Snowy River* and *Neighbours*.

I was still on stage as well. I did a play called *Pastrana*, which was about circus freaks in the nineteenth century. We went on a rehearsal camp in the middle of winter and for the first time in years my asthma came back. I'd had a few too many drinks and I fell in the pool – when I got out, I could feel my chest constricting. I thought I was never going to feel that again, and it was scary. Fortunately, it was a rare event and was more embarrassing than dangerous, although I did think I was going to die and I did get carted off to hospital in an ambulance!

My last TV role was in 1995, in a show called *Correlli*. Hugh Jackman was one of the stars – not that he was anyone back then, but he was fantastic to work with. In fact, that's the show in which he met his wife, Deborra-Lee Furness, which was pretty cool in hindsight. So that was it for acting for me, but I loved the industry and I wanted more.

With *Correlli*, I'd begun paying more attention to what was going on in the background – how the production was handled – and that started to interest me more than the other side of the camera. So I began speaking to people behind the scenes about movie production and tried to learn as much as I could.

It did take a sharp rejection, however, to make me give up my acting career. My manager sent me for an audition for a new Jackie

Chan movie, *Mr Nice Guy*, they were filming in Melbourne. They were after actors with martial arts experience, and as you now know, I did karate as a kid so I figured I'd have a go – even if I was delusional about my karate skills.

The audition was held in an apartment in South Yarra. When I walked in, the first thing they asked me was about my martial arts experience and I told them how I did Zen Do Kai and karate. I was pretty nervous as I did a few stretches. Then I was asked to do a spinning back kick. I'd never done one in my life, so I jumped and tried to do it and I was hopeless. I broke a lamp. They looked at me, stunned, and said something in an Asian language, which must have been something like: 'Don't call us, we'll call you'. After that, I retired from acting.

Obviously, stepping straight into production wasn't easy, so I looked at other things I could do. For a long time I was on the fringes of the commercial film industry in Australia, trying to break in but it seemed impossible.

In 2000 I wrote and produced my very first low-budget film, which was called *Mr Average* and starred Chris Franklin. Once the film was finished I tried to shop it around to distributors. I had Palace Films very interested, but they wanted me to re-shoot forty minutes of it. I started to learn that getting distribution for movies is the chicken and egg scenario and they are the gatekeepers.

I spent more than twelve months trying to get it to the market. I was so frustrated. Then I began looking into the Australian film industry and finding all the movies that were sitting on a shelf because they couldn't get distribution. Over a five-year period there were more than 1000 movies made, with more than five million dollars invested in them, that never got to the screen. We may, at best, get twenty into the cinemas.

I sure had chosen a tough industry to pursue a career.

Alan Finney, who I'd met already and was forming a friend-ship with, liked *Mr Average*. He said it took him back to the days of the Alvin Purple movies in the 1970s – Alan had appeared in both the original film and the sequel – so I was pretty happy with that. A few years ago I changed the name of the movie to *Average Bloke* and now I have to work out what to do with it. I might even load it up on YouTube just so it isn't wasted.

All of that led me to the concept that we needed some people in this country to have a go at distribution, because there were great movies doing nothing. In 2006 I took a chance distributing a movie called *Shot of Love*. It had been known as *Dope* when it was originally released in 2004, but no-one had wanted to touch it and it had never got into the cinemas. They let me handle distribution even though I had no experience, because they needed it out for tax purposes.

It was quite a racy film and it touched on drugs and prostitu-tion – it was backed by the South Australian Film Corporation and I thought it was a pretty good movie. Alan Finney was the Managing Director and Vice President of Buena Vista Australia & New Zealand at the time, which was a Disney-owned distribution business. He's an amazing man and was – and still is – my mentor. When I told him I was distributing *Shot of Love*, he asked me why I'd bother – I said it was because I wanted to give it a go. I asked for advice, and he said, 'My advice is do it yourself. I'm not going to tell you how to do it. Do it yourself.'

So I did. I had a small budget to work with and I paid myself $4000 for six months of work, which was just stupid. But I got *Shot of Love* into the cinemas when no-one else wanted to do it. I learned then that lots of people made movies in Australia without thinking about distribution, so here was something I could do.

It was hard work, but I'd loved it. After *Shot of Love*, a few things started to open up for me. The movie didn't do too well, but I'd done everything that needed to be done and we'd got the absolute best results possible. People were paying attention, including Miramax, who had an informal chat to me about a job in distribution. It paid a couple of hundred grand, but it was in Sydney.

I had to turn it down. Shaun's life was embedded with the Royal Children's Hospital in Melbourne, and I wasn't moving him away from that. Or moving away from him.

Around this time, I got to know the legendary local actor Charles 'Bud' Tingwell. I sent him a script, which we sat and talked about, although it never got beyond that stage. We ended up becoming really good friends. I went to see him at his house in Doncaster pretty much once a week until the day before he died in 2009. When he passed away, he was given a state funeral, which was pretty amazing. His family insisted I sat with them, which made me very proud. He was like a grandfather to me and I'm a better person for knowing him.

Bud had encouraged me to follow my dreams, which inspired me to head to Hollywood in 2007 to work on a movie I had an idea and a plot for. It was called *The Bloke Goes to Hollywood*. I found a scriptwriter to sort out the words and then went to Hollywood to start work on it. I got Corey Feldman and Nikki Griffin on board, along with the wrestling icon 'Rowdy' Roddy Piper. Corey had starred in films like *Stand by Me*, *Goonies*, *Gremlins* and *Teenage Mutant Ninja Turtles* (he played Donatello), while Nikki had a long list of credits – from *Young and the Restless* to *The OC* and *How I Met Your Mother*.

The aim was to film a bit of a trailer to use for more funding. We had the film crew from the TV series *Ugly Betty* and the

Spider-Man movie, so we weren't dicking around. It was a lot of fun and I thought my life was set on its path.

We filmed on the *Queen Mary* at one stage and that was pretty amazing. There was also a scene on Muscle Beach in LA – this is where Roddy came into it. Roddy agreed to do a cameo if we put his daughter, Ariel Toombs, in the movie, which we did.

It was amazing getting Roddy, because I'd been a big fan of his in the '80s, and Shaun was a big fan as well. I remember the day we picked him up in the van and then we had an hour drive to Muscle Beach. Along the way, he told me about wrestling with Hulk Hogan in front of a packed house at Madison Square Garden and how he'd broken just about every bone in his body and how he'd beaten cancer. During our conversation, I could definitely see his charisma and, even though he seemed very humble, I could see why he'd become one of the great entertainers.

Roddy also asked me what my story was and I told him all about Shaun and how hard things had been for me. He turned to me, putting his hand on my shoulder, and said that if there was ever anything he could do to help Shaun, I should let him know. I'll never forget it.

When we finally got to the film set, as soon as the word got around that Roddy Piper was doing a scene, a big crowd gathered. I couldn't believe what I was seeing. People were crying as he signed autographs and spoke to everyone – he was such a huge icon and star.

It was very sad to hear that he passed away in 2015, because he was just about the nicest guy I'd ever met. However, his memory lives on with Ultimate Fighting Championship legend Ronda Rousey. She now wrestles in a tribute to Roddy Piper wearing the classic 'Hot Rod' T-shirt, which was Rowdy's trademark, as well as his iconic leather jacket. She dubs herself 'Rowdy' Ronda Rousey, which I think is also a beautiful tribute. To this day, I still speak to his daughter. In fact, Ariel is an ambassador for the foundation.

I was enjoying my time there, even though I was away from Shaun, who was back home with Penny – but if we work the timeline a bit you'll see that the start of this chapter is before I had custody. I was starting to think that when Shaun was a little older we could move to the US and build a pretty good life. It'd be a different life, sure, but I could make a decent living there. I was good at meeting people.

The plan was always to come back to Australia for a little while and sort out some things. However, Shaun got sick again and we found out he was suffering from chronic heart rejection, which stopped the dream. In the end I had about twenty minutes of the movie – unfortunately we never went any further with it.

Shaun used to blame himself, but that was silly. To me, it was just life. I could still go back one day and follow up some of those possibilities, especially with a couple of good scripts I was offered.

SHAUN

19

AFTER WE WON the restraining order, Dad and I felt like this great big black cloud had lifted. After that we lived with his parents, Nanna and Poppy John, for a bit and then moved in with Dad's girlfriend at the time, Penny. They'd been going out for a couple of years and she lived in this great house in Dandenong.

I absolutely adored Penny. And she loved me. Living with her was so good. She was very welcoming and warm and friendly. I had my own room which Penny's dad fixed up for me. We even had a dog – a short-haired border collie called Dally – which we took for walks every day. Best of all we were happy. Her family were great to me.

Moving houses meant a new school, which I was a bit scared about. Dad enrolled me at Carwatha College. Starting new schools was always a bit scary for me, but Carwatha was awesome. I made some great friends there. When we moved to Penny's I was waiting for another miracle. Being able to go to school made such a difference because all I would be doing was sitting around the house, doing practically nothing, just waiting, hoping for a second heart. It's weird because this can only happen if someone else gets killed in an accident. Not really a nice thought.

Penny was Dad's rock. She supported him through our legal battles and custody conflicts with Mum, and somewhere along the way I think she taught him how to be a father. He was always down on himself and never gave himself credit for the stuff that he did. It was Penny who made him see what he was and what he could do. It was amazing just to see this happen. She gave him confidence, lifted his self-esteem and he was like a different person. So in some ways, my dad and I grew up together.

Sometimes he seemed more like a big, older brother than my father and a few times it seemed that I was the father and Cameron my son. Whatever was going on, it was real special because after this Dad and I were the best of mates. It was all good – none of the nasty, negative stuff we'd been copping for yonks.

Penny's nickname for me was 'Mini-Me', after the Austin Powers movie, because I looked like Dad, only smaller, and we were always doing dumb things together. We had lots of fun times, but sometimes she got annoyed when Dad and me acted silly – like when we had an orange fight. Penny had this mega orange tree in the backyard and one day we ripped some oranges off and played lawn bowls with them on the grass, pretending to be old fuddy-duddies. Then we started pelting one another with them and pretty soon you couldn't tell it was an orange tree anymore. Whoops. Next thing Penny came storming out of the house. She couldn't believe we'd stripped the tree playing games with oranges – she was so mad. She called Dad a big kid, which he was. But we all laughed about it later.

And Dad was starting to make things happen in his career. After he does his pitch to the big movie studios he always asks them,

'What's the verdict?' Then they'd tell him they're giving his concept the green light, or say it's a pile of crap. Sometimes Dad will answer his phone and go, 'G'day! What's the verdict?' Which is why, when he started his own production company, he called it Verdict Entertainment Group.

He distributed a crime drama called *Hobby Farm* in 2010, which was really cool because I got to go to the premiere and hang with my mates. It won awards like best international drama at a New York film and video festival. We were all real proud of Dad after he had the breakthrough with that movie. It always made me feel bad that my sickness consumed Dad's time and energy, which meant he hasn't been able to put in the work to make his company go mega.

Too many times when Dad gets involved in a project or begins to negotiate with a client my illness comes in the way and everything gets put on hold. He says no to so many film projects and he's sacrificed a lot of his life and career for me.

I guess I've always kind of been interested in acting because Dad's in the movie business. I was in school plays and thought it was pretty cool and stuff, and when I was about ten I told Dad I wanted to be an actor. First thing he did was tell me what a tough life it was, and that actors can go for months, even years, without work.

That didn't put me off because I'd seen that happen to Dad, except when he did get those jobs it was like he was a completely different person. After talking about it he said he'd take me to a casting agent and see what they thought. 'Shaun,' he said, 'don't get your hopes up. These guys are pros. They only take people on who they think will bring in the dollars. It's got nothing to do with whether you're a good kid. You have to have something, the looks, the presence, charisma, something they can sell. Fair enough?'

We went to this agent, Peter Derrick, who runs an agency in Moorabbin called Small Fry. In the days leading up to this, I prepared a couple of pieces and worked on them with Dad. So I walked in and did my audition. Peter just sat there and didn't say anything. When I'd finished he swivelled round in his chair and said to Dad, 'Where have you been hiding him?'

'What do you mean?' Dad asked.

'Hey, this kid is amazing!' said Peter. 'I have the perfect thing for him right now – a Coca-Cola ad.'

I went onto the books at Small Fry and this led to me doing extras work and roles in film and television. Peter says I've got the X factor, even if I didn't get the Coke job.

I love acting and probs for different reasons to most actors. It's great fun for me because I can be someone else for a while. No more the sick kid with chronic heart problems. Suddenly, I'm a young punk going to smash your head in, or an altar boy singing in a church choir. Anybody but me. The other terrific thing is that you meet loads of new people, and no matter whether it's an ad, or a TV ep, you're working with really talented people who just amaze you with what they can do with a word, or a look.

I worked on a television film with Guy Pearce and have been an extra on *Neighbours* about five times. There's just something so great about the actors and directors on that show. Every time I worked with them it was a blast.

The first role Peter found for me was a scene in *Neighbours* where I was a student playing a game of basketball in the school gym. A few days later, a cheque arrived in the mail addressed for me. My very first pay cheque! Yippee! I made Dad take me to the bank so I could deposit it straightaway. From then I figured doing a bit of acting would be a better way of making a little bit of pocket money than slaving away at somewhere like Maccas. You know, kids get pimples from working at Maccas. True story.

One of Dad's movies, *The Bloke Goes to Hollywood*, was a comedy about an Aussie stand-up comedian who tries to crack the big time in America. Chris Franklin, from The Hood, was the comic and I know there were some big stars from the US in it as well. But when they were shooting it in LA I became really sick and Dad flew back straightaway. This happened a lot. Without warning I'd get sick overnight and be rushed to hospital. Dad was always there for me. Because he'd do this, I sometimes tried to play things down with my health, but this time that wasn't possible. It upset me because I knew that it was disastrous for Dad. You can't walk off the set of a movie and come back a few days later – it just doesn't work like that.

Time and again he'd be in the middle of filming, or in meetings with the big studios, when he'd hear I was in trouble and drop everything. And never once did he bitch or whinge about this. Not once. His whole career was stop/start – off again, on again. It must have driven him crazy, as well as having to deal with all the crap coming from Mum and Fletch.

Hearing Dad talk about my condition, I was amazed with how much he knew. He really got the science. Dad seemed to know when my lungs were acting up and put eucalyptus on my chest or turn the heating up. He could sense at what point of the day I most needed saline. And, of course, he'd take me to the Children's Hospital when things took a turn for the worse.

SHAUN

20

FOR SOME REASON the PICC line's driving me crazy. This is back to me now. Sorry, I should have explained that first. The docs are a bit worried about this build-up of fluid in my lungs. With the antibiotics going in day and night it should have cleared up by now, but it hasn't. Oh yeah, PICC stands for peripherally inserted central catheter and it drip-feeds antibiotics into a vein in my chest and this will clear it all up.

The PICC line stops me getting a decent night's sleep so I'm now tired and cranky all the time and it gets in my way. I can't even have a shower. That's my dream these days – just to be able to stand under the stream of a shower and feel that water coming down, without worrying about the PICC line. And I shouldn't be sounding so negative because where I was up to in my story was really one of the best bits.

Dad and I were living at Penny's place and we were real happy even if I was slowly going downhill. The wait for a new heart was long and painful. And I know there are lots of people like me in this awful situation where it's like a race against the clock. If that heart doesn't arrive in time then it's game over.

Each day I became sicker and more exhausted. My hands and feet turned blue all the time. Obviously, I was too ill to go to school and it was a struggle to try to stay positive.

To cheer me up, Dad's sister entered me in a competition where a local radio station, Fox FM, was looking to give someone with a hard-luck story something special. When she told them my story they were really amazed. We won the competition, which was a trip for two to Bali. I was ecstatic. Not only had I never won anything before, I'd never left Australia. I called my grandparents and Susanne and Ken. I was babbling on like an idiot, 'I'm going on a holiday! I'm going on a holiday!' How dumb was that. It was a great prize, but as it turned out I was just too sick to go anywhere.

Things were bad. The docs gave me this portable heart to carry around because I started to get bad angina pains. Dad and me called the defibrillator R2D2 after the *Star Wars* robot. All the teachers at Carwatha College had to learn how to use it. If I had a heart attack they had to zap me with this thing and give me a thousand volts or something.

And the wait continued. Then, to keep me going, the docs decided I needed a stent in my heart. A stent's like this tiny wire-mesh tube they feed up through an artery in your groin and snake it up to the blocked area of the heart and blow it up like a balloon. It unclogs the artery and stuff. They do this at another hospital, the Alfred, where they're the experts at this stuff. As a precaution they took me there in an ambulance. We were driving down Punt Road when I had a mega angina attack. Everyone was screaming at the driver to stop.

One of the ambos said, 'What's the pain level?'

'Ten,' I said.

So then it was siren on and we were full bore to the Alfred Hospital. All kinds of scary stuff. Anyway, they did the stent and told me I was the first thirteen-year-old to have one at the Alfred. They probably tell everyone this. 'You're the first two-year-old to have a stent.' Ha ha!

I promise to get off this subject pretty quick as I feel like maybe your eyes are rolling here. Next came the best thing of all. After I'd made it back home, the phone rang. Dad answered. It was the hospital. They'd found a new heart for me. I'll never forget that night. It was August 2008. I was whooping for joy in Penny's lounge room, jumping up and down on her sofa and going crazy. And I had a dentist's appointment booked for the next day and I was stoked about skipping the dentist!

Because of Mum's viral meningitis, she wasn't allowed to visit me in hospital after my second heart transplant. There was too high a risk of her passing on an infection, bug or cold. We were talking again by this stage, so we communicated via the computer, using webcam and Skype.

In the days, weeks and months after my second transplant I slowly became fitter and stronger. I tried my hardest at sport, but it was always a struggle. Even with a new heart I still tired easily, and when I approached exhaustion, my lips would turn that familiar shade of blue. The reality was that games like football or basketball were potentially too dangerous for me. They're too fast-paced for someone in my condition. Which is why I joined a tennis club.

This was more my style as there isn't as much running around involved, or massive numbers of players in your way. Our tennis club played games all over Melbourne. We even made the grand final, but lost. My prize was a chocolate frog. The next season, some Sudanese kids who had just migrated joined the club. At first, having never played tennis before, they seemed more fascinated with the actual ball than with trying to hit it with the racquet. They'd look at the ball in awe as it bounced out of the court.

Being in Dandenong, Penny's place was not that far from the Dandenong Ranges. In the national park there they have the Kokoda Track Memorial. It's meant to be sort of like the real one in New Guinea that the Aussie soldiers had to climb in the war. There's supposed to be 1000 stone steps, and one weekend my Aunt Susanne organised a picnic day there with some different families as part of a YMCA group. My cousins and other kids were there. You could climb the steps, or just stay in the car and drive all the way to the top. Because I was feeling so good and with that new heart beating away I thought I'd try and see how far I could get. It had been hard for me in the past walking on the flat from one school classroom to another, so this was something else altogether.

'You can always turn back when you've had enough,' Dad said when I told him the plan.

'Yeah. Let's do it,' I said.

It was a hot summer day and I remember I was in just shorts and a t-shirt. The steps aren't evenly laid out like ones you see in buildings, so you have to be careful. A couple of times Dad slipped and fell. I was walking in front so I didn't really notice until I said something to him and there was no reply. I looked around and he was a few metres below me.

'I fell,' he said.

'Well, you'd better get your arse back up here again!' I told him.

Every now and then there were these plaques saying the name of a plant or a bird. There were heaps of birds chirping away. It was like a rainforest.

Halfway up, I was close to giving up. My legs were aching and both Dad and I were gasping for breath. Then I made the mistake of looking up to where we had to go. 'Oh my God,' I said to myself, 'it's just getting steeper and steeper.' There was a time when I would have felt, 'Nup that's it,' and just wanted to quit. But for some reason I thought to myself, 'I can do this.'

I kept chanting to myself, 'I can do this,' all the way to the top. When I reached that final step I was exhausted, but it felt incredible. Of course the view was spectacular – you could see all over Melbourne – but that wasn't the best thing. Being able to climb those steps made me so proud of myself. It was the most amazing feeling ever. I must have been at the peak of my physical fitness back then. Now, when we drive past the Dandenong Ranges I point them out and say to whoever, 'I climbed those!' For me, it was like climbing Mt Everest.

CAMERON

21

I HAVE A lot of regrets with Penny. However, it's hard to keep it all together in your life when you have a really sick child, and it's even harder to hold a relationship together. Well established couples often struggle, so we were really going to have to put in. And I didn't.

You can only imagine what the emotional rollercoaster is like with a child as sick as Shaun. To start with, he's up and down with his own health and abilities, but you've also got to watch some of his friends die. For me, I just bottled it up and didn't really cope. Since coming back from Hollywood I was sliding down into depression, and strangely Shaun's transplant triggered a rapid decline. I was in a really bad depression and not doing anything about it.

I put on a lot of weight and I just wasn't doing anything with myself. Shaun was going to school and when he did, I didn't want to go out of the house. I can't explain it. It is funny too, because around that time Shaun wrote an open letter in the *Herald Sun* to Mark 'Chopper' Read, because the news had come out that he needed a liver transplant and he wasn't going to get it done.

Shaun wrote that Mark should do it for his sons, because they needed a father. And this is right at the time I was not much use to either Shaun as a father or Penny as a partner. Maybe he should have written me a letter too. Anyway, that was the early start to a friendship with Mark, who was perhaps Melbourne's most notorious modern-day criminal.

It was 13 May 2009 when Penny and I went to see *Angels & Demons* with Tom Hanks. It was the follow-up to *The Da Vinci Code* movie from a few years before. The next day was my birthday, and after watching Hanks solve all those riddles, Penny turned around to me and said, 'I don't love you anymore.'

All I could think was 'Shit!'

Life was kind of crashing in around me in every way except for Shaun. He was doing well. I was spending a lot of time with 'Bud' Tingwell because he was dying from prostate cancer at the age of eighty-six. He passed away on 15 May, two days after this revelation from Penny and one day after my birthday.

Penny and I tried to work it out a little and I think she sort of got back with me, because she felt sorry for me. But that isn't enough, and it didn't work.

I love her for the person that she is and what she did for Shaun. She took us in when she didn't have to. She gave Shaun a home, which was a big ask given his health. Her parents embraced Shaun like he was their own child, so when her dad died in 2017 I went to the funeral. Penny finds it hard to talk to me, but her sister calls every couple of weeks just to see how things are going. They are everything Olivia's family isn't.

Anyway, the break-up meant we needed to find somewhere to live. I spoke to Shaun about it and he wanted to try to stay at Carwatha College and he wanted to be in a house. I located a place in Noble Park right near the school and we moved in. However, I didn't find it easy being out there near Penny and so far away from the rest of my family. So after about four months, I sat down with Shaun for a heart-to-heart.

I told him I couldn't do it. I couldn't live in that area near her – it was hurting me too much. I told him I wanted to go home, which for me was the northern suburbs. So we got a house in Mill Park and we moved in with a friend of mine called Pat who I'd worked with at O'Brien's Glass in Collingwood.

Pat's child, Liam, was living with him. Liam had Asperger's, so it was an interesting time for us. It was a nice house and Shaun had his own room. We stayed for about a year before we got a house that we didn't have to share with anyone.

With that first move, we needed a new school, so I went to visit the principal of my sister's old school, Lalor North High, and the social worker. As it turns out, I'd gone to school with the social worker's brother and she'd followed Shaun's story as it played out in the media. She knew what was happening and what we needed. They were happy to have Shaun, so that's where he ended up and he had a ball there as we settled down.

SHAUN

22

WE'D BEEN LIVING in Dandenong for about a year when Dad broke the news to me that he and Penny were splitting up. At least this time there was no nastiness or back-biting stuff. It had felt like the first time we'd been a family, so I didn't want to go. Penny was great, though. I was in Year 7 at nearby Carwatha College and stayed until the end of that year. From Year 8 to Year 10, I went to Lalor North Secondary College, which was the same school my Aunt Susanne went to, so that gave me a good feeling. Lalor North is in the northern suburbs of Melbourne, close to where I live with Dad in Mill Park.

At first, getting back into the routine of school after more than six months off was quite overwhelming. The timetable was hard to get used to. There were two timetables, which alternated every week with different class schedules and rooms. They were colour coded to make things easier – week one was green and week two purple.

What I was especially anxious about was how massive the school was. All the classrooms were miles apart and it was a struggle for me to walk from one class to the next. One of the teachers must have complained because I was spoken to about dawdling and being late for classes. There were lots of red faces all round when I gave my excuse. I suppose they think they've heard every excuse under the sun and then you say, 'Well, since my second heart transplant, it's taking longer for me to get my strength back.' They all knew, but in a school that size, they can sometimes forget who's who. They were all very apologetic. 'Just get to class when you can,' one of the teachers in charge said.

Being the newbie meant that I didn't know any of the kids in my classes, so I was a bit out of my comfort zone. But I really made an effort because I loved school and was never the sort of person who gave up easily. Luckily for me, another kid, Kane Davies, started the same time as me. He looked a bit lost too, and we got talking, and we've been best friends since. For some reason Kane's lived all over Australia. His family is always on the move. Before they came to Melbourne they lived in South Australia. He told me he wants to be a helicopter pilot when he grows up.

None of the other kids at school were told about my medical situation – privacy, I guess – but I had to fess up eventually. The girls teared up and the boys wanted to see the scar going down my chest.

'There's another person's heart in there?' they'd ask, pointing to my chest.

'Yeah.'

And I made the mistake of telling them my first heart had come from a little girl. 'So did you feel like a girl?' the boys wanted to know.

'No! It's just an organ. I didn't feel like a girl or anything like that!'

Really, apart from that, my classmates were pretty understanding and supportive.

I studied English, Maths and Science. Science is my favourite subject, probs because we had the best teacher – Miss Radford. She was a blast. She always made the class fun and was really encouraging. Once, we did an experiment in the lab where we burned sugar with a Bunsen burner and turned it into caramel. The smell of it was drool-worthy. In Year 9 Miss Stone was my English teacher and we studied John Marsden's *The Day After Tomorrow*, which I loved.

My grades were never flash. I don't think I ever scored an A in anything. Some of my school reports didn't even give me a grade, because I'd missed too many classes to be assessed. Obviously I never had a perfect attendance record.

The kids at Lalor North were a good bunch, but you know there's always one. When this kid found out that I'd had two heart transplants, he reacted all weird. Started calling me a weakling and stuff. I took no notice – I just ignored him – but that only made it worse.

This kid was pretty cunning. He'd find those moments when there was no-one around and have a crack at me. First, it was the names, and then he started getting physical – an accidental bump, then a bit of a shove and a clip over the ear. Like anyone in this situation I wondered at first if it was me – that I might be doing something to provoke him. Maybe it was my fault. That didn't last long – it definitely wasn't my fault, but I didn't know what to do about it.

If I went to the teachers, then of course I'd have to prove it and all my mates would think I was a dibber-dobber. Eventually, I told Dad. We were at home, and as I explained what was happening he started crying and was really upset. He looked dreadful. He put his head in his hands and sat there for a while.

I was almost going to say, 'Look, it's not that bad, I suppose,' when he cleared his throat to speak. 'You know, it happened to me too. I was bullied at school.'

Dad opened up about stuff he'd never told me before. He said there were many similarities between us. We were both small for our age, I even looked like him, and we both had health problems. He missed a lot of school and failed a grade in primary. I had to repeat at school myself, a year in primary and a year in high school after each transplant. Dad was picked on from his first day in Year 7 at Keon Park Tech when he was thirteen years old. There was a pack of about fifteen kids who regularly ganged up on him. It was both physical and verbal. Bullying really affected Dad. It made him hate school so he never completed his education. Which was a pity because he had some good friends there.

He told me he never felt like he was good enough, never able to feel strong. That was something he carried with him, even when I was born. Having a baby to look after was a huge responsibility, but a kid with heart problems freaked him out. At least he was honest with me, like saying he just couldn't cope. And then when he split with Mum and she started giving him a hard time, he felt like he was being bullied all over again.

After hearing all this, we went back to what was happening at my school. 'You have to stand up for yourself, Shaun,' he said. And with this strange smile on his face, he added, 'We're going to pay Chopper a visit.'

CAMERON

23

IT'S KIND OF funny – my parents tried to keep me out of 'certain' schools to stay away from 'certain' types of kids. Kids like Mark 'Chopper' Read, who was one of the people Shaun reached out to with that open letter in the paper in 2008. When the opportunity arose a couple of years later, it would kick-start a friendship with one of Australia's most notorious criminals.

Shaun had read an article about how Mark needed a liver transplant, but that he wasn't going to have one. He felt there were others more worthy of a new liver than him; however, Shaun felt he wasn't thinking about his two children who needed a father. And that's what he wrote in his letter.

Mark was an interesting person, that's for sure. It's why so many movies and TV shows have been made about him. If you've never heard of him, look him up on the internet. He was given the nickname 'Chopper' as a kid, after a TV character, but most people think it's because he chopped his own ears off. Largely, he did that to get out of H Division and Pentridge Prison, and into

135

a mental or hospital ward for a bit, to stave off an attack he knew was coming.

He'd had a tough life with bullying as a kid, then fired up as a defender and aggressor on the streets. He was in prison as a teenager and he openly spoke about his life to the media and in books that he wrote. Despite many of the things he'd done – and he claimed he'd killed people, 'but only people who deserved it' – he was a strangely moral man, so to hear him talk about accepting death rather than taking a new liver made sense.

But Shaun was having none of that.

'Hi Mark, my name's Shaun,' he said in his letter. 'I've had two heart transplants, and many, many, many operations in my life. I understand that you need a liver transplant. I ask you to please get your liver transplant. You're saying that you're no good, and people don't like you. Don't think about what you've done in the past. Think about the future of your boys. Please get the liver transplant.' Or something like that.

People at the *Herald Sun* were stunned. So they came out and did a bit of a story on Shaun and why he felt the way he did. And that was it, or so I thought.

A couple of years later I met Mark through a guy named Benji, who I knew through a bunch of entertainers called the Debonairs. I met a few interesting people through the regular lunches they held for the music industry, and some of them were way out there. People like the singer Madeleine Qiex, who was a bit kooky to say the least, but I thought she'd hit it off with Shaun, so we arranged for them to meet.

But back to Benji. I'd only just met him when I went to his fiftieth birthday party. After the party, Benji got into his car and ended up slamming into the back of another car on the Nepean

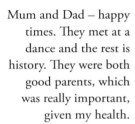

I suffered from chronic asthma during my childhood and my struggles helped me to understand what Shaun was going through after he was born.

Mum and Dad – happy times. They met at a dance and the rest is history. They were both good parents, which was really important, given my health.

Pictures from my acting days. After a disastrous experience in an audition for a Jackie Chan movie, I decided I was better off on the other side of the camera!

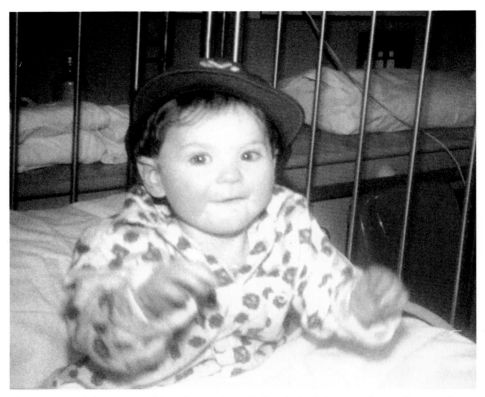

Shaun, around three years old, in hospital. He'd already had dozens of procedures on his heart and physically was developing slowly.

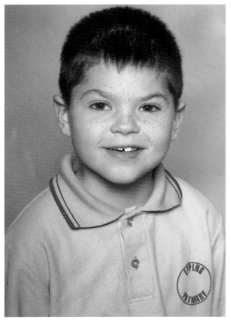

Shaun, aged about seven. Within a year, he'd need his first heart transplant.

Shaun playing his very first football game,
only weeks after having the transplant.
He was so proud, and, despite being half
the size of some of his opponents, he
immediately threw himself into tackles.

Shaun, thirteen years old, looking stylish
at my sister Susanne's wedding.

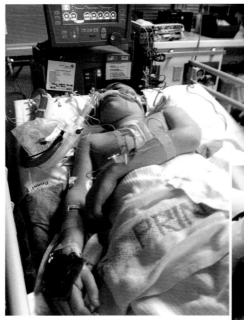

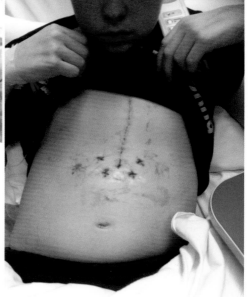

A few months after Susanne's wedding, Shaun had his second transplant. (*Above*) Here he is in the intensive care unit afterwards, and (*right*) showing his scar. (*Below*) It was remarkable how the new heart worked, and Shaun now had all the energy and life he'd been missing.

Shaun having fun – with some local musos and on his own – for Donate Life Week.

Shaun gradually got used to his role as a spokesperson for Congenital Heart Disease. Here he is at a public speaking engagement.

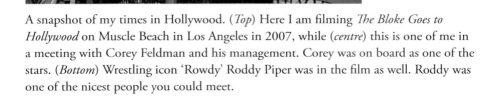

A snapshot of my times in Hollywood. (*Top*) Here I am filming *The Bloke Goes to Hollywood* on Muscle Beach in Los Angeles in 2007, while (*centre*) this is one of me in a meeting with Corey Feldman and his management. Corey was on board as one of the stars. (*Bottom*) Wrestling icon 'Rowdy' Roddy Piper was in the film as well. Roddy was one of the nicest people you could meet.

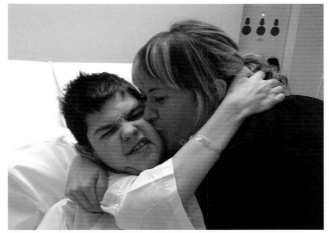

Susanne giving Shaun a big kiss in hospital.

Shaun with Zane Dirani, a self-defence master and natural healer and a great friend to us both. Zane said that Shaun had been chosen as 'one of God's angels'.

After Shaun posted his 'My Final Goodbye' video, there was so much media attention, including a photo shoot with the *Herald Sun*. Here's one of Shaun and me from that day, as well as one of us with Sally. 'It felt like a real family,' Shaun said to me about life with Sally.

Phil Hillyard/Newspix

Shaun with boxing champion Garth Wood at a South Sydney Rabbitohs game. Garth called Shaun his 'secret weapon'.

Mark 'Chopper' Read had a scary reputation, but he was pretty moral in his own way and he was good for, and with, Shaun. Here we are, on a night out at a film premiere.

Shaun and I went up in a helicopter together at Essendon Airport, organised by the local police. Shaun absolutely loved it.

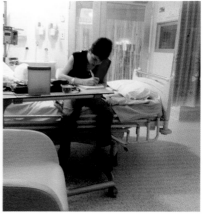

Shaun hard at work in hospital on his memoir.

Shaun had an amazing time as a guest on the AFL *Footy Show*. (*Above*) One of his heroes, Essendon captain Jobe Watson, was on the program and Shaun was thrilled to meet him. (*Below left*) Shaun loved meeting Sam Newman as well. (*Below right*) Shaun and I made sure we got a photo of the two of us on the set.

Tim Carrafa/Newspix

WELCOME

Shaun Miller

★

"JACK"

The morning after *The Footy Show*, Shaun was ready for his cameo appearance on one of his favourite TV shows, *Neighbours*. Here he is with the cast, who made him feel so welcome. He loved everything about the day, from sitting in the make-up chair to seeing his name on his dressing-room door.

Tim Carrafa/Newspix

This was the banner that greeted me when I turned up at Shaun's funeral service.

Shaun's funeral car with an Essendon Bombers stripe on it. He would have loved it.

Shaun's coffin in the back of the funeral car.

Carrying Shaun's coffin on one of the saddest days of my life.

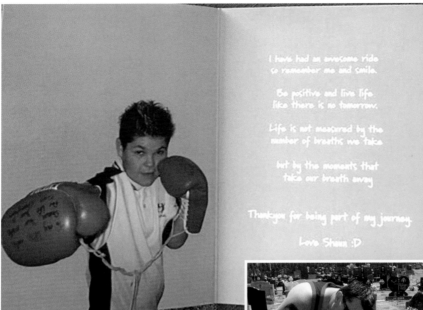

I have had an awesome ride
so remember me and smile.

Be positive and live life
like there is no tomorrow.

Life is not measured by the
number of breaths we take

but by the moments that
take our breath away

Thankyou for being part of my journey.

Love Shaun :D

Shaun's funeral card.

Shaun's headstone.

It was really tough going to Shaun's Kick-Arse Party at Luna Park a few weeks after he passed away. I didn't want to be there, but Sally and I still managed a smile. I love this mural, which was painted especially for the event.

I was so proud when Shaun's book was published. Also in this photo, you can see the tattoo of Shaun on my arm, which I'd promised him I would get.

Launching Shaun's book on the *Today* show.

Six months after Shaun died, I was sitting in the car thinking of him. All of a sudden, the car was freezing, which was confusing when it was 29 degrees outside. For some reason, I picked up my phone and took a photo. When I looked at it, I was amazed, because Shaun's Converse runners were clearly visible. I'd given them away to a needy family four days after Shaun had passed away. I don't know how to explain it.

I took this picture at 4 am in May 2016, as I was starting to see light flashes in front of my eyes. Some people believe orbs of light like this are spirits from the afterlife, and, with some of the things that were going on, who am I to argue?

In 2016, I had a dream in which Shaun told me to start a foundation. About a year later, and after a lot of hard work and a lot of help, I discovered that we'd been granted tax-deductible status – which was basically the green light for the Shaun Miller Foundation to go ahead. As you can see, I was pretty happy. It was an incredibly satisfying and emotional day.

I launched the foundation on *The Footy Show* with the help of *Footy Show* co-host Rebecca Maddern, Jobe Watson and Sam Newman, who is one of the ambassadors for the foundation, a role in which he has been amazing.

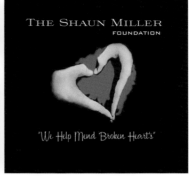

Above: I'm very proud of our logo for the Shaun Miller Foundation and what it stands for.

Left: Here I am at the Royal Children's Hospital, delivering dolls for the kids at the Koala Ward.

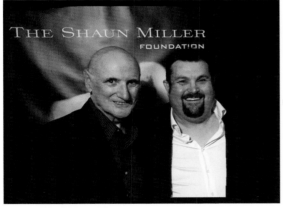

Me and my good friend Alan Finney OAM, who is the Chairman of the Shaun Miller Foundation.

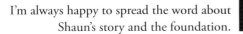

I'm always happy to spread the word about Shaun's story and the foundation.

Me and Shaun had so many great times. He was not only my son, he was my best mate, and he taught me so much more than I taught him. In many ways, I'm still learning lessons from him too.

Highway in Elsternwick. He was hospitalised with some pretty serious injuries.

Shaun had friended him on Facebook and they'd been talking before the crash, so when Shaun found out, we had to go in and visit him. Benji was feeling pretty miserable. He posted on Facebook, 'No-one will care about me, or no-one will help me.'

Shaun read this, and being the empath he is, said, 'Dad, we need to help him. He needs to come and live with us.'

'What?' I said. 'He's virtually a total stranger. I've known him for one week, Shaun. You've maybe spoken to him half a dozen times on Facebook. Why would we do that?'

'Yeah, I know . . .' said Shaun, but he wasn't going to give up easily. He kept at me until I decided to let Benji come and live with us. So, after he was released from hospital a few weeks down the track, we took this stranger into our house. More on that a bit later. Anyway, Benji was mates with Chopper and around November 2010, when we were visiting him in hospital, we met Chopper.

He remembered the article and the letter, and he was quite open with Shaun about his decision not to get the transplant, despite knowing his time was limited. 'Regardless of what you said, Shaun, and whether I took your advice or not, no-one's going to want to give Mark Read a new liver. No-one!'

So Shaun started on his theme. 'Yeah, but what about your children? You're going to die, you know what I mean?'

Chopper was having none of it. 'No, I'm not going to do it, Shaun. I just can't do it.'

Eventually they stopped talking about it, and then the banter really started. Mark wanted to look at Shaun's scar, and he agreed as long as Mark agreed to show him his scars, since Shaun had heard all about some of his injuries. So, as Chopper put it, they had a 'scar-off'. There we all were in the Alfred Hospital, with Benji in a bed and other people around us, because it was a ward, and Shaun and Mark were trying to get one up on each other with their scars. I think Mark won on the stories but Shaun had him dusted in quantity.

Mark pointed and said, 'Okay, ice pick here.'

Shaun would say, 'Drainage tube here. This there.'

They both got down to their boxer shorts.

A seventy-year-old guy in the next bed on oxygen was starting to stress and he ended up freaking out and calling for nurses. There was Mark 'Chopper' Read with all those tattoos and scars on display, and the two of them just standing there in boxers. Chopper ended up conceding – Shaun had him beaten.

I tell you what, though, it was bloody funny to see. And again it was amazing how naturally Shaun built a rapport with someone he'd never met. It was like they'd been mates for years. From that meeting they built a pretty good friendship. I think if they were both alive today they'd still be good mates.

They spoke about a lot of things, and one of those was Fletch. The timing was perfect. For some reason Olivia was making moves to see Shaun again. For a few months he said no, and then one day he consented – but not without a back-up plan.

They met at a shopping centre and were talking away when Shaun saw Fletch. So he pulled out his phone and said to his mum that he had Mark 'Chopper' Read on speed dial, just in case. 'If Fletch comes near me, I'm calling Mark.'

What was really funny was that Fletch liked the Chopper he'd heard about in the news and the movies and the like, but after talking to Shaun, Mark didn't like Fletch. It worked and Fletch kept his distance.

SHAUN

24

I'VE TRIED TO think of how I could explain Mark 'Chopper' Read to my friends in America and other places overseas. And it's no good saying he's like a modern-day Ned Kelly because then they'll go, 'Who's Ned Kelly?'

Chopper is, or was, a notorious Melbourne criminal, no doubt about that. He's the first to admit he's done some terrible things – he was in jail for a long time for murder. He chopped his ears off so he'd get sent to a better jail. But the thing about Chopper is that he has this amazing sense of humour and you can't help but like the guy. He says he's reformed and he's written books and stuff. They made this fantastic movie about him and Eric Bana played the lead role.

So we went over to Chopper's place, although I've noticed that Dad always calls him 'Mark'. Also, Dad says Chopper's never hurt an innocent person in his life – just other crims. While Dad was telling him what had been happening at my school, Chopper walked up and down in his lounge room, like you see those guys do in jail on TV – up and down, up and down. All the time he was listening and thinking. Then he said, 'Mate, once upon a time I would have found this bastard and beaten the crap out of him. Teach him a lesson. But you can't do that these days. No. My advice, young man, is to take it to the powers that be. Okay? This is what those pricks are there for, right? Front up to the head honcho and tell him straight.'

I could see Dad wasn't quite following. 'Sorry, Mark, which head honcho is this?'

'The boss. You know, the headmaster. Shaun's done nothing wrong. You just tell him what you've told me and let them sort it out. Okay?'

On our way home I could see that Dad had somehow expected something different from Chopper, but he didn't say anything. The plan we agreed on was that the next time this kid bullied me I was to head up to the office and let them know. Sure enough, it happened again. Up to the office I went and it was a nightmare. There were forms to fill in, people to talk to, this and that. I told my story to one person, then had to repeat it to another. One of the teachers told me I was the first to ever complain about this kid. 'This is extremely serious,' the teachers told me. 'Are you sure what you're saying happened? Is it possible you misinterpreted his actions?'

Deadset, I'd known when I walked in the door it'd be hopeless. As usual there were no witnesses and they were powerless to do anything. He'd deny it and next time give me an even bigger thump. After I told Dad, he 'ummed' and 'ahhed' and got on the mobile to Chopper. Back we went to see him.

As Chopper listened I could see this big, black look come across his face. 'You're just going to have to go old school on him,' he explained.

'Old what?' Dad wanted to know.

'Old school. Just smack this prick in the mouth next time he tries it on. Okay?' Chopper grabbed me and stood me up opposite him. 'It's all about surprise, young Shaun. This guy will get the shock of his life. So you have to get in the first punch – it has to be a beauty – then follow that up with a couple of others and he'll be history.'

We spent about an hour practising until Chopper was satisfied that I had the perfect punching technique. I must admit that I couldn't really focus on Chopper's mouth or his eyes. All I noticed was the weird space where his ears used to be. You don't really notice something like that until they go missing. I kept thinking to myself, 'Oh my God. He really did cut them off.'

When I finally got it right, Chopper gave me his fedora hat to wear. He said I could keep it. And he suggested I take nutrients and supplements to develop more muscle. 'One final word, my friend,' said Chopper. 'Hit him and he'll feel the difference.'

As luck would have it I went to school all geed up to take this kid on and it turned out that he was away. This went on for a couple of days, which kind of lulled me into forgetting about him. And then I was walking back from the library and I saw him waiting for me. As I got closer I just walked along like I normally did, kind of cringing, until he grabbed the front of my shirt. *Bang!* I punched him in the face, but missed and collected the bottom of his jaw. His eyes almost popped out of his head.

Remembering Chopper's advice, 'Hit him hard and hit him again,' my next blow got him in the guts. I couldn't believe how soft it felt – I half-expected my hand to come through the other side. By then it was all over. He tumbled to the floor. I made a motion as if I was going to kick him and he said, 'Don't!' He never bullied me again. And I swear after that he used to look at me differently – I don't know, maybe with respect.

SHAUN

25

THIRD WEDNESDAY EVERY month is Debonairs lunch day. You have to cough up something like forty dollars, but all the money goes to the cause. It's one of those not-for-profit things supporting struggling entertainers. The Debs members are old rockers and filmmakers. Dad became mates with this guy called Frank Howson – who'd directed famous movies like *Flynn* in the 1990s – after they met at a film premiere and he took him to his first Debs lunch. Since Dad was once a struggling actor, he feels right at home there. This is how Benji 'The Bass Player' came into our lives.

I really liked Benji, even though he was really old – at least fifty, I reckon. One night he went to a party, got plastered, then drove home. Big mistake. He smashed into this car parked on the street. When the paramedics found him he was in a bad way. His ribs were poking out of his chest and stuff. They rushed him to hospital with the sirens blaring. His condition was critical. Benji was a real mess.

Every day he was in hospital, I'd go see him. More than most, I know what it's like being stuck in one of those places. For about two weeks solid, Dad drove me to the Alfred. Benji wasn't handling it all that well and sometimes he'd start crying and say stuff like, 'I don't think I'm going to make it.' All I did was try to be his friend and try to keep things positive. Anyway, he picked up bit by bit and recovered.

When it was time for him to get out of hospital, Benji didn't have anywhere to go. He had no house of his own and no family to look after him. It was really sad. I suggested to Dad that he stay with us, but he didn't like the idea one bit. Word on the street was that Benji was bad news. Obviously he had a drinking problem. Dad didn't want me exposed to any of that, on top of all the crap I already had to deal with myself.

'We need to help this guy,' I said, 'because no-one else will, and if we don't, he'll die.' Still, Dad didn't want to do it. So I pointed out to him that this was what the Debs was all about – helping entertainers get through a rough patch. It was hard to argue against that. In the end he agreed that we'd offer Benji a place to live until he got back on his feet.

We told Benji that he could stay for a week. I think in the end he was with us for about three months. Benji was kind of weird in a nice way. Because I loved having my Froot Loops in the morning he nicknamed me the 'Froot Loop Muncher', which was fair enough.

While living with us, he was going through rehab for his injuries and trying to get better. I tried to help Benji, but I have to admit he was a handful. The thing which we sort of forgot was that he had health problems even before his car accident. After the accident he was put on all these painkillers. Dad was pissed off with him most of the time and there were heaps of arguments. What I tried to do was help the guy and Benji admitted that if the situations were reversed, he'd probably never be able to do what I did for him – not many people would. It doesn't matter whether you're a bad person or a good person; everyone deserves to have someone to look out for them. I'd like to think I had an effect on Benji and helped him pull through.

It was all over after he and Dad had this mega blue. He said Benji was using us and had overstayed his welcome – plus a few swear words, of course. Benji had had enough and packed up his things and took off. I was a bit uncomfortable with how all this happened and didn't want Dad to be angry with him. Sure, Benji didn't handle things too well, but I understood why he was like that.

I tried to convince Dad to give Benji a call and smooth things over. 'Deep down I know he has a good heart. Don't blame him for the way he is. It's just the painkillers that are doing this to him.'

You know, Dad can be bloody stubborn. It took weeks to convince him to ring Benji.

In the end he did it – probs because he was sick of me nagging him.

They patched things up even if they were never going to be the best of mates. I don't know where Benji 'The Bass Player' is these days, although every now and then we get word that he's doing okay. He recovered from the car accident, but he limps and he'll need to use a walking stick for the rest of his life.

Months and months after he'd left, the subject of Benji came up and Dad said, 'Shaun, I'm proud of what you did for Benji – visiting him in hospital and helping him convalesce and stuff. Chances are he wouldn't be alive today if it wasn't for you.' Maybe so. When I get rid of this lung infection I'll have to rock up to the Debs lunch on the third Wednesday and say hi to Benji and the guys.

CAMERON

26

So, Benji came to live with us and Shaun was like a nurse to him. He helped him with his medication, or getting him a Miller's beer out of the fridge and anything else Benji desired. Benji took over the whole house. He was a bit of a termite – he ate through everything. I walked into my bathroom, and he'd stunk the whole place out with cologne. I don't think he paid any bills either, but that's another story.

During the time he stayed with us I found myself taking him to the Alfred for his check-ups, and Shaun wanted to come too. Given the way his life had been, I thought it was strange that Shaun would want to go to the hospital when he didn't need to, but he just wanted to make sure Benji was okay. So I'd pick him up from school and we'd head off to the hospital for someone else. In my mind, I kept saying it wasn't meant to be like this. Benji took over everything in my life . . . even choosing what we watched on TV.

I hated having him there. He left early in 2011 and I was relieved.

*

The relationship with Penny was something unusual for me, and it just happened. After that I didn't really go out much. If I did, I'd just spend my time worrying about Shaun, and in some ways that was a bit of an 'out clause'. If I didn't go out, I wouldn't meet anyone and I couldn't get hurt. I'd never been much of a one for talking to girls anyway, even as a teenager. So all I really did at that time in my life was to spend time with Shaun and pick up some work on film projects.

Shaun didn't think this was enough, and he was always at me. 'When are you going to find someone who loves you?' he'd always say. One night at Susanne's house, Shaun pulled out the big guns. He sat me down in front of Susanne, Mum and Dad and said that this was no good, that I was in my forties, I needed to find someone, and that he was going to set me up with an RSVP account.

I wanted to know how Shaun knew about this dating site, and he said it was always advertising on TV. So he started to work on it and then started hunting for me. He soon spotted a beautiful woman on there with blonde hair, amazing eyes and a great smile. Shaun said this was the one for me and he made me send a message to her, which I really didn't want to do. He kept at me until we did it, but then we didn't hear from her. So I assumed that was the end of the story.

About six months later, I was surfing around on Facebook when she popped up. I called Shaun in, and he said, 'Yes, it's her, Dad. Go for it.'

Shaun spent some time talking to her on Facebook because he wouldn't let it go, at which time we found out her name was Sally. Shaun made me send her a Facebook friend request, and the next day she accepted.

146

Shaun said I had to go slow, that I didn't want to look like some sort of creep. A couple of weeks later we were having a BBQ, and Shaun made a Facebook event under my name and invited her.

Later, Sally told me she got the message and thought it was strange. She showed people at work, and they thought I was some kind of weirdo. The BBQ arrived and we had no messages from her, but Shaun still thought she'd turn up. He was so disappointed when she didn't.

A week or so later, Shaun had been bullied at school and I took to Facebook to vent about how sad it was that kids would pick on someone simply because they had a heart condition. I was just about to log off and play Xbox with Shaun, when Sally popped up and wrote, 'People can be so cruel, you are a great father Cameron.'

Shaun was behind and looking over my shoulder, and he said, 'Wow, Dad, it's Sally,' and he had this big smile on his face. 'This is your chance to meet her now.' I said, 'I don't think so,' but he kept at me until I wrote to her.

Sally and I traded a lot of inbox messages and then eventually I got the courage to ask her out. She knew all about Shaun by now, so at one of our earliest dates at the Pier Hotel in Port Melbourne, I brought Shaun with me. As far as I was concerned, he and I were a package deal, so if she was going to date me she needed to get along with him too.

Sally thought Shaun was so cute and the night was going well. Then the music started and I told her that Shaun was a great dancer, so she asked him to dance for her. He wasn't shy like me, so he got up and started break dancing, spinning on his back and the whole deal. Sally was cheering him on, saying, 'Go, Shaun, go!'

A little later, Shaun went to the toilet and Sally turned to me, looked into my eyes and kissed me. I was now hopelessly in love . . . as was Shaun. So much so, he started talking about his operations and heart transplants, and showing her the scars.

We started dating properly and she began to fall in love with Shaun as well as, I hoped, me. He'd say, 'Dad, she's cool, apart from her smoking,' but she never once smoked around Shaun since she respected everything he'd been through. We'd often go and spend time with her at her apartment in Port Melbourne, and they were becoming quite close, which made it easier for me.

One day, Sally wanted to go for a swim. Shaun wasn't much of a swimmer but she talked him into it. We went to one of those wave pools, and he was walking around with his scars on full display, which he often didn't like to do. That's probably why he didn't swim much. But the wave pool was a lot of fun. They were right out with the waves when Sally got hit by one and her boob popped out of her swimming costume. She quickly covered up, but Shaun saw.

In the change rooms later, Shaun told me what he'd seen and he said, 'Dad, now I really am scarred for life, I saw Sally's boob.' I couldn't stop laughing. I later said to Sally, 'What's this I hear about you flashing my son?' and we all laughed. She was a good sport.

We were now getting ready to move into a new house in Mill Park and Sally's lease was up on her apartment, so I asked her to move in with us. Her work was a fair trek away, but she said yes – except I had to clean her apartment so she could get her bond back. That was easy, and we set up a nice home in Mill Park for the three of us. I was happy, Shaun was happy, and I think Sally was too.

When Benji brought Chopper into our lives, I wasn't sure. He had such a reputation, and I was very cautious. But as I got to know him, I realised not all was as it seemed. As I said, he was pretty moral in his own way and he was especially nice to good people. He was good for, and with, Shaun.

Still, Chopper had a way of talking that just scared the crap out of you – and most of the time you didn't know if he was serious or not. He'd say something like, 'I'm going to go and say hi to that person,' and the way he said it was like no-one else would say it. I can't put my finger on it, but he'd put a chill through your bones.

I remember when Shaun first watched the *Chopper* movie, he asked Mark, 'Did you really do all that stuff?'

Mark replied, 'Shaun, most of my books are probably ninety per cent crap, and ten per cent truth. The movie – what do you reckon?'

'I don't know, what is it?'

'Maybe ninety-eight per cent crap, two per cent truth. They didn't even mention my wife's name in there,' he added, looking at Shaun. He didn't like that movie much, and he donated the money he made to the Children's Hospital.

He tried to explain to Shaun why he ended up where he did, and to make him understand that he was not such a bad guy. Sometimes you don't have much of a chance – it's about your environment.

'I was bullied very badly when I was at school, and my mum put me in a mental hospital,' Mark said. 'I was sixteen years old when I first went into Pentridge . . . When I die, the government owes me a bloody good apology.'

And I think he's right to some degree. His dad had been in the Army – he'd been in Vietnam – and his mum was a Seventh Day Adventist, so his childhood was pretty extreme. After some of the stuff he'd been through, the government put him in an environment like that, and of course he's going to turn out like he did.

We got to know Mark quite well, and we did like him a lot. We went to his house a few times and Shaun would muck around with his son Roy and his Staffies. If you'd told me, after Shaun wrote to the *Herald Sun*, that we'd end up being mates I would have been sore from laughing.

The scary bits reached up every so often. One time was when we were at Sally's brother's place in Williamstown for a party on New Year's Eve. We invited Mark, who decided he liked the pool and jumped in for a swim. He pulled one of his Staffies in at one stage and nearly drowned the thing.

'I love this life, Cameron,' he said from the water. 'I'd love to take Margaret (his wife) and Roy to Queensland, and just live there. Queensland forever.'

He was doing backstrokes and floating and spitting water out of his mouth like he was some kind of fountain. It was quite funny.

Everything was going all right for a while that night, but it didn't last. Sally had a lot of drinks, because she was nervous around Mark. After Mark had jumped out of the pool, she jumped in and then kept screaming at me to join her.

I said, 'I'm trying to talk to someone and you're screaming out, "Come in the pool, come in the pool." I don't want to.'

Mark was sitting next to me and Sally got out of the pool, walked up to him and said, right in his face, 'Who the fuck are you to keep my boyfriend like this when I'm calling him?'

Mark just looked at her. I thought he was going to bang her one. He just shook his head. He didn't say a word. I was quite upset about the situation, so I walked out the door and he followed me. He said he had some things to say to me.

'One, that girl in there,' he said, 'I believe she's wrong for you. I believe that she's gone through a lot of problems with men, and she's too strong for you, as a person. She smokes, she drinks. It's her overall aura.

'Another thing,' he said, moving on and ignoring my protests. 'Shaun's told me things. Things about Fletch. Let's talk about that. Let's go.' Mark hated how Fletch had treated Shaun and he used to talk about what he was going to do to him. I'd always treated that as a joke.

He asked where Fletch lived and if I had a car. He got me to show him my keys and then snatched them out of my hand and pumped his huge arm over my shoulder and we began to walk. We were in Williamstown, pretty close to the West Gate Bridge, and somehow we ended up walking onto the bridge entrance and then up onto it. The traffic was coming at us and people were slowing down and beeping their horns and swerving around us, as there was no pathway and we were on the road!

I said, 'I'm scared, Mark, what are we doing?'

He grabbed me tighter around the shoulder and said, 'Hang on.'

I thought, 'Hang on? There's bloody cars coming at us!'

People kept yelling out to Chopper and saying things like, 'Hey Chopper, what are you doing?' He'd yell back, 'What do you think I'm doing here, numbskull, I'm going for a walk.' He was totally fearless. I was like a deer in the headlights, not knowing what to say or what to do and we were on top of the West Gate Bridge!

I swear to God, Chopper's a big man, and he was leaning right on top of me as we walked. 'I want to talk to you about some things. You work on films and stuff?'

I nodded.

'Why don't you take my story, and make it into another movie?'

'Why?'

'Because Shaun's going to need another heart.'

'What?' I said. 'What do you mean?'

'Go and buy two hearts for him.'

'Mark, you can't go and buy a heart and put it in a fridge or a freezer.'

'No, Cameron, go to the black market, right? Go to the black market, and give them $500,000 and buy a heart.'

I said, 'Mate, it doesn't work like that.'

'It's quite simple to me. Money buys things.'

I didn't know what to say. When I'd finished arguing with him about that, he went on.

'Okay. That's number one. Number two, I'd like to see you get in the gym every day. I just think you need to probably lose some weight and get fitter.'

'All right,' I said, wondering where all this was coming from. He'd obviously been thinking.

'Number three. Where's Fletch?'

'What? Fletch, Shaun's stepfather?'

'Yes, Shaun told me about what happened. I want to do something tonight.'

Now I was worried. 'What would you like to do?'

'Shaun's told me he doesn't want me to do anything, because God will handle it, but I don't believe that. So I'd like to bring a mate of mine, and I'd like to get what's called "a full ten strike-out".'

'Why are you telling me about all of this stuff? I'm not some sort of underworld figure.'

'Just listen. We're going to get in your car right now, and we're going to go pick up the gun, and we're going to pick up two slugs.'

He had me in a tight grip – he was serious. All I could see was something bad happening and me ending up in jail with Chopper. I had to find a way out.

'I know a guy who knows a guy,' he said with some reference to getting guns.

I was thinking, 'Who talks like this?' I thought we were just going for a walk to calm me down. Not because I know a guy, who knows a guy.

'It's time for Fletch to pay the piper. It's time he paid. His time has got to come now.'

'All right, what are you planning on doing?' I pulled back from his grip and I was nearly hit by passing cars. 'What's your plan, Mark?'

'Simple. You're going to knock on the door.'

'Yeah, and . . . ?'

'Fletch's going to answer, or his wife's going to answer, and you're going to say, "Come outside, Fletch."'

'What are you going to do then?'

'He needs kneecapping. Shotgun pellets straight to the kneecaps. I'll just come out from the dark, like this,' he said, pretending to cock a gun. 'I'm just going to go *boom*, *boom*. And we're going to walk away.'

'Walk away? What's going to happen then? I'm probably going to be an accessory after the fact, or whatever they call it in police terms.'

'We're going to use Shaun as self-defence. We'll say we were defending him, because that is what it is. We'll be right.'

And I swear to God, I'm glad I talked myself out of going with him . . . or of him going. 'Please, Mark,' I pleaded with him, 'I don't want to do this. And Shaun has said to you not to touch Fletch.'

'But the boy suffered.'

'But you shooting him in the kneecaps twice, do you think that's going to make Shaun's life any better? I'm going to go to jail, you're going to go to jail. You've already spent twenty-three years in jail. You want to go back there again? Your wife's told you that she'd leave you, if you ever went back. And you've got an eight-year-old boy. Why would you want to do that?'

'I know that Shaun suffered.'

'Yes, Shaun has suffered, but he handled it. He's okay.'

'All right,' he finally said, and we turned around and started walking back down the bridge.

I'd never heard him talk like that before, and it was pretty scary. I had no idea what was going to happen to me, but I sure as hell had to stop that happening. Aside from it being wrong, I didn't want to go to jail.

But as much as he scared me that night, he also did some amazing things. Shaun had a mate from the Noble Park days named Michael. He was a troubled kid and you could see he was going down a bad path.

Late one Wednesday night when he was in the car with me and Shaun, Michael was joking about some of the stupid stuff he was up to which wasn't good. Shaun wasn't happy with what he was hearing, so 'Shaun the fixer' piped up.

'I'm concerned about you, Michael,' he said. 'You're going to end up in jail.'

Michael thought that was very funny.

'You think it's funny, do you?' asked Shaun. 'I'm calling Chopper Read – he'll tell you it isn't funny.'

Michael laughed. He thought it was hilarious. So Shaun rang Mark to give Michael a lecture. It was on the speaker phone and I'll never forget it.

'Shaun wants to talk to you,' I said to Chopper. 'One of his friends, called Michael, is going down the wrong path.'

So Mark asked, 'What's he look like?'

Shaun said he was thin and had blue eyes and blond hair.

'Put Marco on, Shaun,' Mark said, getting serious and mucking up his name.

Michael said, 'Hi, Chopper.'

'Only my friends call me Chopper or Mark,' he said, pausing. 'You can just call me nothing at the moment.'

This conversation was getting pretty serious.

'Tell me something, Marco,' he said. 'Can you fight?'

'I can a little bit,' he said.

'If you go to prison, you're going to need to know how to fight, mate. From what Shaun told me, you're skinny, you've got blue eyes, you have blond hair . . . you're going to be someone's bitch in prison.'

They spoke for nearly half an hour and Michael seemed to listen – I mean this was Chopper Read! Ultimately it didn't make any difference because Michael did end up in jail. He's been in twice now. I got a call from him a year or so ago after he was released. He struggled more than some others with Shaun's death, but he should have just honoured Shaun by sorting himself out. I reminded him recently what Shaun said that day. Michael's got a baby now so I'm hoping he can get his life together.

Anyway, that was kind of how it worked with Chopper. He was a good man with some pretty big flaws. Funnily enough, we got closer to him after that night on the bridge. Shaun liked having him around. It made him feel safe from Fletch and that was all he needed.

Sometimes I'd get a little worried. I found myself being followed by cops at times, and if Chopper was with me they'd pull up beside us and say something like 'Hey, Chopper. How are you?'

Mark would do that laugh we've all heard. 'Ha, ha, ha, ha. I'm good, how are you?' And he'd start some sort of banter with them. They didn't worry him in the slightest. He'd say something like, 'See the bank over there? We're just making a deposit.' And he'd laugh again.

'You've got to stop talking like that, mate, you can't say things like that,' I said to him one day. 'It's freaking me out.'

We met some of Chopper's mates too. One bloke, Frankie Waghorn, really put me on edge. He was a convicted murderer. He was a big man, very scary.

We first met him at the hospital with Benji, and he offered Shaun a Coke and reached out with these huge hands. We had lunch with him and he seemed like one of the nicest guys I'd ever met. When I did some research on him, though, I nearly had a heart attack. I was starting to freak out. Chopper Read, Frankie Waghorn . . .

Shaun thought it was funny. 'Dad, they're just people that have had a hard time. He's very lovable, isn't he?'

'Lovable?' I said. 'He was at Pentridge with Mark. Go and look him up.'

All these people were starting to gather around me. I was more confident I had nothing to fear any longer from Fletch, but what about these people? Shaun always chose to look at the brighter side of everything, though. And that included Chopper and his mates.

SHAUN

27

You know this game called Mafia Wars that you can play on Facebook? Dad was obsessed with it. You play dudes from all over the world and that's how he stumbled across this American player, David, and his wife, Sondra. That's kind of how it all began. They became Facebook friends and it turns out Dad and Sondra and her husband had much more in common than Mafia Wars. They're heart parents too, although their son had died. Dad told her about me and my heart problems, and then Sondra added me as a friend and we've been friends ever since.

I've been writing to Sondra Baker Kilgo since I was fourteen. She lives in Alabama, USA, and has been the bestest friend a person could wish for. Her son, Nathan, was born with TGV – Transposition of the Great Vessels, a congenital heart defect. He had his first open heart surgery when he was three years old. Sondra said Nathan was the most loving child any parent could ever ask for – like a gift from God. When he was sixteen, Nathan's girlfriend had a daughter, Jessica. That means he was a year younger than me

157

when he had her. I can't imagine being a father at sixteen – especially on top of everything else he was going through. Nathan was doing good – raising Jess, going to college, and he was even on the Dean's list, which means he was smart and getting great marks.

But in 2009, at the age of twenty-two, Nathan died suddenly from heart failure and Sondra's world came crashing down. She told me she had nothing to live for, although she had two other kids. Nathan's death affected her mega and she admits she was even suicidal. Sondra hit rock bottom.

She felt really lost and it was especially hard on her when all those who were supporting her started getting on with their own lives. Everybody was there for her in the beginning, but then her husband went back to work, her children went back to school, her friends stopped calling and visiting regularly, and then it was just her. It was the worst time of her life and that's when I came along. It's funny how the universe works.

I'd jump on the net to check if Sondra was online and we'd chat. If I could cheer her up or make her smile then I was happy too. And we'd make sure each of us was doing all right. We always stay in contact, no matter what. She writes on my wall and sends me messages and things. What surprises people about our friendship, apart from the fact that she lives in Alabama, is that I'm a teenager who takes the time to write to a woman he's never met. 'You are just an incredible little person for doing that,' my Aunt Susanne always says to me, but it never felt like that to me – it is just what you do. She's proud of me for this – maybe because she's a mother and understands how much it would mean to lose a child.

One night, when I was in hospital using my laptop, I said to Dad, 'Do you have enough money to fly Sondra over here so we can meet her properly?'

I just wanted her to come over so I could give her a hug. I just wish that she didn't live so far away. Sondra had said to me, 'I talk to you more than I talk to the people who have been living next door for six years.'

She always says nice things about me to Dad like, 'Your son gives me the comfort every day to go on with life. He saved my life, and he gave me a reason to live.'

Sondra tells me I've helped her to deal with the death of her son. She still can't believe that it ended up being a fourteen-year-old boy from Australia who would see her through her tears, but it's like my friend Zane Dirani says: 'Send love and warmth from the heart and may that light show you the path of life.'

She's been through a lot, Sondra, and she's just such an amazing lady. I promised her she'll get the first copy of this book, signed, sealed and delivered. Sondra's a great friend.

I'm pretty sure I've talked about my friend Christian – the one with heart issues who was deadset on getting to the Olympics. We've asked him to give a pumped-up speech at my Kick-Arse Party – which I'll tell you all about soon – because he's so inspiring.

The best thing about Christian is that he's an ambassador for HeartKids. We're now both HeartKids Ambassadors together, but he does so much more for them than I do. He goes around visiting hospitals and talking to teenagers with heart problems. He always tries to do what he can to help these kids because he understands where they're coming from.

Christian is very serious about his role as a HeartKids Ambassador. He's always one of the first to visit me when I'm under the weather, and he's the first person most heart kids run to when they have any questions they might not want to ask their doctor or parents. Sometimes it's just easier to talk to Christian. He says he's learnt lots from us and we've learnt a lot from him too. Everyone loves Christian. He's really easy to get along with and a lot of fun – whether that's doing burnouts in wheelchairs in hospital corridors, playing chubby bunny at camp (stuffing our faces with dim-sims till we feel like throwing up), or playing beach volleyball.

He's only seven years older than me, but a real role model. Going away each year on camp we've seen the best and worst of each other. Sometimes I get the feeling Christian feels sorry for me, probs because I'm so young and what I'm going through shouldn't be happening to a kid – even though he's gone through some pretty sucky stuff himself. He gets the way we have this ongoing battle with medication.

Christian stopped taking his medication when he realised it was banned by the anti-doping mob. He didn't want this to ruin his chances of competing in the Olympics so he stopped taking his tablets, which landed him in hospital. They've since lifted the ban. He admits it was a pretty poor decision, but he was just chasing the dream. On a few occasions, my illness has gotten in the way of me doing stuff, so I know how he feels.

I'm not dumb. I know that the medication I take is the reason I'm still alive. And yet sometimes I just get so fed up with it all. It's frustrating when people say, 'Oh that wasn't a very smart thing to do,' but it's hard to explain. I think Christian understands. It's like he can read my mind.

'You know what it is, Shaun?' he'd say to me. 'In your life, you feel like you've had so much taken away that sometimes there's the temptation to rebel against everything that's going on by doing something like not taking your medication, even though it's crazy. It's the one thing you have most control over, because God knows you don't have control over much.'

Who knows what's going on in my head anyway? I say to Christian, 'I just can't stand taking all those pills. They taste like shit.' And I have to do it day in and day out, a handful of fat disgusting pills which make me want to vomit. All I want is to go to a sleepover with my friends and not have to worry about carrying around a dosette case with meds that are strictly timed.

I have to admit that if I'm having a bad day it's easy to crack. I don't care. I just want to be normal for one night.

Christian starts pointing a finger at me. 'I know how you feel, trust me I do, but it's really dangerous. I know more than anyone that that's not the way to go. It nearly killed me. What you gotta understand, Shaun, is that people worry about you, whether you like it or not. When they nag you about taking your pills, you can't get mad. Everyone has your best interests at heart.'

I get all that. Anyway, there's heaps going on in my head at the moment. One thing I hate with a passion is this stupid PICC line that's driving me mental. A nurse from Hospital in the Home comes every day to check on me and change my PICC line dressing. She doesn't like it when I tell her I wish she'd just pull it out. It's hard to sleep. Dad and me have swapped beds so I can stretch out a bit more. The PICC line just makes me miserable. All I cop is a lecture from the nurse, but I swear it's making no difference to this chest infection.

SHAUN

28

DAD NEVER WENT out much at all. If he wasn't busy looking after me, he was working on one of his film projects. For ages, I'd been thinking he was overdue to start dating some girls. I'd kind of hoped it might just happen, but it didn't. He'd be telling me about this or that actress and I'd be dropping hints left, right and centre about how he should talk to them, but he was hopeless. Too shy, too scared and stuff.

I thought the best way to get him back out there was the internet. One night, after copping a lot of bitching and whinging, I sat him down and made him look through the RSVP website with me. Right there on the very first page was a shot of this beautiful woman with blonde hair and a great smile. I know it's just a photo, but she looked heaps friendly and perfect for Dad. I could just tell.

'Dad, she looks like she'd be good for you!' I said straightaway.

He looked at the picture and said, 'Yeah, maybe too good.' Not the best sign.

'Well, Dad, you never know unless you give it a go.'

I managed to get him to sign up for RSVP, but that's as far as it ever went. Every now and then I'd get onto RSVP using Dad's password and check out what was happening. Nothing, of course. Then about six months later the same blonde woman popped up on Dad's Facebook newsfeed as one of those 'people you may know' suggestions because they shared some mutual friends. Her name was Sally and after a bit of prodding Dad sent her a Facebook friend request.

A month went by and we were having a BBQ at our place. I said, like it was no big deal, 'Hey, why don't you invite Sally?'

So I did a Facebook event for the party under Dad's name and he added her and wrote a personal message saying, 'I'd really like you to come to my BBQ.' All that afternoon I was waiting for her to rock up, but she never came. As typical blokes we never said a word about it, but I reckon we were both disappointed.

Still nothing was happening. Then one day Dad posted a status on Facebook saying, 'Kids picking on my son for having a heart problem. Breaks my heart.' This was when Chopper was helping me with bullying. Sally wrote, 'People can be so cruel!' That kicked the whole thing off. He started writing to her on Facebook and eventually convinced her to go on a date with him. She must have forgotten he was the stranger freak who invited her to a random BBQ.

Having heard all this from Dad, I was real keen to meet Sally and see for myself, so Dad said I could go along on their second date. He was a nervous wreck. It took him ages to decide what to wear, and he was even breaking my balls about looking presentable. We went shopping especially for the occasion and he bought me a new leather jacket.

Now Sally probs found the date a little weird, but Dad and I are best mates. He didn't think it was a big deal because we do almost everything together. The moment I saw them together, I could tell he really liked her.

I was tiny back then. I'd just begun taking steroids to speed up my growth. I still have that leather jacket, but it's way too small for me now. I can't even fit my arms into it. Even though I was fourteen, I probably looked about eight years old, because I still hadn't gone through puberty yet. During Sally and Dad's relationship the steroids kicked in and my shoulders started to broaden and I even began to grow hair on my chin. Sally was there when I grew from a boy into a man.

On that date, I told Sally that I could dance like Michael Jackson. She begged me to do it right in the middle of the pub. She was very persistent and kept bugging me, 'Just do it! Who cares what people think? Do it for me, please, Shaun?' I gave in and started breakdancing in the middle of the pub. Sally absolutely loved it and was laughing, and ever since then we've had a great connection. Dad jokes, 'I think Sally fell in love with Shaun before she fell in love with me.'

The beginning of Dad and Sally's relationship was pretty rocky. By her standards, Dad never had any fun. Sally was a bit of a party animal whereas Dad never went out, never partied and never got drunk. They always seemed to be arguing and I got stuck in the middle. Somehow I ended up being the referee, the teenager solving these two grown adults' issues. I was soon sick of the bickering so I decided to sit them down to give them some relationship advice. It didn't matter that I was fifteen and knew nothing about girlfriends.

I knew exactly what Dad and Sally needed. It was like a lecture. I had a whiteboard propped up especially for the occasion and everything. On it I drew up a family timetable that would structure how we spent our weekends and nights. I delegated chores and blocked out a two-hour period every night for us all to be together. After that, Dad and me would hang out and then Sally and Dad would have 'alone time' and I'd play Xbox, then we'd all go to bed. Sounds kind of bizarre, I know, but somehow I had a feeling my plan might work. I just knew these two were going to be good for each other.

SHAUN

29

In late 2009, Dad became obsessed with this TV show on Foxtel called *The Contender Australia*. He couldn't stop talking about it and wanted me to start watching it with him. As a big WWE fan I was interested in wrestling, but thanks to Dad, I was soon hooked on boxing as well. It was a reality type show where a group of amateur Australian boxers lived together and each week they'd have to face off against one another. Eventually there'd be one winner and he'd have the opportunity to fight Anthony 'The Man' Mundine.

I watched every ep multiple times and was convinced this guy called Garth Wood was the best of them. I turned to Dad, who was sitting with me on the couch, and said, 'See that guy right there?' I pointed to the screen. 'He's going to win!'

Dad looked at me sceptically and was like, 'Sure, Shaun, keep dreaming.' He said that Wood wasn't considered a serious prospect.

And yet every week we watched and many of the best lost their bouts while Wood was still there. It was great fun to watch. I'd be bouncing round the lounge room swinging hooks and jabs and pretty soon I had everyone in the family watching.

When the finals came around about ten weeks later, it was Kariz 'Peter' Kariuki versus Garth Wood. In that match Garth knocked Kariz out cold, and earned himself 'The Contender Australia' title. This meant a chance to fight Mundine – a three-time world champion – as well as prize money and a car and stuff.

Then the program announced the shock news that Garth didn't want to fight Mundine anymore. So I went on Garth's Facebook fan page and wrote on the wall something like, 'Hi, my name's Shaun. I've had over a thousand operations including two heart transplants. You have to do this fight for your family and your friends. You need to beat Mundine cos he's a talker and you need to knock him off his perch!'

I didn't even know if I was talking to the right Garth Wood or not. It was just a fan page so really anyone could have just made it up, but I wrote my message like I was talking directly to him anyway. There were a lot of comments back from other Facebook users who saw my post. Things like, 'Wow, you've been through a lot! That's great that you said that.'

Then a week later we were at home and Dad came into my room with this big grin on his face.

'What are you so happy about?' I asked as he passed me the phone.

'Nothing,' Dad replied.

'Hello?' I said.

Then I heard a voice on the other end I didn't recognise straightaway.

'Hey, brother, how are you?'

'Who's this?' I asked.

'It's Garth Wood, brother,' this guy on the phone said. I was caught completely by surprise. 'Listen,' he continued, 'I've seen your wall post on the Facebook fan page. It's not me – it's some guy pretending to be me – but I did see it. I was going through a tough time when I made the decision to back out of the fight against Mundine, but reading about what you've been through has really turned me around and motivated me. This is all thanks to you, so I want to meet you and say thank you in person.'

The Mundine versus Wood fight was back on! After that I used to talk to Garth a lot on Facebook and sometimes on the phone every couple of weeks.

'Never, never, never give up. Never!' I'd say. I didn't see the point in keeping my thoughts to myself, so I told him he was pretty amazing and that he'd be the one who'd beat Mundine.

Then Dad and I were invited up to Sydney. We met up with Garth at a pizza place in Darlinghurst. While we were there, he offered to pick us up to watch one of his training sessions. He said to me, 'I'll wake you up at five o'clock tomorrow morning and we'll go for a run.'

'Five am?' I asked, confused.

'That's when it all happens.'

'Yeah sure, mate,' I said, 'it's not gunna happen. Never been a morning person.'

I did actually end up going for that run with Garth, and because he was an ex-Rabbitohs player he also took us to a South Sydney rugby league game. Dad and I had great seats. After the match, Garth took us down to the players' dressing room. It was real loud because they'd won and were celebrating, singing their song and banging things and stuff. Even Garth was singing along.

One of the players was crying, because he was getting stitches near his eye. I went over, pulled my t-shirt up and showed him my scar. 'Look what I've had. You got nothing to cry about.' The guy looked at me and said, 'I'm all good. Thanks, buddy.'

Then this scruffy looking dude with a beard, who was watching us talking, wandered over. 'Hi, I'm Russell Crowe,' he said, and he stuck out his hand. He's one of the owners of the club.

'The movie star?' I asked. 'Wow – you look like a bum.'

That did it. Russell just laughed and laughed. Apparently, he wears crappy clothes to annoy the media and stuff. He pointed to my chest where I'd shown the player my scar and said, 'A nice Rabbitohs tattoo right there on the heart would be good.'

'I don't think I can get tattoos because of my immune system, but what about a fake one?' I said.

'Yeah that's all right, but it doesn't last, you know.'

I was enjoying myself so much that I really didn't want it to end. That's why I was disappointed when Garth turned to us and said, 'Unfortunately I have to go now.'

'What? Where!?'

Then he said, 'Don't worry, you're coming too,' and the smile was back on my face.

'Where are we going?' I wanted to know.

All Dad cared about was whether or not there was going to be food there, because he was hungry.

'Of course there's going to be food there, you fatty!' Garth said. I couldn't help laughing. Trust Dad to always think about his stomach – he does that wherever we go.

So Dad and I ended up at this press conference where Garth was speaking to a crowd of journalists and photographers. Garth spoke about his time on *The Contender* and about his experiences and then said to the crowd that he'd been through nothing in his life like Shaun Miller. He was pointing at me and everyone was wondering what the hell was going on.

'This kid's had two heart transplants,' said Garth, 'which is amazing.' People started clapping so I was feeling pretty special. 'He's going to help me through this. He's going to be in my corner at the Mundine fight.'

At the big event we sat with Garth's family, who gave us these ringside tickets. It was a massive night, but before the main fight, there were heaps of other bouts to sit through first. They were all so boring I nearly fell asleep. Then when Garth came out, I woke right up and saw him point at me and grin. I was so excited my adrenaline was really pumping.

The beginning of the fight was quite slow – not what I expected. But Garth was losing and by the fifth round things weren't looking too good for him at all. Mundine was getting his swagger on and throwing good punches to Garth's head, leaving him looking drowsy and disorientated. Even though I couldn't help but feel anxious about the outcome, I was positive that he'd pull through. I knew I had to step up and remind him of what we'd been working so hard towards. If I didn't, he was going to lose.

When there was a break between rounds I turned to Dad and said, 'Put me on your shoulders.' So I was a couple of metres from the ring and climbed up above everyone else in the crowd. At the top of my voice I yelled, 'GARTH! NEVER, NEVER, NEVER GIVE UP!'

Just for a split second, he saw me there perched on Dad's shoulders. Deadset, as soon as he heard me, it was like a wave of energy overtook him. He gave his chest a mighty thump, shot me one last glance and then when the bell went he jumped up and went

SMACK! with his left, throwing a massive hook and knocking Mundine out cold. He'd won. No-one could believe what had happened. He'd beaten the world champion!

The next day was pretty full on. We did a lot of media and ended up at another press conference. Jeff Fenech, another world champ, came over. 'I don't know what you did to Garth, mate, but it was amazing.'

Because I'd been able to help him, Garth calls me his 'secret weapon'. Then he did something awesome. He handed me his *Contender*'s jacket and his boxing gloves from the last fight in the show. On one glove he wrote, 'Thanks for always being in my corner, I'll always be in yours,' and on the other, 'To my little mate Shaun. Your mate for life. You're a true champion. Garth.'

I have to admit this was a pretty special gift, like one of the best ever.

CAMERON

30

WHENEVER SHAUN'S HEALTH dropped down a bit, television became his escape. We both loved watching *The Contender Australia*, kind of a boxing reality show in which the first prize was some cash and a fight against Anthony Mundine.

The boxers ranged in experience from Ben McCulloch with three fights and Garth Wood with four, to boxers with ten times that number. I figured experience would count, but we were down at Mum and Dad's one day, all watching the show, when Shaun made his call.

'See this guy,' he said, pointing at Garth Wood, 'he's going to win.'

Dad and I looked at each other and, while laughing, we started to debate Shaun.

'What are you talking about? That guy has had hardly any fights. He's in the middle of depression. His wife's broken up with him. You think he's going to win?'

'He's going to win – I'll bet anything,' he said.

Ten episodes or whatever later, Garth won *The Contender* and Shaun reminded us of his tip before declaring that he'd like to meet him. Shaun, the little social media whiz, jumped onto Facebook, tracked Garth down and introduced himself to him.

Of course, Garth didn't know whether Shaun was the real deal or not, so he contacted the hospital and they confirmed. Yes, Shaun was definitely the real deal.

Garth was based in Sydney and they started talking on the phone pretty much every day. They talked all sorts of crap, but the serious side of it had Garth doubting his ability to fight Mundine, even though he agreed to the fight. Getting through *The Contender* had left him with some breaks in his hands, and he had to keep putting the fight off.

My sister had told Shaun's story to Fox FM on some sort of competition, and they called Shaun and offered him a trip to Bali and a computer because they were touched by his story. Going to Bali was never going to happen. With his heart, all the disease there and the poor hospital system, that was just too risky. So he convinced them to turn Bali into Sydney and went to meet Garth.

They got along like a house on fire, but Garth kept talking about his doubts about fighting Mundine. Shaun wasn't having any of that, and when they were sitting at a Rabbitohs game together I heard him say, 'Garth, I've had two heart transplants, I've gone through this, I've gone through that. I think you need to pick yourself up and do this for your family, because I believe you can beat Mundine.'

They spent two or three days together, and Garth even took him to training – at 5 am. I tried to get out of it. I just wanted to sleep, but Garth and Shaun paid no attention to that and we were at this gym in Redfern, and the sun wasn't even up. Shaun was loving it, but I definitely wasn't!

The fight with Mundine wasn't until sometime in December, still six months away, and Shaun spoke with Garth maybe three times a week. Each conversation was a pep talk from Shaun, and each week Garth believed a little more. Finally the fight came. The big one.

We flew to Sydney and stayed in some dingy motel near Acer Arena. We were met outside the venue by Garth's mum, who gave us our tickets. We went inside – it was chockers.

When the fight started, Garth was immediately in trouble and was losing pretty badly. During the break after the fourth round, Shaun asked me to put him on my shoulders.

'What for?' I said.

There were lunatics everywhere, guys just jumping up and down, and I thought having Shaun on my shoulders was not a good idea. What if he got knocked off? He insisted, though, so after the round began I lifted him up. Garth was getting hit with lefts and rights, but when Shaun got up there, he yelled out, 'Garth! Never, never, never give up!'

All of a sudden Garth went *bang* and hit Mundine with a right to the temple. He went down and didn't get back up again. Shaun was elated, freaking out. He couldn't believe it.

In the excitement afterwards, Shaun just wanted to go to the rooms. 'I gotta see Garth!'

So we did and the security guard let Shaun in – but not me. No matter how much I argued I got nowhere, and I was left outside for forty-five minutes hoping Shaun was okay. When he eventually came out, I asked what had happened in there. The cheeky bugger said, 'What goes on in the room stays in the room, Dad!'

As we headed back to our motel, I asked Shaun if anyone had spoken to him about being Garth's 'secret weapon', which is how Garth referred to him during their conversations. When he said no, I got all righteous and decided to do something about it myself.

I got on the phone and rang every TV network I could think of, and the guys from Nine came to the motel to have a chat. They could see the story panning out in front of them, so they offered to take us to Garth's media conference the next day at Jeff Fenech's Redfern gym.

Garth and the team were happy to see Shaun there, and Jeff Fenech came up to him. 'You're Shaun Miller, aren't ya? You're Garth's secret weapon. Let me shake your hand.' And he did.

Shaun was over the moon about that experience – he had such a great time.

He really believed in Garth, but unfortunately he was disappointed after that. Shaun said Garth lost his way – he changed trainers and tried to change the way he boxed. 'Why is he changing his style?' Shaun would ask.

He'd beaten Mundine the other way, becoming only the second bloke to have knocked him out. Shaun didn't understand why you'd change. After a while they started to drift apart, which was a little sad.

I spoke to Garth a while back when he was in a spot of trouble. He'd been at a party and he and his friends left to go to a pub and a fight broke out at the pub. He saw one of his mates fly off a balcony and smash his head onto the ground. There was a bloke kicking him so Garth stepped in to help. Probably because he was a famous boxer, the police charged him with affray.

The court hearing was held on a new *Judge Judy*-like TV show where he got to explain himself, and was eventually found not guilty after the judge watched video of the incident. It was a tough time for him, though. He could have gone to jail.

Anyway, we had a good talk. Garth really struggled when he found out that Shaun was going to die, and he didn't know how to deal with it, so he just put distance in there. I kind of understand, but it's a pity for both him and Shaun that they didn't stay strong together.

SHAUN

31

THREE TEENAGE SCHOOLGIRLS make a pact to all get married in the same church on the same day. Life, however, has a rather different plan in store for them! That's the basic plot of the movie *Groomless Bride*.

Even though Dad's the producer he still insisted that I audition for the part I wanted. 'I don't want anyone thinking I'm biased,' he said. 'The other actors, like Natalie Blair and Gemma Bishop, had to audition and so do you.'

Luckily, the director liked my audition and I was set to play the younger son of the character 'Allan', who was played by Chopper. But on the day of the shoot, I ended up in hospital, so they had to do the scene without me.

At 7 West Ward, the doctors realised I'd developed an aneurysm in my chest. When the walls of your blood vessels weaken, a spot can start bulging. This aneurysm fills with blood and stretches the side of the vessel. If this big bulge bursts, you can bleed to death on the spot. My aneurysm was the size of a small tennis ball, so things weren't looking good. When everyone was called to my bedside I knew it was even worse than I thought.

The medical team explained that to prevent the aneurysm from bursting they had to operate and 'shave' it. There was a high probability that the aneurysm would burst during the shaving process and it could be all over for me. However, if they didn't operate, it would eventually burst and end the same.

Before I was wheeled into the operating theatre, Dad, my aunt, her husband Ken and my grandparents said their goodbyes to me. They were crying and looking very down, but I ignored it all and said, 'See you after the op!'

I kept thinking about that epiphany I had before my first transplant, and although I didn't hear any voices, somehow I just knew for certain I was going to be okay.

After a few hours the surgeon walked out of the operation room and announced to my family, 'It didn't burst!'

They were all so happy for me. It was only then that we heard all about the things that could have gone wrong on the operating table. One of the doctors told us that something like ninety per cent of aneurysms burst during the procedure.

I was lying in bed in my hospital room when this weird random dude appeared out of nowhere. And he had with him this massive punching bag on one of those big plastic bases you fill with water.

'They tell me you're a fighter,' he said, 'which is why I brought you this gift.'

I was thinking, 'Who is this guy?' But one look at him and straightaway I liked him. He was real old, like maybe forty, and wore this bandana on his head. Not many can pull off a bandana, but he did.

This is how I met the amazing Zane Dirani. He's an expert in martial arts, but does all this other stuff as well. Sometimes he works as a stunts co-ordinator and actor for movies like *Killer Elite*, starring Robert De Niro, and did the stunts for Dad's film, *Groomless Bride*, which is where he heard about me. Later Dad was telling me about him and Zane talking on the set. When he mentioned my name Zane said, 'Shaun means "God's gift". Your son is an angel.'

That's exactly how he talks. Like Gandalf in *Lord of the Rings*. Then he said to Dad, 'When I look into your eyes I can see that when you were young you were a selfish person who didn't really care.' Dad was pretty taken aback because he'd be the first to admit there was a lot of truth to what he was saying. 'Oh okay,' he replied, 'who told you this?'

'No-one,' said Zane. 'Your son Shaun is an angel, bro, sent to you by God for a reason.'

For Zane, one of the most powerful actions a human being can take is to visit the sick. As soon as he heard from Dad that I was in hospital, he made plans to visit me the very next day. The punching bag he brought in towered over me. He'd filled the circular base with water so it wouldn't topple over when I used it. I couldn't believe he'd carried it through the hospital to my bed – it must have weighed a tonne.

When I asked him about this he said it was more difficult finding out where I was. There were no parking spots left in the hospital car park so Zane had parked his car several streets away. He was pretty sweaty and smelly by the time he lugged this fifty-plus kilo punching bag all the way to the information desk in the children's ward.

'I'm looking for a kid called Shaun Miller,' he told the reception-tionist. Her fingers did a little dance on the keyboard while she tried to discreetly check out the weird dude in the bandana and make sense of him and his punching bag. I think Zane was a bit worried they might not let him in, because of rules or something, but he was determined to find me and deliver my surprise gift.

So Zane said, 'He's had two heart transplants – one when he was eight and one when he was thirteen. This boy's had three hearts and a strong will to live.'

'Oh I know who you mean!' the receptionist said. And looking at the punching bag, she added, 'He's going to love that.'

I probs didn't say much the first time I met Zane. Maybe I was a bit overwhelmed. He didn't stay long. Just a quick hello – he introduced himself as Dad's friend – and he set up the punching bag in my room. 'It's a message to keep on fighting,' he said as he was about to leave. 'I shall see you again.' Then he was gone. Awesome.

That night I told Dad about my strange visitor. Zane was so intriguing I wanted to see him again to learn more about him and to thank him for his present. It only occurred to me after he'd gone that I never said thanks. Dad and I were planning a get-together to catch up with some friends at the McDonald's in the hospital in a few days' time, so I asked him to invite Zane.

CAMERON

32

SHAUN HAD ONE of his regular biopsies, and something happened inside from it. We don't know if they nicked something or not, but without us knowing, an aneurysm started to grow. By the time we found it, it was the size of a tennis ball and it was dangerous, even if he didn't feel it inside him.

This was around the time Shaun was going to play Chopper's son in *Groomless Bride*. They'd both been rehearsing for the film.

So we knew very little about the aneurysm because it wasn't causing Shaun any pain. I was out on set when the hospital called with some results, and they told me about the problem and that we needed to get him into the hospital immediately. So I grabbed him from school and took him in that morning to get ready for surgery the next day.

But the little bugger was having none of it. Mo Dirani, who Shaun had met before his cousin Zane, came in to see him and they left the hospital to have lunch at Crown – they just walked out. The hospital was freaking out – they had no idea where he'd gone. I had

181

to ring Shaun to find out where he'd disappeared to, and in typical fashion he said, 'Don't worry, Dad, I'm just having lunch with Mo.'

I said, 'Shaun, you've gotta have surgery soon.'

'Yeah, it'll be okay.'

He wasn't listening to the ticking time bomb discussion I was downloading on him, which for me was how I saw it all. The aneurysm could have exploded any moment in his chest, so I was stressed. In hindsight, it was a little bit funny. I've still got the photo of him, Mo and a guy called George Gingers and some of the other things he loaded on Facebook that day.

Unbelievable. Not a care in the world.

The doctors always played things close to their chest, but I think they knew more than they were telling me. It was things like this, and earlier in the year when Shaun had ulcers in his mouth so big that he stopped eating for a week because of the pain. There were major side effects to the rejection medicine all over the place, and they were always poking things in his body and looking at his heart.

After the operation to remove the aneurysm, he changed. I think Shaun knew too that his body was slowly shutting down. Maybe it was one operation too many, but he became very short tempered and not tolerant of people, which was just not him at all.

During that phase he revealed a little more to me about some of the thoughts he was having, and perhaps for the first time in his life he wasn't positive and upbeat. He said to me, 'You know what, Dad? Every time I look forward to something in my life, like going to the wrestling or playing football, I have an operation or I get sick. Every time. I'm absolutely sick of it. Every opportunity I get, I get sick, and I have to stop it.'

And I thought, 'He's actually right.'

He'd been rehearsing with Mark and he was having a ball – then the aneurysm hit and stopped that. So I understood what was going on in his mind. Then one day in November, he just snapped out of it.

CAMERON

33

ZANE DIRANI IS a bit of a big deal in martial arts. He is also like a brother to me, which is a promise he made to Shaun. He said he'll always watch my back and that he'd even take a bullet for me – which I believe he would, 110 per cent.

I first met Zane when I went to the after party with a mate for the film *Killer Elite* in 2010, but it wasn't until a year later that we started to build a friendship. May seemed to work for us – we initially met in May 2010, then in May 2011 we next worked together and our friendship became deeper. That was when he heard how sick Shaun was.

He wanted to give Shaun one of those standing speed-ball punching bags, so we organised a time for him to drop around while Shaun was still in the hospital. This was about a week after the operation for the aneurysm. Shaun had been cut down the chest and had a bunch of tubes coming out of his chest, neck and groin.

Zane walked straight in, kissed my forehead and gave me a massive hug. It hurt a little. Then he sat with Shaun. He looked deep into Shaun's eyes, then said to me, 'Cam, can I speak to you for a minute outside?'

I wasn't prepared for what Zane was going to say to me.

'Bro, do you know what you have in the room?'

I said, 'You mean Shaun?'

'No.'

I looked at him, trying to work out what he was on about.

He went on to tell me that Shaun was an angel – he felt it. I was stunned. He turned and went back into the room to talk to Shaun, and told him the same thing.

'Bro, you are an angel and in one year you will have a message to the world.'

Shaun just nodded and said, 'Yes, I understand.'

We'd later discover Shaun and Zane had a lot in common. When Zane was twenty-three, he'd had a tumour on his spine, and after going under the knife twice to have it removed he was told he'd never walk again. He had to be moved every day so he wouldn't get bed sores, and they had to feed, bathe and clean him.

Zane was completely powerless and the future didn't look bright. The way it was going, he felt the doctors were right. Then one morning Zane says he saw a strange light encasing his bed and felt his foot twitch – and just like that he could move it again. Zane had won his battle with cancer.

Up to that point in his life, he'd been training as a boxer and his dream was to be world champion, but he took a different path after that. Zane became a martial arts instructor and teacher, and started tapping into his spirituality. He also makes a living as a stunt co-ordinator and extra on movies, like *Killer Elite*. All that allowed him enough time to do volunteer work.

We learnt over time so much about Zane and his beliefs, and if more people listened the world would be a better place. Whether you are Muslim, Jew, Hindu, Christian or whatever, it doesn't matter. We all bleed the same blood and we are all messengers of God. We all have a purpose and we all carry a message to share before it's time to go.

Shaun, in Zane's eyes, was chosen as one of God's angels. He told Shaun he had a message and he had to give it to the world. It would take a while for me, and Shaun for that matter, to understand, but we eventually did.

Zane was great with Shaun. He knew how to lighten him up when things were serious. Like when Shaun was in hospital and he told Zane one day that he was worried about me because I needed to go to court to get the restraining order against Fletch renewed. Zane asked Shaun if he wanted him to make him laugh – of course Shaun said 'yes'. So Zane got me to stand in front of him and stood in front of me and twisted the front of my shorts and they dropped to the floor and I jumped backwards. Everyone laughed, especially Shaun.

One of Shaun's other visitors, Kyle, who was the brother of Shaun's mate Zavier, wanted a go. He was huge, maybe six foot two and 130 or more kilos, and he said Zane couldn't make him move like that. I tried to talk Kyle out of it, but he thought I was faking. Zane hit him with a Bruce Lee-like punch, which he later said he didn't feel, but he flew into the air and smashed into the wall. It was like something out of the wrestling. Not only was Shaun laughing, but this was his mate who'd done that, and he swelled with pride.

Then we got serious again. Shaun told Zane the whole story of his life, especially how Fletch had treated him. Zane looked at Shaun and told him he would always act as his protector – another one – and healer. You could see Shaun relax. But no matter how much Zane could help, we still had to go to court. Shaun asked Zane to go with me, which he did.

During that day at court, I shared everything with Zane about all the stuff that Fletch had done and said over time. Shaun was scared even to say Fletch's name – that's how bad it was. Zane and I were sitting in the waiting room together at the courthouse, with Zane sitting really close to me, dressed in all black and wearing a red bandana. We walked into the court but unfortunately the case was adjourned until a week later.

Afterwards, Olivia phoned Shaun. He rarely answered her calls but he did this time, because he was interested in what she had to say. She wasn't one for pleasantries and began yelling at him, asking, 'Did that father of yours hire a hitman?' Shaun started laughing and she hung up on him. Zane did look like a hitman that day, and the impact was obvious.

When we went back to court, this time Fletch brought rein-forcements in Olivia's father. Zane was with me again. After listening to the evidence and reviewing the case, the judge ruled that the AVO was not going to be lifted.

I was happy but I wanted to get out of court fast. Fletch looked furious and that always made me worry, AVO or no AVO. As we were leaving I had a funny feeling, and I said to Zane that I thought we were being followed.

He said, 'It's okay, bro, don't stress.'

We picked up the pace, but as we were walking to a set of traffic lights we could hear Fletch and Olivia's father a couple of metres behind us, with Fletch making stupid threats. It was pretty stupid of them, given that it was breaking the orders – which could result in a jail term – and that I had Zane with me.

When we stopped at the street corner, Zane was still telling me to relax – that they were just trying to get me to start something. Then all of a sudden I felt Zane's arm around my arm. He lifted me up and put me on the opposite side of the traffic light pole behind him. To this day I still don't know how he did it.

Then he turned to face Fletch and just said, 'Gentlemen,' and looked at them. Fletch said, 'Give us that little fucker Cameron,' but Zane refused point-blank. Zane was imposing, so they turned and walked away, which I'm glad they did.

Thankfully, there were no further issues with Fletch, and he and Olivia drifted out of my life. Today I have nothing to do with them at all, which is a great outcome.

SHAUN

34

THE SALLY I know these days is a completely different person to the one I first met a few years ago. On her first date with my dad, she told him she didn't have a maternal bone in her body. Sally was a lovely and warm person but quite selfish – with no cares or responsibilities. But really, she never had to until she met us. I think she spent most of her free time partying and being a 'good time' kind of girl. But just as Dad learned how to be a father, Sally learned how to be a mother.

One day Sally and I were talking and she started going on about this place she loves – the Melbourne Sports and Aquatic Centre. She thought it was bad enough that I'd never heard of it, but then she discovered that I couldn't actually swim. Dad had tried getting me to swim for years, but I always made excuses. I hated that I couldn't swim, but pretended it was no big deal for me.

'You know what, Shaun,' she said, 'it's going to be my mission to teach you to swim.'

We all headed off for this aquatic centre, and while she was real excited, I was like, whatevs. While Sally had a swim, Dad was reading a book and I was in the stands playing on my phone. Every now and then Sally was waving and trying to get us to go in. Then she got out of the water and was standing near me. She knew what was going down.

'It's okay, Shaun.' She gave me this look that went right through me. 'Come on,' she pleaded, 'go and get into your swimmers.'

Every excuse I came up with, Sally shot down in flames. When I still didn't budge, she said, 'You know what, Shaun, you wouldn't be alive without those scars, so wear them with pride.'

Sally talked to me about my insecurities. While I was embarrassed about the fact that I couldn't swim, the truth was that I was too self-conscious about the big scars on my chest to ever show my body in public. When I was in public I wanted to be a normal kid and didn't want people seeing my scars and wondering what the hell happened. She made me see those scars as something to be proud of. So, I went into the change rooms and came out, scars and all.

The aquatic centre has a wave pool – basically a shallow kids' pool with a machine that makes the water slosh back and forth. It feels like you're at the beach, but minus the sand and wind, which I hate anyway. Sally coaxed me into the wave pool, assuring me that I could stand up with my head above the water if I was scared.

As soon as I was in there, I absolutely loved it. I couldn't believe that this was what I'd been missing out on for so long.

After that we went to the aquatic centre quite a few times and once Sally was even able to get me to float. The trick is to hold your breath and pretend you're a balloon. Although I never got as far as swimming proper strokes, the wave pool was good enough for me. Once I became more confident, Sally convinced me to go down the water slide. It was fifty metres long and I was only just tall enough to be allowed on the ride. I measured myself on that height thingy. However, the slide was kind of scary and I never went on it again.

Sally also helped me deal with the issues on Mum's side of the family. While I could talk to Dad and my Aunt Susanne about anything, I sometimes felt they were too involved to help me. There was too much pain there, especially for Dad. He'd been so hurt that when I brought it up it felt like it was happening all over again. Sally was an outsider and able to discuss it without being emotional. And she helped me deal with the guilt I felt about what had happened with my mother and them. Like, whenever we had contact, Mum blamed me for the restraining order and said Fletch couldn't get a decent job because of what I'd done and that because of me they'd lose their house.

I could never forgive Fletch for what he did to me or how he treated my mother, but I wanted to try and make peace. I discussed with Sally the possibility of having the restraining order lifted so that I could improve things between me and Mum.

Sally talked it over with Dad and convinced him to let the restraining order go if Fletch agreed to apologise. Knowing how much bad blood there'd been between my dad and my mum, I thought this was nothing short of a miracle. That was the difference Sally brought to our lives. She tried to bring out the best in everyone. She was able to persuade Dad to draw a line over the past and do something good for the future.

Removing that restraining order was really important to my mum. I called her immediately and explained what we'd discussed – that Dad would accept an apology and the restraining order would go. As we hadn't spoken in quite a while, she was surprised to hear from me. She listened and said she'd tell Fletch, but sounded pretty happy to me.

While all this was going on, Fletch was obviously there listening and she was telling him about it.

Fletch picked up the phone and yelled, 'Shaun, you and all the Millers can go to hell!' Then he hung up on me.

Immediately, all my memories and fears came flooding back.

SHAUN

35

THE DAY OF the get-together that Dad had organised at McDonald's arrived and I was the first one there. Then Dad sent me a text saying he was running late because of work. It turned out that the others who were meeting up had stuff on as well. Only one other person showed up that day: Zane Dirani. While I munched on chicken nuggets, he had a cup of coffee. 'Like, what do you do, Zane?' I asked him. 'I do many things,' he replied with a smile.

Zane was one of sixteen children. Although he was born in Sydney, the family later moved to Melbourne. Of the sixteen kids, twelve are still living: four brothers and seven sisters. I wasn't game to ask what happened to the four that died. His birth name is actually Hasam, derived from the Arabic 'Hasanad', meaning 'good deeds'. When he was four years old, his mother started calling him Zane, which means 'benefactor' or 'doer of good', because she noticed how kind he was to the other children.

Zane left school at the age of thirteen. Even at that age he was already tall and, as he idolised Bruce Lee, he focused on training

193

and fighting. His talents took him into the world of boxing and he dreamed of being a world champion fighter. He fought in the ring over twenty-five times, never losing a bout. At eighteen, he fell in love and married. During the birth of their first child, his wife developed a malformation of the uterus. When she gave birth to their second child – both of them were girls – she was no longer able to have kids. His wife asked for a divorce because Zane was still young and needed to have a boy to carry on his name. Zane didn't want to remarry or have a son, but he gave her the divorce anyway. 'My deeds will carry on my name,' he told his wife. He bought a house for her and their children and continued on his life's journey, but he has always kept his promise and never remarried.

He told me that day at McDonald's: 'The ultimate truth for me is being a righteous man. I want to show people the path to righteousness, to make a difference in society by touching hearts.'

Zane believes we are born potential beings who journey through life to reach our higher self, and this happens when we have knowledge and discipline. He says that all human beings are unified and equal. He also talked about energy therapy and how he can see beyond what the average person sees. I didn't really get half of what he was saying. He told me he can read people just by looking into their eyes.

'What do you mean "read people"?' I asked.

'I'll give you an example if you like.' Zane looked into my eyes and said, 'Shaun, you have a reputation to live up to, but deep down you are hurting. It's not because of what you have been through, but because you want to release your pain. And yet you know that you can't because of the people around you. You have massive fear as you don't know where you're going after here. Even though you are sick, you are more mature than normal kids. You have been brought up mostly by one father, but you've had many mothers. No-one has looked deep into your fear, especially when you were hurt. And I'm not talking about your heart surgeries. But I won't go into that unless you want to talk about it yourself.'

The man was amazing. I was getting teary-eyed as he told me stuff he couldn't possibly have known. We'd only known each other for minutes, but it was like Zane knew me better than anybody in my life. I nodded and said, 'I want to talk about it.'

Then I shared with him everything about what had happened with Mum and Fletch. Obviously, I was still real scared of Fletch. Even though we had that restraining order, and even though I nearly gave it up to mend the bridges with Mum, I was still worried that someday he'd try to get even with me. Zane saw all this. He looked at me, smiled, then grabbed a strand of my hair and said, 'Shaun, from this moment onwards, as long as I am breathing, no man will ever touch a hair on your head.'

For the first time in my life I truly felt safe. Zane has been my protector and my healer ever since. Oh yeah, and he can do 150 push-ups nonstop. Deadset. I've seen him.

My idea to make peace with my mother and Fletch had backfired, I guess – big time. And I was recovering from my aneurysm surgery and had to stay in hospital for a few weeks. Although I was alive – barely – I was exhausted. All I wanted to do was sleep, which I'm sure Dad was happy about because he didn't have to fork out for the massive internet bill I usually clock up during hospital stays. Also, I was drugged up and half-asleep/half-awake most of the time.

At one point I opened my eyes and there standing beside the bed was Mum. I hadn't seen her in ages and kind of wondered if I was hallucinating or something. I was on heaps of medication so I was pretty much out of it most of the time. She held my hand and told me she loved me. Then she said, 'Shaun, I just need you to sign this.' Next thing there was a pen in my hand and I was signing a piece of paper. The problem was that I was so groggy I had no idea what I was supposed to be doing. Mum said, 'Thank you, Shaun.' And then she was gone. I was really whacked and wondered if this was for real, or a dream, or what.

For the next few days I didn't know what to make of it. A week or so later, I was having a session with the psychologist and I remembered this 'dream' about Mum's strange visit. As we were going over it, I noticed that he was looking real worried but trying to do the poker face thing. He knew the background with this restraining order shit and his alarm bells seemed to be going off. I was worried that I might have done something really wrong.

After that session everything cranked up a couple of notches. The psych rang Dad and he was onto his lawyer to check a few things out. The lawyer said that, even if it wasn't a dream and I had actually signed something, nothing I signed was legal because I'm under eighteen – not to mention that I was out of it at the time.

Anyway, something soon came in the mail to say there was going to be another hearing and I could see Dad getting all worked up and worried. I think just the thought of having to come face to face with Fletch again made him almost physically sick. All that trouble had been years ago and we'd all moved on and this was like the Arnie Schwarzenegger dude in *Terminator* – he was back causing everyone grief.

So I had a brainwave. 'Hey Dad,' I said, 'take Zane with you. That guy's amazing. There won't be any trouble if he's there.'

I got on the phone to Zane and gave him a heads-up. He didn't say a word. Just listened then said, 'Not a problem. I'll be there.'

The day of the court case came round, but I was too sick to go. Dad tells me he and Zane were sitting at the courthouse waiting for our lawyer when in walked Fletch. And, of course, he took one look at Zane standing next to Dad and figured this dude with the red bandana in incredible physical shape ain't a lawyer.

Dad later told me that Fletch then mysteriously disappeared, but I knew something had happened because even before Dad and Zane arrived back home, I had a phone call from my mum. 'Did Cameron hire a hitman?'

When I started laughing she hung up. Apparently, Fletch figured Zane was a hitman and bolted. I probably would have shit myself if I was him as well.

About a week later they were back in court. This time Fletch brought reinforcements – Mum's father and some other friends. And Zane was again there to give Dad back-up. After listening to the evidence the judge said that the restraining order wasn't going to be lifted. Dad was really stoked about this, of course, and obviously Fletch was heaps pissed off, but who cares.

As Dad and Zane left the court, they noticed that Fletch and Mum's dad were heading in the same direction. Pretty soon they realised they were actually following them. Dad and Zane picked up the pace but the other two were catching up – and the car was still a couple of blocks away. As they were heading towards an inter-section they could hear Fletch behind them making threats. All of which was pretty amazing considering Fletch was actually breaking the order. How dumb could you be?

They got to an intersection and the traffic signals went against them and Dad and Zane had to stand there while Fletch caught up. When Dad told me what happened next, it was like something out of a kung-fu movie.

Dad was standing there waiting nervously at the intersection listening to the threats being made by Fletch as he got closer and closer. Then he felt Zane somehow snake an arm around him, lift him, and put him down on the opposite side of the traffic light pole. It was incredible. In one move Zane lifted him and removed him from the action.

'Cameron, stay here,' Zane ordered. Then he spun around – those deadly arms at the ready – and walked towards Fletch and Pa. 'Can I help you gentlemen?' he asked. What Zane said to them wasn't even threatening. Just his energy alone was enough to shake them up. Whatever the grand plan was, they abandoned it there and then. Fletch scurried off and, thanks to Zane, he never came near us again.

SHAUN

36

JANUARY THIS YEAR we had a family holiday in Adelaide, which was pretty cool. The day before we were going to leave I hooked up with some of the Adelaide heart kids and hung out at a shopping centre and caught a movie. But the next day I was as sick as. At first I was thinking it was something I ate and I tell you I was so bad I almost couldn't get onto the plane to come home. Then I was back in the Royal Children's. They reckon these stomach pains were some gastro bug and gave me antibiotics.

If I could be healthy enough to study properly at school, I'd love to follow Susanne's footsteps and do Science or go into something like nursing. Having spent so much of my life in hospital, I really get what those nurses do. They make a difference. I rocked up to school for the first day of Year 10 in January and don't really know if I'll ever be back. I always wanted this year to be better than the last, but when I look back on it now, it seems this was when things started to go wrong for me.

It was great to be back at school catching up with all my friends, but as the day wore on I became more and more tired. By the afternoon I was so exhausted that I was struggling to walk. 'How could this be happening on the first day of the term?' I said to myself. Eventually, I had to ask Kane and some other kids to help me get to the school office, where they called Dad to pick me up.

When we arrived home I went to bed straightaway and slept from three o'clock in the afternoon to eight o'clock the next morning. Next day my tiredness was still there, as well as a new sensation – mega stomach pains, right down low.

This went on for weeks and weeks and then months and months. I was in and out of hospital like ten times and I was losing weight big time. The pain never really went away and I was so sick I almost needed a wheelchair. At times I rated those stomach pains nine out of ten. Again the doctors looked, but couldn't find a problem. I just knew there was something wrong with my guts, for sure. Not the start to the year I'd counted on.

Then in February I volunteered to do this thing with Donate Life, which is the Australian Organ and Tissue Donation and Transplantation Authority. What a mouthful. This dude called Shane Laffy, who's had a liver transplant, asked if I wanted to do something with him and Derryn Hinch, the radio guy who had just had a liver transplant as well. I was still struggling, but I really wanted to do it. We went round to the Austin Hospital where Derryn Hinch was and they took photos with us standing next to his bed. That photo appeared in a story in the *Herald Sun* and hit home the message about organ donation.

By March I was clocking in at thirty-seven kilograms. Mini-Me was morphing into Micro-Me. Just eating was painful. And I'd be taking a combination of heart medication, painkillers and antibiotics.

One time in hospital I vomited up about a litre of green gunk (sorry about that) and had to take all the medication all over again.

The danger here was that I reckon I was so sick that my body was probably not absorbing the medication I need to prevent heart rejection. I was so sick of being sick. I'd been in pain plenty of times before but nothing quite like this. I was begging them for morphine and when they did a scan of my lower body it showed I no longer had any stomach lining. Eventually, they discovered I had a ruptured appendix. It had blown up to three times the size of a normal appendix. Now they got why I was in so much pain.

So it was another operation. For some reason they couldn't do a key-hole operation so I copped another big scar. But before they could whip out my appendix they had to pump me full of antibiotics to neutralise any toxins that might have been released during surgery, which meant heaps of diarrhoea. Post op I had drainage tubes coming out of everywhere, which I hate, hate, hate.

But the pain was still there. Then the left side of my body suddenly swelled up. Back into surgery. Gallstones were found and removed. More antibiotics, more drainage tubes, more diarrhoea, more misery. Things were so bad they gave me an adult nappy. The doctors wanted me to eat. Were they kidding! All I wanted to do was crap and vomit. There was talk of force-feeding me through a naso-gastric tube, but to everyone's great relief I finally ate one small triangle of a sandwich.

The thing with my appendix was that it took a lot longer to recover than expected and that delayed when they could do the biopsy. I was in hospital most of January, all of Feb, and into March. Finally, in the middle of March, I was out of that place. Yippee! But the day after I got out, I went to a funeral.

Maddy's best friend, Paige, was a heart kid too, one of us. We all used to hang together at Heart Camp and stuff. Sixteen years old, Paige had one heart transplant and about eight open heart surgeries. She was hanging out at Maddy's doing a sleepover weekend when she suddenly became real sick.

She couldn't walk two metres from the kitchen table to the sink, and couldn't move much so she just lay in Maddy's bed. Maddy and her mum looked after her the best they could, but she wasn't getting any better. They were all worried so Maddy and her mum took Paige to hospital Sunday evening.

By the time Maddy came home from hospital that night she was chatting to Paige on Facebook. Paige said she'd been admitted up to the ward and was feeling fine. As Maddy had to wake up early for school the next day she said goodnight and logged off Facebook at about 12.30 am. It wasn't until the next day that Maddy found out Paige had a cardiac arrest sometime after they were chatting on Facebook and was gone. Just like that.

Paige's funeral changed me. That was the moment I first had the feeling my heart was being weird. Something just wasn't right. Nothing dramatic – like no-one could tell by just looking at me – but something was wrong. This isn't something I can explain exactly but my heart was beating kind of awkward. The doctors didn't know it, but I did. When I looked down into Paige's coffin and saw her resting there, eyes closed, I turned to Dad and whispered, 'I'm next.'

He didn't want to hear any of that talk. Neither did my mate, Nick. A few days after Paige's funeral I visited him in hospital because he was recovering from knee surgery.

'I'm scared of dying, Nick,' I said. Freaked him out, that's for sure.

'What? Don't talk like that,' he came back at me. Usually we were positive to each other, especially when one of us was in hospital. I was always the one who cheered up the other sick kids, the one who raved nonstop about the Bombers and wrestling and stuff.

Nick had this look on his face – like what I was saying was crap. I guess being negative and bringing up the thing no-one ever talks about was too much. Inside I was kind of angry about this. It was like people wouldn't let me have down days. There was stuff that I needed to say and if you couldn't tell one of your best friends then what was the point? I might have been down, but I never give up.

'Sorry,' I said, 'but I feel like it's coming. My time is coming up.'

Poor Nick. My confession was too much to handle. He didn't know what to say. Like Dad, he refused to believe it. Zane was the only dude I could say all this stuff to. He'd listen and then out of his mouth would come this stuff which would blow you away. He's amazing.

And so, guys, it doesn't end there. Sorry it's so damned yucky, but there you go. I was back home after my appendix surgery, only I wasn't getting better. Overnight I developed a racing heart and it was back to Emergency. To see what the hell was going on, the doctors decide to do a biopsy. That's why when the doctors did the biopsy I was nervous, because I knew what was coming. Even then I tried to kid myself that things were okay.

They'd intended doing the biopsy way back in January, having detected a bit of heart rejection, which is usually treated with medication. This little look at my heart was put on hold when my appendix stuff happened. So when they finally did the biopsy all those months later, that's when all this stuff started happening.

The doctors realised from those biopsy results just how bad my heart was. My instincts had been spot on. The arteries around my heart were hardened and narrow and slowly shutting off my blood supply. The doctors didn't understand why this was happening. You can fix heart rejection with medication, but you can't fix anything when the arteries are all blocked up.

I already told you how Dad collapsed when he was told the biopsy results. None of the doctors and nurses can look Dad in the eye anymore. They're incredibly upset by the news. See, I've been part of the hospital for such a long time and they've always been there for me every step of the way, especially Dr Rob and Nurse Anne, who've watched me grow up.

Nearly all of them were avoiding the issue, which is kind of funny in a way, because they're always going on about dealing with stuff. Suddenly when it's a bit personal, they tear up. It's hard for them too. No-one was ever better treated by a hospital than I was there. They've always been there for me and I know if there was any way they could save me, they'd do it.

Dr Rob is my fave. When he told me the biopsy results, he just sat down next to my bed and gave it to me straight. No fuss. A real friendly caring guy. Funny, though, he deadset looks like Mr Burns from *The Simpsons*, but he's nothing like him, of course. Dr Rob is the best.

In a strange way I was okay when I was told the diagnosis. Something I'd been believing came true, and, sure, I was sad about that, but it made me get serious about doing all those things on my list, like writing this book.

Maddy came to see me when she heard the news. When she arrived she simply sat at my bedside and we held hands. 'I won't say anything,' she said, 'but I'm here for you.'

We were both scared. Neither of us knew what was going to happen. And poor Maddy was still grieving her friend, Paige.

CAMERON

37

IN EARLY JANUARY 2012, Sally came to me and said, 'Cam, I've been offered an amazing opportunity to work in Prague for twelve months.' Honestly, I wasn't surprised, because she was amazing at her job. Her employer, KIT Digital, a video management software and services company, had offered her a position as a creative director. We sat down as a family and then went to dinner at Taco Bill in Greensborough. As it was all settling into our heads, Shaun turned and said to Sally that she should go – he'd be okay and he'd look after me. And he was right: it was a massive opportunity.

On the way home, Shaun wanted to drive. He'd just got his learner's permit and I think he wanted to show off a little to Sally – after all, he did get ninety per cent on his learner's test, so clearly he knew what he was doing. And that's exactly what he did. We found a big car park and he drove around like a pro with the music thumping. Through it all, Shaun either forgot to, or decided not to, tell Sally he had a biopsy scheduled for just a few days away – 10 January.

Before that came up, Sally left.

Sally's company knew about our situation and they agreed to fly her back to Melbourne four times a year, so we started looking forward to those visits. Shaun hadn't been well before Sally left, so I took her off to the airport on my own. As he said his goodbyes you could tell Sally didn't want to go, but Shaun promised her he'd stay healthy and happy and try not to spend too much time in hospital.

She told Shaun she was always there for him, and all he had to do was call. As he gave her a big hug, he accidentally called her Mum. Sally smiled.

Unfortunately, from almost the minute Sally landed in Prague, things went downhill for Shaun. He had a horrible stomach pain which no-one in the hospital could understand. But he kept sending Sally messages on Facebook and Skype telling her everything was good, that he was off to school or whatever. However, most of January he was in and out of hospital. His biopsy was cancelled until they could work out the stomach issues.

Shaun did go away for Teen Camp Heart Kids to Sydney on 23 January, but because of this stomach problem it wasn't much fun. When I picked him up from the airport, I took him straight into the Children's Hospital where they did every test they could think of, and came back to tell us they thought it was just gas. There was a suggestion it was all in Shaun's head, but he was sure it wasn't. Shaun and I didn't argue much, but we did have an argument over that, because to me it seemed logical. They'd done all the tests they could think of, and they couldn't find anything.

In the end, I knew it wasn't just gas, but I didn't know what it was. So we tried to continue a normal life. Then one day in the middle of February when he was down at my parents' place outside Geelong with Kane, a mate from school, I got a phone call saying that Shaun was in so much pain they were taking him to Geelong hospital.

A scan was done there and finally we knew what was going on. His appendix had blown up to the size of an orange, and the consequent swelling in his stomach was huge. The doctors said that with all of Shaun's other issues it had been hard to pick it earlier, but now his appendix had a small pinhole and was starting to leak. It had to come out.

Because of Shaun's history, they threw him in an ambulance and sent him to the Children's Hospital on some pretty high doses of painkillers. I told Mum I'd meet them there.

That operation wasn't without its problems. While they were poking around and running scans they found gallstones as well. No wonder he was in pain!

It could have been calcification from the medication he'd been taking. Anyway, he got through that okay and felt better – even if it meant one of his routine biopsies had to be skipped.

One of the hard things about heart kids is that a lot of them die, so we went to quite a few funerals through the years. But there was one in March 2012 that had a lasting impact, and not only because of the funeral itself.

Paige was one of the girls in Shaun's little group. She'd been away to camp with him and generally fought the fight with him, and the others. At the funeral, Shaun approached her coffin. He looked into it for a while, pausing and thinking.

When he came back and sat next to me, he said, 'I'm next, Dad.'

I was shocked. 'You're not going anywhere, Shaun.'

I sat there for the rest of the funeral stunned at what he'd said . . . and scared.

We had to go straight back to the Children's Hospital after the funeral, because the wound from the appendix surgery was weeping. However, there was no particular indication from the hospital to reinforce Shaun's negative view. So in my eyes, it was just situation normal for us.

Looking back now, though, it was clear his body had had enough and was gradually breaking down. I was, of course, completely oblivious. I didn't see any of it.

When he said to me he was next, I think he'd already started preparing himself to die. I just wasn't prepared at all.

That's why I don't think he ever cried about it. He might have done it silently without me, but he never did in front of me. Not once.

Looking back, I think he would have been used to this feeling from the time he was born. Basically he would have known that his time was likely to be short, and that he'd already had a lot of chances in life. Some people in his situation only lasted three months, most didn't get past five years and here he was at seventeen. In a way he was very lucky, and that was how he looked at it.

After the operation, Shaun was not happy. He had all these tubes in his stomach, which made me pretty sad. Also, he was now throwing up his rejection medication and that wasn't good. Deep down, I think we both knew there was more wrong than just appendicitis and gallstones.

As soon as he was ready, Anne Shipp, Shaun's heart transplant coordinator, ordered the biopsy he had missed. That took place on 23 April. Sally was getting ready to fly back to visit me and Shaun, so surely all would be good.

When the results came back from the biopsy, Dr Rob, who looks after a lot of the heart kids, asked to talk to me. Dad was in Shaun's room at the time, and Dr Rob was straight to the point when he took me aside. I'd known something wasn't right with Shaun, but I wasn't ready for what he was going to tell me.

'Cameron, we have really bad news. Shaun has chronic heart rejection and he doesn't have long to live.'

I couldn't believe it. When it is said to you, it really hits you. We'd heard similar things in the past, but this time it felt different. I was choking on my tears when I asked, 'How long?' Dr Rob said between one and twelve months.

He suggested I didn't tell Shaun, but I said, 'No, we're mates and I tell him everything. No secrets.'

I left his office like a zombie and I couldn't stop crying. Then, as I was walking back to Shaun's room, suddenly *my* heart felt strange and I hit the deck. I collapsed.

Later Shaun told me he heard a loud thump. That's how fast I went down – I'm lucky I didn't injure myself. As I lay on the floor I thought I was going to die and I had a doctor and a heap of nurses around me. Dad rushed out and just held my hand. They did a whole lot of tests – it felt like it was taking forever. Eventually I felt a bit better and stood up and went to see Shaun.

He asked if I was okay, and I said I was. Then I began to tell him the news about his diagnosis. He stopped me, saying that the doctors had been in to see him while I was down, and they'd told him. I asked him exactly what they'd said.

'They told me I have chronic heart rejection and the blood vessels around my heart are becoming narrower and narrower, making it difficult for blood to circulate.'

There was nothing they could do to help him. Stents wouldn't work and even another heart transplant wouldn't really make a difference, even though you'd want to try. Sally was still in Melbourne, and I rang and told her the news. I think she was in shock. I could hear her crying, 'Not Shaun, not Shaun.'

After a few days in hospital, the doctors said there was not much they could do and we could take Shaun home. On the drive back to Mill Park, he kept saying, 'Dad, I need to do this message.' I had no idea what he was talking about. When we got home Sally was there, waiting. She hugged him straightaway and started to cry. We just stayed in the lounge room most of the night in shock. Shaun went to bed for 'a rest' while Sally and I watched TV.

Little did we know what he was up to.

SHAUN

38

THIS KIND OF random, crazy-looking woman rocked up to the hospital. She said she was Bev Killick and it was pretty easy to figure she was a comedian – I was laughing in no time. It turns out that Dad met Bev a few years ago through his mate, the comedian Chris Franklin, who took Dad to some of her gigs. What with catching up at Debonairs events and at clubs and stuff, they've stayed in touch a bit. So of course Dad filled them in on everything going on with me and told them about my biopsy result with the really bad news, which is why Bev came to see me in hospital.

She gave me this amazing t-shirt, specially designed by 'The Hood' – a bunch of local comedians who've banded together. Their full name is The Comedy Brotherhood of Australia. They'd written on it a whole stack of the best one liners ever, like this:

'Hey Shaun, I pushed the plunger down on my coffee percolator the other morning and the cafe over the road blew up!' – Matt King

'Ordered a pizza the other day, half American, half Mexican. By the time it got to my place all the Mexican stuff was on the American side' – John Burgos

'Forget what's on the t-shirt, you should see what's on my underpants!' – Darren Sanders

'Mate of mine said he couldn't do a cartwheel to save his life . . . I thought, when would it?' – Carl Barron

Bev says the t-shirt was done by this graphic designer and it's a one-off. There's going to be no reprints for that shirt. The only person who'll ever have one of these is me. How cool is that!

Chris and Bev and some others started The Hood. Apart from being funny, it's not all that hard to become a 'Hoodie'. Through Chris and Bev, The Hood heard about my situation, and to cheer us up they made me and Dad members, which is a blast, I reckon.

Bev handed me a stack of DVDs which the guys in The Hood wanted me to have to pass the time while I was in hospital. We were chatting heaps, and when I told her about an idea I had of throwing this massive party, Bev suggested that we involve The Hood. Imagine that – a line-up of all these great comedians.

Then she asked, 'Who's organising this thing?'

'Well, Dad, I guess.'

'Hell, he's got plenty on his plate,' said Bev. 'Leave it to me.'

You just know that with Bev looking after the party it's going to be more than great. I knew she'd keep it real. This party is really important to me, and it has to be done right. I couldn't think of anything else but my party. Not the tubes hanging out of my arms, not the tablets, nothing. 'Let's do this,' Bev said.

One of the DVDs in the big bunch Bev left with me was this guy Dave Grant. Dave was better known on the live circuit, although he did make a few television appearances on shows like *Rove*, *Hey Hey It's Saturday* and *The Footy Show*. Rove McManus said he was the 'Godfather of Melbourne Comedy'. You should hear this guy. Be warned, he uses the F word big time. This one's heaps funny. It's one of my faves:

'I'm a father but I'm not a smacking father, not like our parents with the wooden spoon. Your legs are going, "Yeah, I remember the wooden spoon!" My mum had seventeen different wooden spoons and I never saw one cake in that house. NOT ONE CAKE! And the way she basted my arse, I reckon she would've made a great pav – you know what I'm saying here.'

Dad told me Dave Grant was a top stand-up man in his day, but passed away from pancreatic cancer in 2010. The guy was amazing. He added this to his material:

'Cancer. Fucking turned fifty and got cancer. Wanted a fucking Harley, don't know what happened there. It's funny, I've dropped twelve kilos, but you don't lose your sense of humour when you've got cancer. I've got a sign on my car that says, "Lose weight now, ask me fucking how." Fuck cancer!'

It wouldn't have been more than an hour after Bev left that the doctors told me I could go home. I rang her straightaway. 'I'm outa here! I'll be home soon!' We started talking some more about the party and Dave Grant. Bev reckons The Hood feel a special connection to Dave, like he's their spiritual guide. Sometimes Bev will feel a presence in the room, or something unexplained will happen and she'll just know that he's around. We had a good laugh about what all the goody-two-shoes types 'up there' would make of Dave Grant.

Bev said that Dave was known for his tagline, 'Look after each other, brothers and sisters, that's what it's all about,' and he took under his wing a lot of up-and-coming talent like Rove McManus, Dave Hughes and Merrick Watts, to name a few. Just from watching his DVDs, I know I would've really liked him. It's a shame we never got a chance to meet. He sounds like my type of guy.

These DVDs are kind of perfect for me. After I got home Maddy and me spent a few days just chilling in front of the TV, working our way through all the discs.

SHAUN

39

ANZAC DAY ARRIVED and I was still in hospital. By then, everyone had heard about my biopsy results and I had heaps of visitors. They all crowded into my squishy little room to cheer me up. For yonks now, Collingwood have played Essendon on Anzac Day, so people turned up dressed in Bombers jumpers or at least in our club colours, black and red. Everyone was huddled around my bed and excited about watching the game on the small TV I had in my room. Maddy dressed up in Bombers gear just for me and she looked great.

Everyone was pretending to be in good spirits. Normally this'd be a fun day for me, but the truth is that I was feeling down. Really down. Everything was starting to sink in and those biopsy results were getting to me. While my family and friends were cheering when the Bombers scored, I just wasn't into it at all. I'm sure they were faking it too.

As I lay there my eyes were locked onto the screen but my mind was elsewhere. What the doctors had said was running through my head over and over again. And I'm not ashamed to admit that I was scared and feeling sorry for myself. They'd more or less said I could die any minute and there was nothing anyone could do about it. I wasn't in the mood for any kind of conversation so I just continued to stare at the TV.

In the background I vaguely heard someone talking about my big party, and a few seconds later I felt my phone vibrate. It was a text from Maddy, who was only sitting about a metre away. 'Can I be your date on the night?'

When I read that, my gloomy mood did an instant 180. I looked up at Maddy and she was looking back at me. She had a smile on her face but her eyebrows creased in a way that told me she was unsure of herself. I grinned and texted back. 'Yes, yes, yes!'

It's just so funny that we were in the same room while we were texting and none of the others had any idea this was happening. The game had suddenly become real interesting. At quarter-time we were down nine points to sixteen, and at half-time we were still down twenty-four points to thirty-six. At three-quarter time we were still behind fifty to sixty-two, but we went berserk in the final term and we were neck and neck with Collingwood. It was unbelievable stuff and in the end we lost by one point, seventy-nine to eighty.

When the game was over, everyone started to leave. Dad offered to drive Maddy home, so we said our goodbyes and there I was – once again all alone in my hospital room. I just sat there thinking about Maddy and smiling to myself. For the first time in a while, I didn't give a single thought to my bad heart. Maddy had asked me if she could be my date. I was stoked.

On the spur of the moment I grabbed my phone and started texting her. We'd been good friends, even close friends for so long, yet we'd never really said how we felt about each other. I had a question for her that I'd wanted to ask her for, like, forever. I typed it out but then wondered if I should send it or not. It might be a dumb idea. 'Should I or shouldn't I?' I asked myself. I held the phone in my hands for a few moments. I was so nervous that my palms were all sweaty. 'Well,' I finally told myself, 'I'm not going to be here for much longer. I have to live like there's no tomorrow.' On impulse, I just pressed the send button. 'Will you be my girlfriend?'

Straightaway I regretted I'd done it. What if she replied 'LOL' or even 'You're kidding, right?' In a bit of a panic I switched my phone to silent and flipped it over so that I wouldn't have to see if something popped up on the screen. Then a few seconds later I changed my mind and checked my phone. Still nothing. It was pure torture. I kept fiddling with my phone.

Only a minute had passed, but it felt like a century. Finally, there was a message. I quickly opened it and read, 'Why are you asking? I thought I was your girlfriend?' That made me so happy. For the second time that day, I felt like I was on top of the world.

Sometimes Maddy and I act like absolute idiots when we're together. We get up to all sorts of weird and stupid things. She recently made a video montage out of all the photos of us together. There are some really funny ones like the one of us doing the 'duck face' and the one where I'm dressed up as a girl at camp. For our three-week anniversary, Maddy gave me a card that said: 'Happy Three Weeks!' We don't know when I'll be going, so we say 'I love you' to each other a lot, just in case. We've kissed. But we haven't done what Dad calls the 'Curly Wurly' yet. I'm going to wait until she's ready.

Even though Maddy and I have been together for a month or so, it feels like we've been together forever. We've been such good friends for seven years that we know each other so well now. We can really be ourselves around each other. When I'm feeling down, she'll be there sitting next to me. She's really caring. Sometimes she'll sit beside my bed and won't say a thing, but she doesn't have to. Knowing that she's there for me really helps. She'll give me a back rub as well and her massages are tops.

Everyone loves Maddy. She's just like a part of the family now. Sally especially liked that Maddy and me hooked up. Even Sondra from Alabama loves Maddy. They've also been talking through Facebook and have become close. Maddy was talking to her about what she was going to wear to my big party. I don't know why Maddy was stressing so much. I told her, 'You'll look beautiful in anything. I'll love you no matter what you wear!' Sondra said the exact same thing.

But Maddy's heaps fussy. She complained to Sondra that she's looked everywhere for a dress to wear to my big event, but she can't find anything she really likes. It's going to be a special night so she wants to look extra special. She looked around a big shopping centre and still found nothing. Then Maddy asked Sondra if she shops online. 'Yes! I shop online a lot!' Sondra replied.

I think Maddy is going to try that next. She felt better about it after speaking to Sondra. Sondra was full of compliments and told her that she had good taste in clothes and all that as a bit of a motivator. She also said, 'You will find something. Just keep looking and stay positive. It will pop out at you when you least expect it.'

Susanne always says that Maddy and I are a good match. She really is perfect for me. When Susanne saw the video montage that Maddy made for me, she had tears in her eyes and quoted this guy called William W. Purkey:

You've gotta dance like there's nobody watching,
Love like you'll never be hurt,
Sing like there's nobody listening,
And live like it's heaven on earth.

SHAUN

40

EPIC STUFF-UP. A new nurse from Hospital in the Home rocks up and checks the PICC line and discovers it's faulty – it missed the vein and it's been drip-feeding antibiotics into tissue, which explains why I'm still feeling pretty crap. Instead of knocking my lung infection out, the antibiotics haven't been doing a thing. They say we have to head back to Emergency and have the PICC removed and replaced, so it's like a shock to them when I say it ain't happening. No way. Because of this bloody thing in my arm, I can't do anything. That's the dream at the moment – not getting to Disneyland, but just being able to stand under a shower without having to worry about this crap PICC line.

Out come the big guns. The nurse is on the mobile and puts Nurse Anne on the line. There's no ifs or buts with her. I'm listening but not listening, if you know what I mean. I've heard all this stuff a million times. She wants to talk to Cameron. He just nods and listens for ages, then says, 'I think he knows the consequences.' Dad says to Anne, 'Just a minute,' and then to me, 'You know what could happen? Without the line in, the infection will just keep getting worse.'

I pleaded with him: 'Just a day. Just a day without that thing. That's all I want.' Then there's more back and forth, but we stuck to our guns and the hospital agreed to leave it out provided we were in there tomorrow.

It's taken me a while to get used to all the media going on around me since I uploaded my video to YouTube. That was about two weeks ago. Not because I'm shy or anything like that, it's just that things have been nonstop – go, go, go. Dad's getting stacks of calls, and people are very interested in my story, including *60 Minutes*.

I know some of my family feel all this media stuff isn't good for me, that it's too much for me to handle and all that. Even the hospital is getting shitty, saying I need to focus on my health. The thing is – I've been sick all my life. I don't have much time left and for once I'm going to do what makes me happy.

The Melbourne rapper B-Mike saw my YouTube video and was inspired to write a rap song especially for me. It's called 'Stay Strong' and I play it over and over. Absolutely love it.

Yeah, Shaun Miller, seventeen and you're so mature
Even if your heart is sore, man, I know it's pure
Shed a tear when I saw you on YouTube
You make it look easy and I know that it's hard
Every day because I've seen every one of your scars
Praise to your dad for always being around
Showed you how to be a man and swear it's profound

Man you gotta just get up, don't ever think to let up
You know we got your back so little homey keep your head up!

It's hard and it's tough, man, you gotta stay strong
Feeling out of luck, man, you gotta stay strong

Your time is never up, man, you gotta stay strong
St-st-stay strong st-st-stay strong
You feel like you alone, man, you gotta stay strong

You fear that you'll be gone, man, you gotta stay strong
St-st-stay strong st-st-stay strong
We believe in you, Shaun, you just gotta stay strong

I've met so many people in these last couple of weeks and the whole experience has been a blast. I've spoken to *Today Tonight* and the guys on *The Project* and done interviews with the *Herald Sun*, Kyle and Jackie O and Neil Mitchell from 3AW.

After talking to this radio station in New Zealand, there was a message from Rachael Leahcar they played to me. She was one of the stars from *The Voice* here in Australia. She said, 'Hi Shaun, this is Rachael. I just wanted to say "hi" and that I think you're a really amazing person, and um, I heard about your video and some of your appearances and I really hope that you're staying positive and always remember that miracles can happen.'

That was real nice of her. I watched *The Voice* so I knew who Rachael was and I was really excited when I heard her special message. It meant a lot to me, because anyone that knows of her knows she has struggled a bit in life as well. Rachael is legally blind, so I think she can relate to me when it comes to your body working against you. But this didn't stop her from chasing her dreams. She's an awesome singer and I hope she wins. That would be something. And how cool is it that her name is the same when spelt backwards?

Everyone knows that I'm a massive Essendon fan and I watch *The Footy Show* religiously. So when Dad told me I'd been invited on to watch them film the show, I was just blown away. And it turns out that Jobe Watson, the captain of the Bombers and one of my heroes, was going to be on.

Once they began filming, Dad and I were sitting in the stands and Sam Newman started talking about me to the audience and invited me up to meet the panel on stage. I shook hands with Jobe and the rest of the guys on the panel and Sam asked me to take a seat.

'So how come you go for the Bombers?' Sam asked.

'Um, I just like the colours red and black,' I said.

The audience thought that was funny and Sam said, 'Well, that's as good a reason as any.'

He then spoke to the crowd about what I'd been through and turned to Jobe. 'He's doing it tough, but the thing that has inspired him is YOU,' Sam said, pointing at him. He then added, 'It must be humbling for you, Tim, to know that a man in his circumstances . . .'

I interrupted Sam with, 'TIM!?'

Everyone just burst out laughing. Sam had made a mistake and called Jobe 'Tim', which is his dad's name. Quick as a flash Jobe said to me, 'I'm glad you picked up on that.'

I was even asked my opinion on the Essendon versus West Coast Eagles game that was coming up. 'Now, Shaun, give us a reason – why are the Bombers going to win?' Sam asked and then pointed out that one of the West Coast star players was sitting there.

'Oh, I better hide my head then,' I said and held up the jumper they gave me to cover my face. Then I said, 'The Bombers are going to win because of our captain, Jobe.' The audience were clapping so I added, 'And Aaron Davey. He surprised us all.'

'Aaron Davey?' said Sam.

'Yeah, Aaron Davey.' Realising my mistake I then said, 'Oops, I mean Alwyn Davey.'

'Hey, if we can call him Tim,' Sam shot back, pointing to Jobe, 'you can call Alwyn Aaron, okay?'

It was a lot of fun. They were so friendly and made me feel real welcome. At the end of it, I made sure I said a special thanks to the Royal Children's Hospital and my heart transplant coordinator and my doctors. From the set I could see Dad clapping loudly in the audience. I could tell he was proud of me.

After the show I went backstage and met the cast and crew and all the guests. Then, Jobe Watson invited me and the family on behalf of the club to the Round 10 game against the Demons at the MCG. He said he'd take us down to the dressing room to meet the team. With that he reached into his bag and pulled out a footy and jumper for me to keep. It was getting late and I had a *Neighbours* cameo the next day, so Dad thought we'd better go. We didn't make it home until early that morning and I had to be on set at midday.

Even random dudes come up to me off the street. I'll just be walking with Dad minding my own business and people scream out to me, 'You inspire us!' When I'm not with Dad, people will go up to him and say how much I've been able to change their attitude toward things. Dad told me that once, when he went down to the corner store to buy some milk, this kid walked in with his bike to buy some lollies.

He looked at Dad and said, 'Is your son Shaun? The one that's been on TV lately?'

Dad was shocked that this little kid actually recognised him. 'Yep, Shaun's my son. Why?'

'Oh, you know what,' the kid began to say through tears, 'I hated school, I hated my life, I hated my mum and I hated my dad, but Shaun's inspired me to be positive and keep going. I was this close to dropping out of school, but I've decided to finish.' You don't really expect stuff like that from strangers, let alone kids.

Dad had another funny encounter. The other day he ran into a guy he knew from school. They shook hands and this guy said, 'Mate, your son has touched so many people.' Then Dad remembered exactly who he was. He was one of Dad's hardcore bullies from back in the day.

CAMERON

41

WHEN WE GOT home, Shaun disappeared to his room. We didn't worry; after all, he needed to digest the news as much as we did. We gave him his space. This was when he recorded his farewell video and loaded it on YouTube. It went for two minutes and fifty-four seconds and it went viral. Today it has nearly seven million views in its original format (there are also versions like the one dubbed in Portuguese with one million views), but back then I wasn't sure about it. In many ways I didn't want it loaded at all, but now I'm pleased he did.

We really had no idea about the video when he came out of his room and sat on the couch with us. 'It just hit me, Dad,' he said. 'I know I will die soon.'

We knew it too, even if we didn't want to accept it, so all three of us just sat on the couch and hugged for ages. Sally was heading back to Prague the next day, and this wasn't easy for her. But Shaun wouldn't let it be any other way. She had to continue her life – that was the point of the message in the YouTube clip.

The next morning when we finally woke, Shaun said he had a lot of missed calls on his phone. I checked my phone as well, and also had lots of missed calls. Shaun said maybe it was his video, so I got him to show it to me.

'Hi guys, I have some bad news I want to tell you all,' he started, clearly choking back tears. This was hard to watch – it still is to this day. 'I have chronic heart rejection and I won't be around for as long as I thought. But I want to say, this has been an awesome ride and I have no regrets. Live life to the fullest because you never know what is going to happen. I just want to thank all my family and friends who have been my life. Please don't cry for me, I will be okay. I ask all my friends to make sure my dad will be okay. I will miss you guys so much, I love you all. I know this is bad news, but good news came as well. I now have a girlfriend called Maddy, and I am so happy at the moment. Nothing can bring me down. I hope I left footprints in all your hearts because I am going to miss you all and I love you dearly. Bye, love from Shaun. See ya.'

It hit me pretty hard. We had a talk for a bit before looking at the phone calls. The video already had 100,000 views, and within a few days it was more than a million. To me, it was pretty powerful and very Shaun. Even in the greatest adversity, it was others he was thinking about.

Then he told me about his bucket list. He wanted his story published and he wanted to go to Disneyland in America – but with his health that was never going to happen. However, the video opened some doors for him, and we did get his story published with his book in December 2012, and we're doing it here again with this book. We're even making his story into a movie, which is something that has given me great purpose and put me back in touch with all those Hollywood connections I was building years earlier.

Soon, the media were ringing and they all wanted a piece of him. The first person we spoke to was Neil Mitchell from 3AW, and Shaun talked about everything, including the bucket list. By the time he'd finished his interview, a lady had rung to offer to fly him to Disneyland and my phone was going nuts.

The Royal Children's Hospital wasn't happy with us. They didn't like the headlines around the world and they said Shaun just needed to concentrate on his health. But do you know what, despite all the great work they'd done for Shaun, at this stage I didn't really care how they felt.

Shaun was enjoying himself and was such an inspiration. 'I am going to die and I have spent most of my life sick and I don't have much time left, so I'm going to do what makes me happy.' And this was what made him happy – talking to people, making new friends and having a laugh.

The day after all this media frenzy started, I went to school with Shaun and had a chat with them about him. The staff at Lalor North High had been amazing. We knew they'd miss him, but we pulled him out of school and set about doing as much as he could with what time was left.

Over the next few days, Shaun was interviewed all over the place: *Today Tonight*, ABC, the *Herald Sun* and Kyle and Jackie O, which was an interesting interview. Kyle told Shaun on air he hadn't cried for five years until he saw Shaun's farewell video. Later, Shaun told Kyle he was getting some haters now, to which Kyle said, 'Don't worry about that – I'm the most hated man around,' and they had a laugh.

Things like Shaun's video bring out the best and the worst in people. He was copping a lot from people claiming the video was a fake. He countered that with another video, called 'I'm not a fake', where he showed all his scars and the like. While he cared, he also didn't. For him, the video was very personal – it was just that a lot of people had tapped into it as well. If they were touched and took the positive messages, then all good. If not, well, that was their problem.

SHAUN

42

THERE'S ALWAYS BEEN something about *Neighbours* that I love. I just can't explain it. It's been going since 1985 and the stars it's had are amazing. Kylie Minogue, Jason Donovan, Natalie Imbruglia, Holly Valance – the list goes on and on. I grew up watching *Neighbours*. It's like watching yourself grow up, I guess. I used to say to Dad, 'One day I want to be on that show.'

My agent managed to get me some work as an extra on *Neighbours*. Another time, when he scored me a speaking role, I was sick. That was that until a HeartKids gala lunch where I was introduced to one of the cast, Jordy Lucas, who I have to say is so hot. In the show she's Summer Hoyland, a journalist with the *Erinsborough News*. Jordy was involved with HeartKids because she adopted it as a charity, and as we were chatting I was telling her how I wanted to be an actor.

What happened then is that Jordy and some of the others on *Neighbours* saw my YouTube video and rang up Peter, my agent, and said they had a part for me. I was rapt. Dad was going to be in it too. I was doing a cameo playing a teenager called Jack from Erinsborough High in episode 6450. There'd been that many. I reckon I've seen all of them.

I rehearsed my lines the whole way to the studio. We turn up to shoot the episode and they'd given me my own dressing room, which was really something. They also made a sign on the door with my name on it. This just blew me away and Dad looked like he was about to burst into tears. They didn't have to do *any* of this stuff. And I knew they might think it was good publicity, but having my name on the door told me these guys were one-offs. Little things like that showed they knew I was doing it tough and they wanted to help my dream come true.

And the cast and crew were fantastic. Jordy came over and took me round, introducing me to everyone. Then we had to do a *Neighbours* cast photo and we walked up a hill for that. On the way back down I was struggling a bit and said to Dad, 'It's getting worse.' I went into the first-aid room for a little nap. After a rest and something to eat, I rehearsed my scene with Alan Fletcher, Jordy, Sachin Joab and the drama coach.

After that I had another rest in the first-aid room. Dad said, 'Are you okay to do this? If you want, we can call this off.'

'Dad, are you kidding? This has been a dream of mine, a proper talking role on *Neighbours*. I want to do it.' There was a knock at the door from the first assistant director. I bounced out of the bed and said, 'Let's do this. Bring it on.'

The scene we did was set in the local coffee shop. It was packed with people and I was sitting at a table with Dad, having a milkshake. Ajay Kapoor, a local politician who was having a tough time campaigning, entered the coffee shop, walked around and then approached our table.

AJAY: I hope I can count on your vote.
JACK (me): It depends, what's your position on underage voting?
AJAY (laughs): You're not eighteen, are you?
JACK: Sorry, mate!
AJAY: Well, maybe you can get your dad to vote for me.
JACK: Maybe.

That was it. That was my scene. I did it in two takes. And the people from that show *The Project* on Channel Ten were there filming as well. The first director called the cast and crew on set and made a speech. 'Guys, I've been working on *Neighbours* for twenty years and all the stories we deal with are make believe, but this story is true. And, Shaun, I dip my hat to you. You are one tough hombre. Why didn't we cast Shaun three years ago? He's a natural.'

People started clapping. Then Jordy came over and she said, 'You know you're a great little actor.' How about that? If my health hadn't become the issue it did, I would've gone into acting seriously. When you have all these things in your personal life, it's fantastic to walk onto a film set and pretend you're someone else altogether. I wasn't after pity from the *Neighbours* cast. All I wanted was a chance to have some fun and maybe remind them that life is precious. Anyway, they all knew my future wasn't looking all that bright and when Dad and I were saying goodbye to everyone, it was a bit emotional.

It's not vanity, but I'm so happy I didn't have to do *Neighbours* and *The Footy Show* with this PICC line in my arm. I just don't want people feeling sorry for me, or thinking I'm going to die any second.

CAMERON

43

THE YOUTUBE CLIP reached some pretty amazing sections of the world, and we were getting emails and the like with offers of help, not just from people in Melbourne and Australia, but from all around the world.

One of these offers was from the Texas Heart Institute. They offered us a backpack mechanical heart till Shaun could have his next heart transplant. And that's when he turned to me and said, 'Dad, I've gone through enough in my life. I don't want to be walking around with some backpack and wires through my heart and everything like that. I've had enough. It's time for me to go.'

In my mind, all I could think was why? They were offering a $250,000 machine to keep him going in case it took a while to find a new heart – and he was turning them down.

'Give it to someone else that's worthy.'

This stunned me. 'But you are worthy.'

'Dad, don't you understand? I've had enough. I've just had enough.'

He was quite headstrong about this one. Shaun's life had been a long series of battles and I don't think he had the energy for another big fight. As a father, this is the last thing you want to hear from your son, and my heart was breaking.

'I want to go out with a bang in my life.'

So he started talking about his Kick-Arse Party for the first time. Bev Killick is a comedian mate of mine and she's bloody funny. She came in to see Shaun a week or so after the video, and she gave Shaun a few DVDs of the people she worked with, like Carl Barron and Dave Grant. She even had a special t-shirt made for him, a one-off.

She's an amazing woman, and she asked Shaun what she could do for him. Shaun threw the party idea at her – 'a kick-arse party at Luna Park' – and she grabbed it and ran with it. Later she said to me, 'I looked into his blue eyes and his lovely smile, and I melted. I couldn't resist putting it together.'

From there she organised the whole party, and got everyone to volunteer, including comedians like Chris Franklin.

As you can imagine, it took a bit to get this together, and unfortunately Shaun didn't make it. But we had the party anyway and he would have loved it. It was so him.

Once we knew that Shaun was not going to have another transplant, we tried to make the most of all the opportunities that were flowing in. We tried to get as much in his life as we could. And believe me, there were plenty of people ringing with things for Shaun to do.

Around 11 am one Saturday, I took a phone call.

'Hi, I'm Sam Newman.'

'No, you're not,' I said and hung up the phone, thinking someone was playing a joke.

A couple of seconds later, he called back. 'Cameron, it's actually Sam Newman here, from *The Footy Show*.'

I changed my tune. It sounded like him, so I gave him some time.

'I've watched Shaun's video,' he said. 'And there's certain people in the press that are calling Shaun a fake. We'd like to stop that. And we'd like to bring him on the show.'

'Okay,' I said. 'What's your plan?'

'There's no plan,' said Sam. 'Let's just get him on the show next Thursday. And we'll go from there.'

Shaun was stoked, but his first thought was that he didn't want to go on TV as a sick kid. The day before the show he was lying in bed at home with a PICC line in his arm through to his heart to help him recover from a lung infection. He had a plan.

When I got up on the morning of the show, Shaun was Skyping Sally and she was working through the logistics of all the things he was trying to do, including *The Footy Show*. So we took him back into the hospital and he said to a nurse, 'I want you to take my PICC line out. I'm going on *The Footy Show* tonight.'

'Oh, look, I don't think that's wise, Shaun. You've still got the lung infection . . .'

Before she'd finished, Shaun had cut her off. 'I don't care. I'm not going on TV as a sick kid.'

It was brave and understandable, but he *was* a sick kid. He was so tired and lethargic I had to wheel him back to the car in a wheel-chair. Deep down, I didn't know how he was going to get through it, especially given that *The Footy Show* didn't even start until 9.30 pm and normally ran for a little more than two hours.

He was allowed to bring a couple of mates with him, so Josh and Kane came in with us, which was good. By the time we got to the studio, Shaun was fading. He had trouble walking to the studio from the car.

We made it to the set of the show, and we had great seats. During an ad break, Sam came over for a chat. He knew a bit of the background but he asked me more, and checked if it was okay to show Shaun's scar. I didn't care, so it was up to Shaun.

'Don't ask me, mate. It's his chest, and it's his life . . . you need to ask him.'

So Sam said, 'What do you think, Shaun? You going to be okay to show your scar?'

'Yeah, of course, Sam. I'll be fine.'

I thought Sam was going to come to the table and chat to Shaun. However, after the ad break the host Garry Lyon introduced Shaun from the main desk. Jobe Watson was up there too, and Garry announced that Shaun was a big Bombers fan. 'Come on up, Shaun. Come here and meet one of your heroes.'

Shaun jumped out of his seat and ran up there with as much energy as he could muster. I couldn't believe it. All of a sudden he had energy to burn.

They started talking to him – Garry, Jobe and Sam were awesome.

'I just want you to think about this for a minute,' Sam said. 'You wouldn't understand what is happening to this lad. Stand up, Shaun, I just want you to show them. Lift up your shirt.'

Shaun lifted his shirt and showed his chest.

'This man here, this young man, has had two of someone's hearts put in his body. And he's staggering and he's in trouble. If we reckon we know what adversity is and we complain about traffic or getting over the West Gate Bridge, just spare a thought for this young man, Shaun.

'He's doing it tough, and the thing that has inspired him is you (he was pointing to Jobe), and it must be humbling for you, Tim (it was a slight faux pas – Jobe's dad, Tim, was a former champion footballer as well), to know that a man in his circumstances . . .'

'TIM?' Shaun kicked in. 'Jobe.'

He was pointing at Jobe. He was so easy and natural.

Anyway, Shaun was invited on air to Essendon's Round 10 game to meet the Bombers coach, James Hird, and the boys and Jobe had a jumper and footy for him. You could see the emotion in Shaun's face – he was really touched by it all. They did the preview of the game, Shaun gave his tips and then he wrapped it up with some thank yous to the hospital, Anne and Doctor Rob.

I was so impressed.

All through this I was worried about how much he was taking on. But he was pretty headstrong and he was in control and chasing experiences.

I remember earlier that day we went into TLC for Kids in Brunswick, which is an awesome outreach centre for sick kids and their families. When we got into the boardroom, Shaun turned to Tim from TLC for Kids and the woman who was with him, and said, 'I don't have very long left to live. You sit there, you sit there, and let's talk. Let's get this out of the way.' He didn't really want to be there – he had other things to do with his time, so he took control.

It was where his state of mind was at – he was packing it in. He'd said to me a couple of days earlier that he was going to go out with a bang, and he was making sure that happened. The day after *The Footy Show*, he went on *Neighbours*. We didn't get home until

3 am from *The Footy Show*, and we were due at *Neighbours* at 11 am. 'Don't worry,' he said, 'I'll be okay.' Sure enough, he was up at the crack of dawn and he started practising his lines in the car.

The *Neighbours* crew had met him before – he'd done some extras work with them in 2010 – but this time it was different. He was there for a different reason. He knew he wasn't building a career – he was just making sure he ticked a few things off the experience list. This speaking role was one of them.

Shaun was talking with the cast and crew at one stage, almost like a little Q & A session, and they were all captivated by him. Alan Fletcher, who plays Doctor Karl Kennedy, led the chat on the set.

They loved him and they would have got him back again if they could, but sadly that wasn't possible. What I saw again was how easily Shaun could engage with people. It was all about his charisma and his intelligence. Despite his lack of education, it was the way he could talk to people and joke with them straightaway. In some ways it made them forget he was so sick some of the time.

It was a great day for Shaun, but he did start to fade as it went on. Even before he did his scenes, we were walking in the little park area on the set – you can see him walking with Jordy Lucas in a YouTube clip – and he had a Coke in his hand, chasing some energy. They'd already got him a small pizza too. He looked at me and said, 'It's starting, Dad.'

I knew exactly what he meant by 'starting'. The arteries were beginning to close off, and he could feel it in his body. He was lethargic and kept falling asleep in the green room.

'Look, Shaun,' I said. 'You don't have to do this, mate. You don't have to prove anything to anyone.'

'No, Dad,' he said, 'I've always wanted to do this. And I need to finally tick it off my bucket list.'

When they came and asked if he was ready, he sparked up and off he went. They even gave me a role as Shaun's dad – maybe they wanted me to be near him. He carried it off sensationally.

With that, it was all over. They showed us the scene in the editing suite, which was great. Otherwise, Shaun would never have seen it.

SHAUN

44

Zane came to see me in hospital. I was back to get the PICC line in. The guy's a legend. Have I told you how he doesn't seem to walk from A to B like a normal person? Suddenly he's there and you're wondering, 'Where did he pop up from?' When the doctors gave me the bad news about my heart, he was one of the first ones I wanted to see. He gave me a massive hug and kissed me on the forehead. All my visitors were crying and stuff, but not Zane. Always the cool dude. I've never seen him worked up over anything.

'Smile, brother,' he said to me when I was in hospital for the PICC line, 'never shed a tear because tears are for people who can't express their emotions. Speak, say what's in your heart and always smile. A smile is a deed – a charity that lights up the world. The first time I met you, Shaun, I saw a smile that could light up the night sky.'

For some reason I said, 'Are you a Muslim? Someone was saying you're a Muslim.'

He smiled, of course. 'Muslim, Jew, Hindu, Christian, what does it matter? We are all messengers of God. Life is a journey. We all have a purpose and we all carry a message to share before it is time to go.'

And when he says this stuff, Zane looks right into you, and it's like, if you're thinking something he's going to know what that is. 'Shaun, you're one of God's chosen angels. You have a message to give to the world.'

Then just as quickly as he arrived, he'd vanished – like into thin air.

Dad wasn't handling things too good. Every now and then I'd catch him giving me this weird look. Then one day, when we were alone in the hospital, he crouched beside my bed and whispered, 'Look, Shaun, I'm forty-one years old. I'm happy with my life and where it's taken me, but it freaks me out that soon you'll face death alone. I can't bear the thought of that. If you want me to, I'll go with you. Okay?'

It took me a few seconds to realise what he was saying. Insane stuff. 'Don't you dare,' I said, grabbing his hand. I meant it.

Nothing more was said, but you can't hide anything from Zane. A few days later he was back and realised what was going down. He just knew Dad was a bit suicidal.

'Cameron, you are selfish,' Zane said to Dad one morning at the hospital.

'What do you mean?' asked Dad.

'I can see in your eyes that you're thinking bad thoughts.'

When Dad fessed up, Zane made him promise not to do anything stupid. See, although I was a long way from dead, Dad was grieving. He told Zane that if there was a God, he hated him. So Zane lectured him on all this stuff.

'Cameron, when you were still with Shaun's mother, even though you didn't know it, you were all about yourself, man. You were a lost soul. Then, she fell pregnant and that was a gift. Shaun was a gift. He entered this life to awaken you. How could it be right that God created a child born sick? It was all part of the message. You have never left your son's side. It has taken you seventeen years to live up to yourself, but you have done it. Now Shaun's job is done here. His message to you is done here.'

I've been thinking a lot about the 'message' Zane talks about. After the response to my YouTube video, I hope I've inspired people to stay strong and be positive, no matter what hurdles they face in life. The really important message for me is to spread the word about people getting behind organ donation. Around three-and-a-half million Australians have some kind of cardiovascular disease and over a third of them will suffer from heart failure. But last year only sixty-four heart transplants were conducted.

There just aren't enough organ donors and patients have to go on these huge waiting lists and hope they get lucky before their disease kills them. It's like being on death row, I reckon. And boy, oh boy, I know how much impact being an organ donor can have on someone else's life. It's a truly amazing gift – the best there is. This book is going to help me get that message out there – make sure you sign up so that in the event of your accidental death someone else gets to live.

When I told my Aunt Susanne about my newfound purpose in life, she said it reminded her of this film called *Pay It Forward*. It's a pretty old movie – it took me a while to remember it. It's about this person who does favours for complete strangers simply out of kindness, and in the hope that they'll show kindness to someone else.

Mum sent me a text the other night. 'I love you, I love you, I love you, I love you.' I haven't replied. I haven't seen much of Mum's side of the family in the last few years since all the Fletch stuff happened. Right now I'm just focusing on getting better. I'll make sure I deal with that later, because I want to tell them I love them.

Then this afternoon Mum came to see me in the hospital. The doctors have figured out that I have to have an operation to get this fluid off my lungs. So I was getting my head around all this crap and the nurse came in and said, 'Shaun, your mum is here.' It caught me by surprise. I was looking at Dad and I could tell he was thinking, 'Your call, mate.'

The nurse was standing there waiting. I know she's my mother and everything, but I can't forgive her for what happened. 'It's up to you, buddy,' Dad said.

'I have enough on my plate without dealing with her stuff.' I told the nurse to ask Mum to leave because I didn't want to see her. Harsh, I know, but there you go.

Change the subject. Think of something positive. You know that the idea was to have a Kick-Arse Party with all my friends and that we all have a great time. Well, Bev the comedian thought about this and then rang Luna Park. She asked about maybe hiring out a function room or whatever. Then she explained my situation to this lady called Atlanta, who asked for time to think about it.

Ten minutes later she was back on the phone to Bev. 'Forget about that function room,' she said, 'you guys can have the whole park.' For free! There'll be unlimited access to rides, free food, free drinks, free entertainment – everything. I suggested that we charge people to get in and donate the money to HeartKids. With the unlimited rides, I chose ones specifically with heart kids in mind. They can't really go on the high-speed ones, so I picked ones they'd feel safe going on. It's important they don't have to worry about all that stuff at my party and just concentrate on having a good time.

Unlike most kids my age, I love stand-up comedy. I'm talking about the real proper Aussie stand-up kind. I don't know why – maybe it's just that I really get into a comedian putting themselves out there and having a go at making people laugh.

And there's some music that I really want played at my party so I can do 'The Shuffle'. Bev says she's lined up a DJ to play 'Sexy and I Know It' by LMFAO. I love dancing to that and 'Moves Like Jagger'. Really, I just love dancing. I could dance all night, but what I'm really looking forward to is just sitting back in a big plush chair and watching comedy acts and everyone else dancing and having a good time. When I tell Bev this, she says she's organised this mega chair for me. Kind of like a king on his throne, ha ha. And Justin, the guy who designed my t-shirt, is doing one for sale to the public with The Hood logo on it, and it'll include Dave Grant's famous finisher, 'Look after each other, brothers and sisters.'

It's all systems go now and Bev says she's on a roll with the party. 'At the moment,' she says, 'The Hood is all about Operation Shaun Miller.' She's lined up sponsors and pulled off the most amazing things. Like a twenty-five-seat stretch Hummer's going to take the heart kids to Luna Park.

The date we've decided on is 15 June. I chose this date because I just know I'll still be here for it. At one stage, there was talk about pushing it back, but I said to Bev it had to be 15 June, or else I might not make it. For some reason, I have a good feeling about Friday 15 June. It's all just so surreal. It's coming together better than I could have ever imagined – and the best thing is that it's all for a good cause.

SHAUN

45

When Dad messaged Sondra in Alabama, telling her about my biopsy results, she just didn't want to accept it. She kept asking Dad all these questions and didn't understand why I couldn't have a third transplant. It must be hard for her with everything that happened with Nathan. Sondra wanted to find a donor in the US who could give me another heart, or wanted to find a doctor who might be able to help me.

After my YouTube video went viral, a few people overseas contacted Dad and suggested possible ways to fix my heart. One email was from Tom and Amy Martin who live in New York. They saw an article about me and wondered if the Texas Heart Institute could help. Dr O.H. 'Bud' Frazier and Dr Billy Cohn have performed a number of experimental heart transplants. These doctors even did one for former US Vice President Dick Cheney. The Martins also linked us to an article, 'No Pulse: How Doctors Reinvented the Human Heart,' which was published by *Popular Science* magazine.

A few hours after that email, Jason Beaumont, a radio jock in New Zealand, came back to us. We'd done a radio interview with him and he sent an email saying he'd got a phone call from a lady in the UK called Nina Lather. She's a lawyer who has friends working in cardiac medicine and thought she knew of a procedure to stop my heart from failing. Jason passed on her phone number to Dad. It's amazing that these people are all trying to help, but I knew it'd take a miracle.

Susanne called Nina to say thank you to her. Nina said she saw my story in the news in England and was touched by the way I spoke and wanted to help in some way. Coincidentally, she'd read the exact same article about the Texas Heart Institute that Tom and Amy had mentioned in their email, and the work of Dr Billy Cohn and Bud Frazier. Then Nina rang the Texas Heart Institute. Living in the UK, she didn't realise that it was five o'clock in the morning in the US. Incredibly, Dr Bud Frazier picked up. He happened to have just come out of surgery and happily discussed some options with her – that's when she contacted us to say we should speak to Dr Frazier too.

The next morning Susanne rang the Texas Heart Institute and guess who answered the phone? Dr Frazier. Susanne says he's a beautiful man for giving up his time to speak to her. Basically, he says there's no simple solution for my condition. Ideally, I need a long-term, totally implantable, continual flow pump, but this technology isn't available yet. Even though my arteries are blocking up, Dr Frazier thought I might be able to get a ventricular assisted device implanted for a few years until another transplant becomes available. The thing is that involves at least two years of living with tubes on the outside of my body which are connected to a battery pack I'd carry around. No thanks.

I'm stunned and amazed with how all these nice people from all over the world have heard my story and wanted to help. There was this one guy all the way from Brazil by the name of Diga Policiano, who wrote me a song called 'Don't Wait for the Next Sunrise'. He got what I was saying about living life for today. I reckon he's awesome.

My family have been touched by how many people have reached out to me. Susanne says it's restored her faith in humanity that so many have been so generous and willing to give up their time to write to me and offer me advice and stuff. The thing is that I know for sure it ain't going to happen. Not because no-one cares, but because I don't care. I could not be honest to their faces and tell them this. The reality is that there's nothing more that can be done for me. I know if there was a way to save me, the doctors at my hospital would do it. For one thing, these are just ideas and we can't be 100 per cent sure they'll even work. And another thing, I detest tubes.

I hope you don't think I'm being ungrateful, but if they offered me a new heart tomorrow I reckon I'd say no thanks. I've had enough. I'm ready to say goodbye to swallowing mountains of pills, heaps of injections and endless hospital visits.

I just want to go float on a fluffy white cloud where no-one will stick needles in me anymore and where there is no pain.

SHAUN

46

No wonder I was having trouble breathing. They drained three-and-a-half litres of fluid from my lungs. So here I am back in hospital where it all started. This lung infection which has kept me here really sucks. The doctors don't want me leaving until it clears up.

'Going against the doctor's wishes is just going to make you sicker,' said Zane. I've been hearing this all my life and am so over it. But I knew he was right, even though I didn't want him to be. Dad was the same. 'Just stay a few more days and then you'll be okay to go home.' Well, a few days later I was still in the hospital.

You know, I just remembered a funny thing. When I was in the back of the ambo on my way to hospital I heard Dad was on the phone to Bev, so I yelled out, 'Tell Bev not to worry. I'm going to be okay. I'm going to be here for my own party, for sure. I'm going to make it. Go ahead with everything as planned – it's all going to be okay!' The ambo guys were looking at me like I was mad.

Even though Sally's working in Prague we keep in close contact. I forgot to tell you. On 10 January 2012, the day I was originally scheduled to have my biopsy, Sally flew off to Prague. Her company, Kit Digital, offered her a twelve-month contract as a creative director at their Prague headquarters. Massive opportunity for her. The company knows about our situation and will fly her back to Melbourne four times a year to visit me and Dad. I was real disappointed I was way too sick to go with Dad to drop her off at the airport. So I said goodbye and promised her I'd be healthy and happy and not spending too much time in hospital.

'If you ever need me, Shaun,' she said, 'you know I'll be there, no matter what.' Sally's been the best thing that's happened to our family. You know one night before she left I accidentally called her Mum. She just smiled and said it was okay. She was happy to be called my mum.

Sally and me speak on Skype a lot and Facebook each other when we can. In one of my messages I said, 'I'm sorry if I don't always respond to you. I'm just so tired but it doesn't mean I don't love you. You've been a real mum to me. Love you lots.' When Sally heard about my biopsy result she booked a flight back to Melbourne, which is great news. Can't wait to see her.

And Dad won't leave the hospital. He's funny. Every now and then he gets this random look on his face and goes, 'I love you, Shaun,' and gives me this big hug. And I say, 'I love you, Dad.' I see him tearing up and remind him that I have a party to go to.

One thing about hospitals is you have plenty of time to think. And having thought about the future quite a lot, there's only really one wish I have, which I don't think I've mentioned before. That wish is that Dad can finally focus on his career and achieve the things we all know he can. He deserves that. Whenever I get sick, he puts everything on hold and is there for me. So when I'm gone, I want him to really go for it, but I'll still be keeping an eye on him from one of the seven levels of heaven that Zane talks about. For sure. And I just want my mum to know that regardless of our battles, I love her. Remember me and smile. Be positive and live life for today, because you never know what tomorrow will bring.

You know I've been dead a couple of times – well, technically anyway – and I think this is why I was never really scared of death or dying. Someone smart once said, 'Life is not measured by the number of breaths we take, but by the moments that take our breath away.' Spot on. Somehow, I feel that whatever happens on the other side, I'll be okay.

This is the final chapter in Shaun's book. He died at 2.30 pm on 26 May 2012 in the Royal Children's Hospital.

CAMERON

47

Tuesday 22 May

Shaun said to me in the car, 'You know they'll make a movie about my life one day, Dad.' I thought it was a weird thing to say and really just ignored him.

Wednesday 23 May

During the early and mid-parts of May, Shaun was in and out of hospital with that 'lung infection', but I was starting to work out it wasn't a lung infection at all. This was his heart shutting down, and the fluid and congestion on his lungs was from that, not a bug of some kind. I don't think I was seeing it too clearly at the time, but I'm pretty sure Shaun did.

He was tired most of the time now, and we spent a lot of time sitting around and talking. While the lung thing was really beating him up physically, he was quite sharp mentally. Early in the afternoon, Shaun looked at me and said, 'Look after my legacy for me.'

I was dumbfounded by this, and it took me many years to understand. I mean, what legacy was there at that time, and what was he talking about? I parked my thoughts but never forgot the statement.

It was around dinner time, and he'd been lying on the couch all day, when all of a sudden he seemed to zone out and started staring at the roof. He had a look on his face that scared me – it was strange. I rang my mum, who was at my sister's house at the time, and then I rang Zane, who came straight over.

I told Zane what was going on. He took one look at Shaun and asked us all to go into the kitchen for a bit. After about ten minutes he came out, looked me in the eyes and said, 'Bro, I don't know how to say this, so I'll come straight out and say it. Shaun doesn't have long now.'

We'd been told he had between one and twelve months. This was only three weeks so it was a big shock. I preferred the twelve-month option, but that was just dreaming. I trusted Zane, but I was speechless for a bit. 'Maybe one to three days,' he said. 'They are coming for him.'

I asked Zane recently what was going on – what he saw that day – and he said the angels of death were coming for Shaun. They had their hands all over him, which is why he looked so scared. Zane went back in and sat with Shaun for a bit and talked. Shaun now looked calm and at peace.

We had this Burmese cat that wouldn't leave him alone. It'd sit on the couch and just watch Shaun – it was almost like it knew how sick Shaun was. It was funny. Up until this point it had been really aggressive, but it changed during this time and has remained a beautiful and passive cat ever since.

I think the angel that Zane was talking about touched the cat, and the cat was looking over him.

Thursday 24 May

On one of his heart camps, Shaun had made friends with an athlete named Christian Williams. Christian paid Shaun a visit at around 11 am and they sat and talked while drinking that purple vitamin water that Shaun loved so much.

Christian was good for Shaun, and whenever Shaun spent time with him or spoke to him he'd always be on a high. This day was no different. But he was struggling, and a little while after Christian left, we spoke about going back to hospital. I told Shaun that if he got any worse we'd have to. He agreed that was okay, even though he'd rather be at home.

As I've mentioned, his slide had started soon after the aneurysm with the 'lung infection', and Shaun was slowly shutting down, which is why I wish the medical people at the hospital had been straight with me about what was going on. I kept thinking, 'Once we get that sorted, I can get my extra months with him,' but that was never going to happen.

He was getting weaker. He'd cough and his stomach would hurt because there was so much fluid in his body that everything was squished in there. Shaun had also become more stubborn and was happy to ignore the doctors a bit, which is why we needed to have that agreement about going back to hospital.

There was a time earlier in May when he'd been in hospital. The doctors didn't want him to go outside because they said it was dangerous for him. But he wanted to breathe some fresh air, so he asked me and Zane – who was visiting at the time – to take him outside. They showed me on the computer how bad the lung infection was and said, 'He's not allowed to go anywhere.'

Zane asked, 'What would you like to do, Shaun?'

'I'd just like to go out and breathe some air.'

I told the doctors and they said, 'No, that's not going to happen.'

Zane came out with Shaun, looked at the doctors, and told them Shaun was going outside with him. 'No, that's not going to happen,' they said again. You had Zane in the bandana and looking very mean, and he was serious. It was a bit of a Mexican stand-off, but they had no right to stop him, so eventually they stepped aside and let it happen – again saying they thought medically it was a bad idea.

Shaun's view was essentially 'I'm dying, anyway, so what's the difference?'

So Zane took it upon himself to make sure Shaun was able to live the way he wanted to live in those last few days. Just like one night when Zane had climbed the building to get into the hospital because Shaun wanted to see him and the front doors were closed. At least that's how I was told it happened.

Anyway, back to the story. About an hour after Shaun and I had made our pact on going to hospital we had to call an ambulance. However, not only the ambulance showed up but the fire brigade too. Apparently when you call the ambulance for a transplant person, the fire brigade also comes. It was strange, but Shaun thought it was pretty good.

We went in the ambulance to the Children's Hospital and then sat in the Emergency ward for ages – well into the next day. While I was there, someone rang the ward pretending to be a relative of mine. She found out that I'd been waiting in Emergency for twenty-three hours, so this person ended up calling a radio station, and complaining. Derryn Hinch then got involved and started talking about it on radio and trying to get the hospital on the line. It seems they didn't like that.

So on Friday the 25th, we finally got a bed.

Shaun had to have a little bit of surgery to get some fluid off his lungs. He returned to the room with drainage tubes in each side, and every time he breathed, fluid would pump out. That was when I knew for sure that it wasn't a lung infection and that he was in big trouble.

Friday 25 May

I remember Zane telling Shaun in hospital that tears were for people who couldn't express their emotions. I must have been having a lot of trouble with emotions at the time, because I was crying a lot.

Zane's advice was 'Say what's in your heart and always smile.' I thought I'd try.

Shaun knew I wasn't dealing with things too well. How could he not? I kept looking at him and I'd start crying. I told him that it freaked me out knowing he was facing death alone. 'I can't bear the thought of that,' I said. 'If you want to, I'll go with you.'

It took Shaun a few seconds to realise what I was saying to him, and when he had a grasp of it, he was firm. He didn't want me to take my life. He said I had a lot of my life left and I needed to go on. So, for the moment, I decided that was what I'd do. I would battle on, and I still do that today. We did agree I should get a tattoo of him on my arm – and I do have that.

After all, Shaun was fighting too. The lung thing was pretty bad, though, and he was sleeping a lot while they were trying to fight it. As I've said, I knew there were big issues with his heart, just by the amount of fluid they were draining. That was a clear indication that his heart wasn't doing its job.

By late afternoon on 25 May, Dad was in there to spend time with Shaun. He'd spoken to the doctors and Shaun, and he said I should go home and get some rest. He was there and he'd call if I was needed.

Saturday 26 May

I did go home as Dad suggested, but I can't say I returned to the hospital on Saturday morning all that well rested. I went straight to Shaun's side and let him know I was there. He liked to know I was nearby most of the time, except when he wanted me to go and get him some McDonald's. Every so often he'd look over to make sure I was there – and I was.

I was in-boxing Sally all day with updates, not that there was much to say. But given she was on the other side of the world, it was like she was there with me holding my hand or something.

I believe Shaun had picked the time and day he wanted to pass away. He wasn't talking much and I thought it was just the lung infection and the impact that was having. He had draining tubes in each lung, and every time he took a breath, water was pouring out of him.

As expected, some of the few words to come out of Shaun that day were for him to ask me to go and get him some Maccas. As I walked back up the corridor at 2.30 pm there was a code blue – which means someone is in cardiac arrest – in the Koala Ward, a specialist ward at the hospital for kids with cardiac or renal issues. I knew who it was.

Panicking, I ran along the corridor as fast as I could. Shaun was in full cardiac arrest with doctors working on him. The whole room was full.

I was screaming, 'Save my boy – please don't let him die!' I was yelling at the top of my voice and crying. I was taken outside by one of the nurses who'd known me and Shaun a very long time. I looked her in the eyes and said, 'Tell me Shaun will be okay.'

She had tears in her eyes. She said she couldn't be sure of that and hugged me.

Once I had control of myself again, I walked back in. It had now been thirty-five minutes of CPR, and during one of the heart compressions I heard a loud snap. After all of Shaun's operations and heart transplants, his bones were not all that strong. His breast bone had snapped.

After forty-five minutes, I was taken outside the room and asked if I'd like to put Shaun on life support – but they said he'd be brain dead.

I couldn't deal with that. With everything Shaun had been through in his life, I couldn't do that to him as well. So I said no, knowing what it meant. I walked back into the room and knelt beside his bed, screaming.

Shaun's journey in life was over. As much as I knew it was coming, it hurt.

The doctors told me that Shaun was gone. Then everyone walked out, leaving me with Anne, Shaun's heart transplant coordinator and friend, and we sat there silently. I look back now and I was thankful she was there for Shaun through his life – and for me that day.

After a while she stood beside his bed and said, 'Beautiful Shaun, no more pain,' and she patted his hair and tidied him up a little. She said Shaun always liked to look good.

I now had him in my arms, and I couldn't see my life without him. Now came the next hard part – telling everyone the news, when all I wanted to do was lie next to him. I didn't know why such a beautiful boy had to leave this world.

The word got around fast. Within an hour, the media were outside, and the hospital went into total shutdown mode, because of the cameras and media hysteria. By 5 pm it was all over the news and internet. Shaun, the inspirational boy from Australia, had died. On 26 May 2012, my son had passed away.

CAMERON

48

THE NEXT DAY we had lots of media at our place in Mill Park to interview me, which was hard. We decided as a family to have a public funeral, but we did draw some boundaries. I had calls from certain media outlets wanting to run the funeral live on air, to which I said 'no'. Shaun was news everywhere, which was both overwhelming and flattering. Without trying, he had touched so many.

As soon as she heard the news, Sally flew back from Prague. I think even to this day she's upset at never getting to say goodbye. She arrived by cab on the Monday and fell straight into my arms, saying, 'I can't believe Shaun is really dead.'

We had to get through a few things before we could make it to the Kick-Arse Party, which was still going ahead. First we had to bury Shaun.

I kept putting it off. I had all these excuses for not doing it on this day or that day. One day when I was in Shaun's room,

Dad came in and said the date had been picked – thankfully he was stepping in to help me.

He knew where my head was and he said, 'If you do anything to yourself' – meaning kill yourself – 'I'll go as well, so you'll have that on your conscience. Not only will you kill yourself, you'll kill me.'

Shaun passed on the Saturday and after that I didn't visit him until Wednesday. I wish I'd gone earlier. My head was all over the place – I was a mess. People were just pressing me on everything, including organising the funeral.

On top of that, some strange things started to happen. I poured his favourite drink – purple vitamin water – into his Essendon cup and the next day it was gone. Also, I'd had an infected toe for more than a year – which Shaun hated because he thought it was revolting – and it cleared up overnight. Sally couldn't believe it.

Shaun had prepared me for some of what to do for his funeral. 'I want to be buried in the country, and I want to be buried in a suit.' He'd already done that part for me, but then you've got to choose a coffin and all sorts of other things. In death, just as in Shaun's birth, they can tell you as much as they can, but nothing prepares you for what you have to do.

It felt like forever before we could see Shaun at the funeral home. I asked the funeral director about embalming Shaun, as embalming preserves the body from decomposing. But when I first saw Shaun's face, I couldn't believe how good he looked. It was just like he was sleeping. There was no make-up on him and he looked like an angel.

The funeral director said to me and Sally, 'I don't want to embalm Shaun.'

I looked at him, stunned, but, looking down at Shaun's body, he added, 'After what he's been through, I don't want to give Shaun any more needles.'

I respected the funeral director's wishes, because I could feel he had some sort of connection with Shaun. I later found out that when his daughter was young, she'd had heart problems.

The next day, I went back in there, and he said, 'I need to talk to you.'

I said, 'Why? What's wrong?'

'Something happened overnight. We had Shaun positioned in a coffin, and he's totally moved himself.'

'Show me,' I said, and he did. 'That's the way he sleeps,' I added, looking at my son, still somehow hoping he was just sleeping.

'He's moved his entire head to the other side.'

'Does that happen very often?'

'No. We took him out of the fridge and he'd moved his entire head.'

After that little exchange, which clearly freaked the funeral director out, I had to dress Shaun – Sally helped me with that. When you're dressing a dead body, you're expecting it to be stiff with rigor mortis, but he was so limber it was like he wasn't dead at all. I could open his lips and his eyes and bend his arms and legs. I finished it off with some gel to make his hair the way he liked it.

You might think that dressing the body would be some kind of morbid feeling, but the only way I can describe it is that there was a beautiful energy, which was extremely powerful. Shaun always told me that death is a beautiful thing – I believe that now.

Although we drew some boundaries, we did do the public funeral. I wish we hadn't. We should have just done a private thing for us. The funeral felt like a bit of a circus. When I arrived at the church, there were people everywhere and TV crews all over the place. It just felt weird. There were so many people in the way, when we were leaving the church with the coffin, we had to walk 100 metres or so to get to the hearse. Even at the cemetery there were people I could see who no-one knew – this part was meant to be private.

I was very touched that Shaun's school had said that anyone who wanted to could go to the funeral. So, as we walked out with the coffin, we were greeted with a sea of blue.

We'd heard that Olivia's family was going to start a fight at the burial, so there we all were, standing on different sides, with Shaun acting as a peacemaker, even though all he'd asked for was for me to protect him.

It was a very strange day. Then, to back it up a week later with the Kick-Arse Party was both tough and surreal. Shaun had organised it, it was his party, and he was supposed to be there – and he wasn't.

I didn't enjoy the party much – all I wanted to do was sit in a corner and cry. I was struggling. However, from the minute I arrived – after being interviewed by Channel Nine's Brett McLeod at the entrance to Luna Park – to the time I left, I had my brave face on.

It was amazing, though, and Bev and her crew did such a fantastic job. They'd even turned the party into a fundraiser, which raised thousands of dollars for HeartKids. There were *Star Wars* characters everywhere and the heart kids were on the rides. It was mind-blowing to see. B-Mike sang Shaun's song, 'Stay Strong', and there were all these different comedians on a stage.

It was a bit of a blur, but despite my mood it was a great night. At the end, we let off all these balloons and I swear to God I felt Shaun's presence there.

For me, though, this was just the start of a rough patch.

CAMERON

49

As soon as the Kick-Arse Party was done, I had to knuckle down and get Shaun's book, *An Awesome Ride*, ready. I had to organise photos and approve the text and then prepare for the media that was being planned around its release.

I was in a rush to get the book out – after all, it was one of Shaun's wishes. However, I should have paused for a few moments and taken some time to grieve. If I'd done that, maybe I wouldn't have kept spiralling out of control.

I think the *Herald Sun* had said in an article about Shaun, 'Why does such a beautiful person have to die the way he died?' That was how I felt. I didn't know what was going on.

I did try to take my own life a couple of times. One of those was when I tried to hang myself in the backyard. Another time, I swallowed all of Shaun's remaining medicine – and remember, he was taking a lot of pills. I'm surprised I managed to get them all down, but I did. Mum found me and I was taken to Northern

Hospital, where they pumped my stomach. Can I tell you that is not a pleasant experience at all.

I wasn't sleeping much either. I was a wreck.

Still, I had to put on a performance for the book publisher. I had to go back to my acting days. Away from that, I was just going through the motions.

As you can imagine, when you don't deal with your grief and you bottle it up, it can explode. That's what happened one night when I'd been arguing with Sally, for no particular reason except that she was the one near me, and it was very late at night and I was very vocal. I decided to go for a walk.

Meanwhile, Sally had called the police because she was worried about me. They rolled up alongside me in a divvy van and got out. I was mad at the world, and the world was starting to notice.

The officers said they'd had a number of complaints about my behaviour and not just from Sally. I can't remember what I was doing, but I can imagine – I was angry with the world. There was a small exchange and then the officer leading the discussion said something that got my back up. I can't remember what, but I got very abrupt after that.

One of the officers pulled his mace and batons out, before the other one said to his colleague, 'Don't you know who that is?'

'No, I've got no idea.'

'That's Shaun Miller's dad.'

He'd seen me on *The Footy Show*. As soon as he mentioned this, the tension started to drop. They backed off a little and I calmed down.

'Cameron,' he said, 'do you think Shaun would want you to behave like this?'

I said, 'Look, it's very hard.'

'I know it's hard. But you need to keep on being strong now. You need to walk in Shaun's shoes.' The officer was really good, and he seemed to understand enough. It was like he was talking me down off a ledge. 'I'll tell you what I'll do. I'll take you home and we can just settle down.'

By now, Sally had run down the street to me, so they put us both in the back of the divvy van and took us home. That was an experience. It isn't very comfortable and there are no windows, so it's pitch black too. I've got no idea how anyone manages to sit in there with handcuffs – thankfully I've never had to find out.

Sally was trying everything she could for me – she was leaving work early and working from home most days – but even that wasn't enough. Unfortunately, I still had some more falling to do. I was also worried what was going to happen after the book was released when I had nothing else on Shaun's list to fix.

For now, though, the book was keeping me going and I was determined to get it out for Shaun. But it was a bitter-sweet time for me. All that publicity and the appearances when it was launched in December – that was Shaun's job, not mine.

I was also paying no attention to Sally. My grief was all consuming and it was like a tsunami coming at me in giant waves that I felt were drowning me. I didn't know what to do, and I was hurting Sally without realising it. In some ways, I can't believe how she stood beside me.

But even Sally's support and love were no use to me in that state. I used to just sit in Shaun's room, talking to him, rocking backwards and forwards. I'd spend every night like that. I wasn't sleeping and I wasn't thinking straight. But somehow, no matter how hard I tried to self-destruct, I couldn't do it properly. Things weren't getting better, though. I wasn't sleeping, because I was now having night terrors. I kept reliving Shaun dying in my arms over and over again.

On 27 December, nearly four weeks after the book launch, it came to a head. It was 4 pm, I was standing in Mum and Dad's kitchen with Dad, and I had a knife in my hand. 'I can't, I can't, I can't do this anymore,' I said. 'I've got to the end of my tether. I can't do this anymore.'

He told me, 'Put the knife down.' He said it four times. 'Put the knife down.'

When I had, he said, 'I think you need to have help.'

Dad took it into his own hands and less than an hour later I was being taken by him and Mum to a psychiatric hospital. That was a shock. Primarily, Dad put me in there to help me try to get some sleep, but even though I went in as a voluntary patient they can pretty much do as they want with you. And they did, to a certain degree.

This place was very confronting. It was just like something out of *One Flew over the Cuckoo's Nest*.

I had everything taken off me – my mobile phone, my wallet, the lot. All I was allowed to wear was tracksuit pants and a t-shirt. I had to say goodbye to Mum and Dad, and they shut the door, and that was it.

I had tea that night and everyone was staring at me. It was a bit freaky. The door to your room had to stay open unless they closed it, which is kind of strange with all these people walking around all the time.

They gave me some medicine, and this big bloke – a staff member – came into my room to make sure I'd taken it. I'd been there less than three hours and they'd already prescribed lithium.

I'd never taken it before and I didn't want to start then. So I told him.

'You either do it now or you do it the hard way,' he told me.

'What do you mean?' I said.

He basically said to me, 'I'm gonna belt the shit outa you if you don't have it.'

I was starting to fear for my time there. I was a voluntary patient, but I felt like I had no choice. Anyway, I took the lithium. It knocked me completely out and it was disgusting.

The next day, I got up and was all groggy. I don't know whether someone did it as a joke, but there were all these magazines in the common area with articles on Shaun, and people were now pointing at me. I was so groggy I thought for a while I was dreaming. I wasn't.

It was a scary place. There were guys from prison in there, and they were all juiced up on something, and a lot of the other patients had big problems too. I felt like my problems were pretty mild.

So then they introduced me to my cocktail of drugs. I had lithium for the night and, during the day, Seroquel, which is for things like bipolar disorder, and Epilim, primarily for epilepsy. They said they wanted to deal with my mood swings. If the lithium had hit me hard, you should have seen me on these.

Dad came in on the third day. He said I was on the couch dribbling and I could barely speak. That's how it felt too, like I was in some sort of vegetative state.

I got assessed by the psychiatrist in there. He said they'd looked into my family history and found an uncle who was bipolar, so that's what they were thinking for me. My uncle Robert, who'd passed away a month after Shaun, had been hospitalised previously for depression. In one of his visits he had shock treatment, and they now wanted to do that to me.

I had to fight. 'Just because my uncle had shock treatment, that doesn't mean I need it.'

There was no way I was going to let it happen. They weren't wiping my memories of Shaun. Dad stood by me on that, and it never happened.

This was a strange and dangerous place. I now had my focus on getting out. It was like a circus in there. One of the guys tried to escape. He put up a pile of chairs to try and climb out a high window, and fell down, smashing his head open. Women were offering sex, and guys were offering to buy my Seroquel.

Then there were the blokes from the prison – I had a few run-ins there. One of them wanted clean urine, so I gave him some, but that didn't keep him happy. I was also on valium and he wasn't supposed to have any of that in his system, so he became threatening when he realised my urine wasn't going to work for him.

Another one started on me too. He'd been on ice and, for whatever reason, he just didn't like me – he couldn't walk past without bumping me. 'There's something about you I don't like,' he said. 'I'd love to take a fork and stick it straight in your eye.'

I tried to talk to him reasonably, but with him being on ice that was going nowhere. 'You don't know anyone, do you?' he asked, making sure it was okay to hurt me.

'What do you mean by "don't know anyone"?'

'Who do you actually know?'

'I actually know Mark "Chopper" Read.'

'Chopper? You know Chopper?' he said, and then asked a few questions to check. Once he was convinced I did know him, he eased up on me and I didn't have to watch my back as much.

Another day I was talking to a lady who'd lost four kids in a car accident. She said, 'I've spent the last six to seven years in and out of places like this. Cameron, don't let it destroy your life, because I let it destroy my life.'

Then the wardens, or whatever you want to call them, wanted to talk to her, but she didn't want to go with them, so they got physical. They grabbed her by the wrist so hard they broke it, and then stuck her in 'The Hole' for a spell. I arced up, and they threatened me with the same, so I went quiet.

I asked her later about The Hole, and she said they stripped her naked and left her in there on her own. She said when she was in there, she was throwing her faeces around the room. Which to me was pretty full-on.

All I could think was, 'I'm just not meant to be in this place.' That was the lowest I got. I was around really ill and dangerous people, I was sleeping all day because I was so drugged, and Dad said I was a dribbling mess.

I went to bed on New Year's Eve and I cried my eyes out. That night, I swear I felt Shaun's presence, and then an arm came over me and hugged me. 'I've got to get out of this place,' I was thinking. 'I can't deal with this.' And I started to work on getting out.

I spoke to my dad about it. Mum couldn't bear to come in, so it was just him. He wanted me out too, but he wanted to be sure I was getting to a point where I wasn't going to harm myself or anyone else.

I put on a lot of weight while I was there – about twenty-five kilograms in that short period. Yes, twenty-five kilograms. The Seroquel will do that to you, they say. You eat a lot because of it, and then, given that all you do is sit there dribbling, the weight piles on.

In all, it was ten days of hell, and I was so relieved when I got myself discharged. After I left I decided to keep taking the meds, so

I was still a bit of a mess. However, at least I wasn't in the hospital anymore and I was in a good enough place not to stress Dad out too much.

For the next two or three years, my life was all about trying to survive and trying to cope. That was the goal until I could function a little more. One good thing was that I did a real estate course. But although I passed, I couldn't do it for work, because I couldn't bring myself to do all the tricks they wanted to sell the houses. It wasn't for me.

In 2013, I went to Thailand with my friend Phillip. He was in the army and was married to a Thai girl named May. I went and sat with the monks there, and even though I hadn't said anything about Shaun, they wanted to help me with the 'boy who died very, very, very quickly'. They did this big ceremony and it made me feel very refreshed. It's a powerful thing sitting in front of the monks while they chant. I had a really good time in Thailand and, for a while, I felt like I could take on the world.

But I couldn't. 2014 was much the same – what was I going to do? Should I go back to glazing or something else that I'd done before, but which didn't grab me? Everything I'd ever done was for Shaun, and at that stage I just didn't want to go back and repeat the past.

One night, in May 2016, everything changed. And all because of a dream. Shaun was talking to me and he said, 'Start a foundation, Dad.' I woke up thinking, 'How do I start a foundation? I don't know anything about a foundation. I wouldn't know what to do.'

But I knew I had to do it. So, four years after Shaun's passing, I started looking into it and I had my purpose. The Shaun Miller Foundation.

CAMERON

50

AFTER THREE YEARS that had mostly been a prescription-drug-induced blur, it had taken a dream to kick-start me back into reality.

I jumped on the net and quickly learned that foundations are quite a specialised field and not many law firms in Melbourne can help you establish one. I tried to get lawyers to do it pro bono, but I guess when they do that sort of work they get asked that all the time – so that wasn't going to happen. I started to realise it was actually going to cost money, and not small amounts of money either.

I got in contact with a lawyer named Darren Brown, who explained it all to me. There are many different types of foundation, so what exactly did we want to do? We could set up one that was budget-priced, but that wasn't going to look after Shaun's legacy. The one I decided on was the most expensive structure and foundation.

Then I had to work out how to finance it. I paid a deposit and got to work. I went to my accountant of twenty years – Sam Pavano – asking him for advice. His wife had been suffering from

MS and he didn't hesitate when I explained what I wanted to do. He liked the idea. 'Okay, I'll put up some money as well,' he said. 'Let's kick it off.'

At the time, I didn't realise how long it takes to put a foundation together. It took us a good year and a bit, at a cost of more than $20,000.

One interesting detail was that you need someone with an Order of Australia to sit on the board of the type we were setting up. I knew that my friend Alan Finney had one, so I gave him a call and he agreed to join the now evolving Shaun Miller Foundation. Things were going okay.

At the same time, I'd decided I wanted to make a film about Shaun's life. A lot of people had read his book and said it would make an inspiring movie. So I started working on *The Awesome Ride* with a producer named James M. Vernon. He had a long list of credits, including as executive producer of the Mel Gibson film *Hacksaw Ridge*, and he was pretty full-on with his ideas and energy.

James wanted to do a launch for the movie in the media, no doubt to try to drum up some money. Alan felt this was the wrong way to go, because Shaun's foundation was involved. As a result, he pulled out of the foundation, so I lost my Order of Australia on the board.

Alan also had some health issues at the time, which was another factor in him pulling out. However, we sat down and had a chat and Alan decided he was back in, as long as we did things 'properly and transparently'. I said that was okay by me. I wanted to do this right and I needed people like Alan with me. He agreed to be a director of the foundation, with Sam as chairman.

Because I'd been dealing with CHD all of Shaun's life, I'd spent a lot of time with other parents and I knew more than most about the personal cost to them. As a result, we decided to focus not just on the children with CHD, but their families too.

With the foundation, clearly one of our goals is to help find a cure, so I spoke to the Victor Chang Institute. I went to Sydney to sit with them to see what we could do. I came away quite inspired, but also even more aware of how big a job was in front of us.

As I said, it took a year to get it all up and running. Even today, the compliance requirements are quite onerous. But with all that done, the Shaun Miller Foundation was conceived in 2016 and born in May 2017.

We had a public launch, which Jobe Watson helped with. He's the patron of the foundation, and a number of other ex-Essendon players are involved as well, which is great. Today the foundation is growing steadily, and we have a few plans for promotions that will raise money.

My struggles taught me that there is little support for parents when a child dies. I was given a box of Shaun's things by the hospital, but even though they'd become such an important part of our lives, the message from them after that was 'Sorry, there's nothing more we can do for you.'

We'll provide options for parents by building care houses – Shaun Miller Houses – in each capital city in Australia and probably Los Angeles as well. We're working on how to build these houses and what facilities we'll provide, and I expect that by the time the movie is out in 2021 we'll be well underway. We have funding locked away for some of it, but we'll be relying on proceeds from the film to finish the project.

CAMERON

51

WHEN I STARTED working with James, he was inspired by the message and the possibilities of how that would translate in a movie on Shaun. But over time we drifted apart, because of what some people would call artistic differences. I've always been conscious that this is Shaun's legacy, and I didn't want the film to drift away from that. So, unfortunately, James left the project.

Soon afterwards, I contacted Alan and had a discussion about the foundation 'owning' the movie, so that any profits would be directed there. He was totally on board with that and we started working on the other parts of making a film, such as producers and money. We lined up Scott Goldman, who'd produced *My Sister's Keeper*, starring Cameron Diaz and Alec Baldwin, and then Village Roadshow gave us some advice and encouraged us to add an Australian producer too. As a result, we spoke to David Lightfoot of *Wolf Creek* fame and enticed him onto the film. Now we had our core team.

I found a new scriptwriter, Stephen Coates, to replace the one who'd been working on James' vision, and dropped him off a copy of Shaun's book. Three weeks later we had a fantastic script. One of the most amazing things about it was that parts of it hadn't actually been in the book. We hadn't talked about any of it, so I didn't know how he'd found the words.

His explanation was simple. 'When I got up every day and sat down to write, I'd put my headphones on and I'd hear voices in my head. I can't say where they were coming from, but it felt like Shaun was talking to me.'

Films always take a long time to put together, especially ones that are from autobiographies. Faith Martin, who is one of the best casting agents in Australia, has said that the hardest part is going to be casting Shaun, because the actor will need to have his charisma, fun nature and looks. Alan Finney and I have spoken in depth about the movie and how we're looking for a marquee cast, because this isn't just a film – it's a film for the foundation and for the CHD community around the world.

But the concept of the movie is evolving all the time. As this book was being finalised, a major player from Hollywood started talking with us and, if he becomes involved, will want a new script again, one which uses this book as its base rather than just Shaun's. You can't become too attached to anything, but you have to keep an eye on what you are trying to do, and for me also an eye on Shaun's legacy. I'm confident we're on the right track and that we will have a great movie, even if it has taken a lot of time and effort to get there.

Our plan is to start principal photography sometime in 2020, with the movie to be released in cinemas in 2021. But before that happens, we're going to take the film to the Cannes Film Festival in France, as all movies go there looking for buyers, to try to put the film on the world stage.

*

Before I finish the book, let me tell you about a very special person we call 'Hollywood' – he's my street angel. I met Hollywood three years ago through a mutual friend.

In one of our early conversations, I started to tell Hollywood all about Shaun and asked him if he believed in the afterlife. He said, 'Absolutely, I'm a Christian. Look at the big cross around my neck.' I didn't know what to make of Hollywood at first, with his light blue eyes and blond hair like Rod Stewart.

Hollywood, who is thirteen years older than me, is old school when it comes to friendship. When you become his friend, you're one for life. We soon developed a strong bond and he had a protective side to him when it came to me. He started taking me out to music venues and over time he opened up about his life in the music industry. He'd been around for a while and had been on the TV show *Countdown* and toured with acts like INXS, Jimmy Barnes and The Ramones. His stories of touring and his feats as an amateur boxer were amazing.

Hollywood is very interesting and charismatic, but he also had a breakdown over the music industry when he was young, so he's vulnerable like the rest of us.

I've seen him on stage now and he is a fantastic singer and guitarist, and his friendship has been a truly positive experience. He's given me a lot of confidence to pursue the things I want to do, and he has been one of the great drivers behind the foundation. When I told him I needed some money to get it up and running, he came to me with $3000 to start the journey.

Last year I introduced Hollywood to my parents. My dad liked him straight away because he knew he was real and had my back. My dad is a very private person and for him to welcome Hollywood is a really big thing.

Today Hollywood is my closest friend. Looking back at things, he's helped me so much with my depression and missing Shaun.

He comes to the cemetery whenever I want to go and he is very supportive – but he can be a hard arse as well and he'll tell me if I'm in the wrong. A true mate.

In 2018, he told me about a song he wrote twenty years ago and played it for me. I was amazed by some of the words, but I asked him, 'Can I add some of my lyrics?' We spent all day working on it and the end result was 'Show Your Heart', which we're using for the foundation. My dream is for Ed Sheeran to sing it one day. I'm very proud of writing this song with Hollywood.

I know he'll always have my back and I'll always be able to count on him.

'Show Your Heart'

Don't fall apart on me tonight
Stand up, and be counted for
Hold on, Shaun can set you free
In him, shone the light of eternity.

See the ships out in the harbour
Setting sail for the promised land
Hold on to dreams that live inside you
Show your heart and make a stand.

Stay strong, love is by your side
Life is simply an awesome ride
His light can open any door
His light will shine forever more.

Chorus
Show your heart and make a stand (x2)
Cos life is an awesome ride (x4)

EPILOGUE

It still hurts. Losing Shaun was the hardest thing I've ever faced and am ever likely to face. I went to some pretty deep lows and there were many times when I thought I couldn't go on.

Today I feel like I've become a public person. It's going to be weird when firstly this book is published and then the movie comes out, because I'm not sure how much attention I want on myself. But it's going to be good for the foundation.

I've got over the hardcore grief. It still hurts on birthdays and anniversaries, but I can handle it now. Seeing other people with their kids hurts too, but I am okay.

It took a long time for me to work it out. Shaun was always teaching me, but I wasn't listening. He was the master teacher, so to speak, and I'm now an A grade pupil. I'm finally listening to his message about living life to the fullest, because that's what I do now.

I enjoy – well, that's not really the right word, but you know what I mean – talking to other parents about what they're going through, and I think I help. I believe my journey is with the foundation, and everything we're doing is just to bring awareness and to assist others.

When you're in the sort of situation I was with Shaun, you're dealing with hospital appointments and a million other things. It's ongoing and it's all the time. That is your life, and you can forget yourself in the process.

Living your life to the fullest – enjoying the ride, as Shaun would say – won't happen when you don't look after yourself. I look back at all the years with Shaun and it's almost like he was training me for this. When he was told he was going to die, he had to push that training forward.

Today, I hope I'm making Shaun proud.

AN AWESOME RIDE THROUGH OTHER EYES

SALLY DEVERS

When I was first approached by Cameron, I had no idea I was going to end up in a relationship or anything like that. There was the stuff on RSVP, but then there was the inbox asking me to go to a barbecue. I didn't think anything of it, and just sort of ignored it.

Then there was another one saying, 'Are you going to come?' I distinctly remember turning around to everyone at work and going, 'Some weirdo's asked me to a barbecue.' I didn't go, and can I add that it was very sane that I didn't.

Not long after, someone picked on Shaun at school and I commented on Facebook – I think I wrote 'arseholes' or something like that. Cam then inboxed me and that's when it started properly.

We had a first date on our own and then on the second Shaun came with us. It was amazing. He was so little then. He'd just turned fourteen and he looked like he was eight, with his little leather jacket on. Shaun had a much older mind than even fourteen, though. I used to say – and it sounded better when he was alive – that he had a wisdom that you can only have from being dead as many times as he'd been dead and been to the other side. He had this strange ability to relate to anyone on their level. He had me hooked from that first date.

I honestly feel like Shaun needed me. Cameron needed me too, but not as much as Shaun. I definitely needed them as well, and I think the RSVP and Facebook happened for a reason.

The other side of Shaun's family, his mother's, had not been good for either Shaun or Cam and the mere mention of any of them would set Cam off. He was so blighted by the anger that he couldn't hear Shaun's side. Shaun didn't hate his mum. I think apart from Fletch he didn't hate anyone.

But he had a sister there living with his mum, and there were other family members too that he missed, and he figured he could even have dealt with Fletch if he knew his mum would protect him. It would have meant so much to Shaun to have a relationship with them all. It never really happened because they were hard work, but we tried . . . well, Shaun and I tried.

I loved Shaun and I would have done anything for him. When I was in Prague we were Skyping every single day – I spoke to Shaun more than I spoke to Cam. The relationship I had with them was a beautiful experience for me, because I'm not a mother and I'm still single, so that was it for me.

I just think that was my chance at that sort of lifestyle. I was a party girl as Shaun openly says and then he and Cam settled me down, and made me grow. I'm a different person now.

I smile a lot, and the reason I smile and I'm happier than most is because of Shaun. He had a thousand operations and still smiled every day. I still hear him in my head telling me all the time there was someone worse off than me. He loved and he taught me to love life. So when something is tough, I just think of Shaun and his outlook and I can deal with anything.

I moved in with them less than six months after meeting Cam, and I think we all had a special connection. I'd like to think if things hadn't happened the way they did after Shaun died, Cam and I would still be together, but that was a tough time.

My whole life changed, and it wasn't just instant motherhood. I'd moved from Port Melbourne to Mill Park — about forty kilometres away — and catching the train into work took me an hour and a half. I'd never even lived in a house before in my life — I'm an apartment girl. I love that little vibe, but it was a big change. And while it was amazing, it was really hard too. But Shaun just made everything better, he really did.

It's kind of funny that even though Shaun had all these problems, you never really thought of him dying. He was like Superman, so it wasn't as if you were counting days or anything. I was a big-sister type of friend to Shaun for a long time, but when push came to shove he actually asked me to be his mother for the rest of his life, which I was hoping was going to be a long time.

When the opportunity came along to work in Prague, it was such a big thing for me. I really struggled with the idea, but Shaun was adamant I had to do it. I had it written into my contract that I could come home four times a year, which they only agreed to because of Shaun's health, but I never imagined he would deteriorate the way he did.

Pretty much when I got on the plane it was all okay, but by the time I landed he was in hospital. It was one of the times when I was home that he got told the bad news. We went home from the hospital that night, and Shaun went into his room and did the video. He wanted to load it onto Facebook, but it wouldn't load, so I suggested he try YouTube because it was more a video site . . . which he did. Then he came out and said it had 'hit him'. Cam said, 'Who hit you?' That was quite funny at a serious time.

I wasn't going to stay in Prague now, but I did have to go back and pack the apartment. I planned a month there, and I was going to return in time for the Kick-Arse Party, but it happened so quickly. As soon as the media attention started, that was the time for me to head back to Prague. They had things to do in Melbourne and I had things to do over there so I could move back. I'm not a limelight person or anything like that, so I was quite happy not to be there and to let them have the spotlight.

We were told Shaun would have six to twelve months and he died within a month. It was not fair. He used to talk about how every time he was looking forward to something, his health would take it away – this time it was the Kick-Arse Party that he missed out on. In hindsight they shouldn't have organised that party. It was just a fucking jinx.

It was five in the morning in Prague when I found out Shaun had died. I think I was on the plane within hours – I knew Cam was going to need me. The flights took forty-four hours and they were the worst forty-four hours of my life.

The next few months were a nightmare. Cam was 24/7 in terms of my attention. I was working in Southbank in the city, and I'd have to leave early because Cam would ring saying he was going to commit suicide or something. I don't think he was ever really going to do it, but I couldn't take that chance. It was bad enough losing Shaun, I didn't want to lose him as well. It was happening every day, so eventually they let me work from home. In the end that was no better for them, though, and I ended up losing my job.

Five days after Shaun's funeral, Maddy and Kane, two of Shaun's best friends, cooked dinner for us to try and help. They were just trying to make us happy, which was lovely. But Cameron was broken-hearted and it got too much for him. That night took a bad turn and he had to go for a walk, and eventually the police were called. That could have turned ugly, but they were great.

What I was doing really was maintaining Cam – I wasn't fixing him. You know we were good in our little bubble for a while, and we had it a little under control. He was okay – smiles and hugs and laughter.

At the same time, Cameron's parents were having their own grieving process. They didn't really even speak to anyone and they didn't ring much. But I had to send Cam to his parents for a few days, because I needed time to work on my CV and find a new job. I couldn't do that with him there. I knew it wouldn't be great for him, but I didn't think he'd go downhill as fast as he did.

This was at Christmas time, which wasn't easy for Cam to deal with. It was Boxing Day when he was institutionalised and his parents basically – I think in a loving way, not in a nasty way – just cut me off from him. No-one rang to ask me how he'd been over the last seven months, when no-one else had been there to help him. I think they just wanted to let me live and be happy, or maybe they just needed someone to replace Shaun in their lives, someone to look after, and Cam now filled that hole.

When he was in there I had no contact with him because he was blocked from everything, and his parents didn't tell me anything. They took him out of my life step-by-step, which is essentially how our relationship ended. We never actually split up or anything – he just didn't come home.

But we're great friends, always will be.

Cam's not usually a finisher and he's normally not good at following through. So to see him today is seeing a different person. When I met him he was a director and he'd started movies but he never finished them. He was good at getting people to do things – he's probably a bit selfish in that sense. But today he is so focused and driven. I've never seen that in him before. I think Shaun would be proud.

ZANE DIRANI

IT WAS MAY 2010 when I first recall meeting Cameron Miller. I was at a wrap-up party for a movie and it was more of a greeting than anything more at that time. I saw more than the outer image of Cameron and I vowed to spend some more time getting to know him.

Then a year passed. In May 2011 we were on the set of *The Groomless Bride*, of which he was the producer and I was the stunt co-ordinator. One day, Cameron mentioned he wanted to produce an action film. Being the founder of Zul Je Nan Self-Defence and Zul Je Nan Self-Empowerment and Physical Wellbeing, I decided to write a script which was the start of a great brotherly relationship, although at this time we had not gotten personal.

I overheard that Cam had a sick son in hospital. My belief in life is there is no greater deed than to visit the sick of family or friends. The next morning I met with Shaun Miller in hospital. It was a quick 'hi' and I gave him a gift of a stand-up punching bag.

It was my message to Shaun that he was a fighter. A week later I visited again, and then spent time with Shaun alone.

Shaun opened up to me and shared that he had been physically abused by his step-dad, Fletch, and almost choked to death. When I heard these words I saw the fear in Shaun's eyes. At that time he was renewing a restraining order against Fletch. As a believer in human rights, and helping a fellow being, I made a promise to Shaun, who was having nightmares at the time. My promise was as long as I am breathing no-one would hurt him – and that is how I became Shaun Miller's protector.

I then went to court twice alongside Cameron while they were presenting the restraining order and I made sure that Cameron was not threatened or hurt by Fletch.

Once Shaun was out of hospital he had his sixteenth birthday and that was great. Then I had to spend time with my own father who had been sick too. I was beside my dad's deathbed in hospital for two weeks, when he suddenly started to get better.

As soon as he came home, I was able to resume some normal life. I was on Facebook and read a post from Cameron saying that filming for his movie was no longer working in Australia. I lost contact with him then, and assumed he had gone overseas to finish the movie and taken Shaun with him. I was at peace knowing that the restraining order had been renewed.

Then May 2012, yes, amazingly May again – and, yes, I am a man of numbers but that's another story – I got a call at 10.47 pm and it was a young man's voice. It was Cameron, which was a surprise. I thought he was in the States, but he said he was home and that Shaun had been given bad news from the doctors.

I knew right away they needed my support, so I was at the hospital an hour later. Sally, Cameron's girlfriend, came around twenty minutes after I arrived and we were both there for Cameron and Shaun. I was asked many questions about life and death and was happy to put all at peace and Sally said, 'Thank you, Zane, you are like a modern Jesus.' I am no different to anyone, but I do respect the fact that the Miller family trust me and I respect Cameron for not deserting Shaun as his mother did. If you were to ask me to define love I would answer you by referring to Cameron's unconditional love for his son Shaun.

I was happy to see the spark in Shaun's eyes and smile when I was explaining to him about heaven and how we all carry a message, and that life is a journey we travel with a purpose, and that we are here for a reason and have a message to share. I explained to Cameron that he was a gift to Shaun and Shaun a gift to him. That night I left knowing they were a little more at peace.

Shaun later went back into hospital for a lung infection, and came home again before a final visit. I saw that the media was causing them distress. The last media organisation that came to interview the family was *The Project*. Cameron, Shaun and I spoke about it, and we sent them away. Shaun didn't like letting people down, but he just wasn't up to it. I advised Cameron enough was enough with media, and he pulled it all back, knowing how it was affecting Shaun and everyone around him. Cameron and I posted on Facebook thanking all media for their interest, but Shaun was no longer able to do any interviews. There were other children in the world who were dying and being killed, and perhaps it was time they turned to them and let other stories be told.

The hospital was not happy with Shaun's YouTube clip, so no doubt they were happy now. Cameron and Shaun were happy that their message had gotten across to live life to the fullest and to be an organ donor, but the hospital felt it was making it hard for other heart kids.

With Shaun now suffering from a lung infection I showed Cameron some different exercises and natural remedies to help Shaun to get rid of phlegm and mucus. It was now time for them, so I gave them space and helped look after the Kick-Arse Party for Shaun.

Cameron has had a very hard life, but he is not a man to give in. And he did not, he stood by Shaun's side until the end, and now he is doing the same thing in a different way. The Shaun Miller Foundation is just a measure of Cameron and what he is trying to do, and he has my full support.

I would like to personally thank you all for your support to the Miller family – it has meant a lot to them.

Live life as if you were to live forever,
Be pure body mind and soul as if it were your last,
In the hearts you touched you will remain alive till the end of time.

MY BEST MATE, SHAUN – NICK WILLIAMS

MY NAME IS Nick Williams and I met Shaun Miller at the Royal Children's Hospital when my dad had to go back home and I had to stay in the hospital alone. I was born in Adelaide on 24/10/1995, the same year as Shaun, who was born on 13/01/1995.

My birth was complicated as I was diagnosed with Multisystic Bilateral Renal Dysplasia and given a total of three days to live. My parents were advised to plan a funeral rather than spending money on baby's clothes. However, when I was born my renal doctors had a different idea.

It was Dr Paul Henning who explained the plan to my parents. They planned to keep me alive with a special diet long enough to go on dialysis. They said if I could stay off dialysis until I was at least six months old it would double my chances of survival. I am not going to go into any real details as that would be a book in itself and this book is about Shaun's life not mine. Anyway, after several operations I finally had a central line catheter inserted at the age of ten months.

As sometimes happens when chronic illness disrupts a family, my parents separated and I went to live with my mother, but after complications became too much for her to handle, I ended up living with my father. Dad and I were living together when I received my first kidney transplant at the age of five (Dad was the 'living donor'). I had been on haemodialysis, peritoneal dialysis (due to access problems with haemodialysis) and then haemo-dialysis again, before the actual transplant at the Women's and Children's Hospital in Adelaide.

Sometime after my transplant my father met a lady named Vivienne in an MSN chat room who was at the time living in Victoria. She came to Adelaide with her two youngest children for a holiday and when she met Dad they moved in together. This entailed collecting furniture and clothing for her and the kids from Victoria and a whole new life for Vivienne, Tamara and Troy, who became my mum, big sister and big brother, and I had become part of a family – something which is as real today, if not more so, as it was back then.

At the end of 2004 with my health problems under control Vivienne wanted to move back to Victoria as she was missing her grandchildren. We eventually moved to Bendigo, where we were temporarily housed with my big sister Lee. Monthly trips to the Royal Children's Hospital in Melbourne became the norm. Sadly, however, in the middle of 2005 I lost another mother, when Vivienne passed away after complications with deep vein thrombosis.

Although my biological mother was, as far as I knew, still alive, she had not come to see me since I was four years old in 1999. Over the next couple of years the trips to Melbourne continued – usually monthly and sometimes weekly, depending on how my health was going. Another setback happened when I somehow picked up a bladder infection, which eventually caused my kidney transplant to fail. Dad and I would have to move to Melbourne but in the meantime we made many trips to the Royal Children's Hospital.

Often I would go down for a check-up, a day trip, and because my blood test results were not good I would be admitted. It was one of these times when I was admitted that Dad had to go back to Bendigo, as we were not prepared for an extended stay and I was due to have surgery the next day. Dad went home in the afternoon to come back the next morning. At this time I was alone and with Dad in Bendigo, and the extended family living there, I had no visitors and was scared because of the upcoming operation.

There was a boy around my age in the next bed, Shaun, who came over and befriended me and cheered me up. He introduced himself by saying, 'My name is Shaun. I have had 1000 heart operations and two heart transplants. What are you looking so sad for, buddy?' Shaun being himself said this with a bright smile on his face, as he always did when he was trying to cheer someone up. Shaun had been through his own tough times and was always sensitive to the feelings of others. Because of this natural empathy Shaun had, he always made others feel comfortable and with his naturally sunny disposition I was always happy to spend time with him, as were many others.

Shaun and I became friends on Facebook and good friends in real life and one day Shaun's dad invited us to his place for a BBQ. Dad did not have a car at the time so Cameron came and picked us up from home and dropped us off afterwards. When we could, Shaun and I went on activities together.

If Shaun was in the hospital when I was too, we would spend time in the Starlight Express Room, sometimes playing table tennis or Mario Kart with Captain Starlight from the Starlight Foundation, before Dad and I had to catch the train home again. Shaun and I, with another friend Paige, went to the Christmas Party at the Starlight Express Room, where we went on Starlight TV with Captain Starlight.

Even though I went on peritoneal dialysis after our move from Bendigo to Melbourne, Shaun was able to visit and to sleep over at my place. At times I was also able to sleep over at Shaun's place, but not as often as I would like, as I had to be on dialysis twelve hours per day – but by manipulating my treatment I did have some days off. Shaun and I would watch the WWE pay-per-view events on Foxtel and even go to the football at the Telstra Dome (later to be renamed Etihad Stadium and now Marvel Stadium).

Shaun even stayed at our place some weekends so his dad could have some time out. But I could never stay at his place for more than one night.

In 2009, Shaun and I kept meeting at the Royal Children's Hospital and spent as much time as we could in the Starlight Express Room. In April 2009, Shaun and I went to the State Library before going to a game at the Telstra Dome where we watched Essendon playing.

Through the rest of 2009 and into 2010, Shaun and I kept up our activities, including going out to lunch – Shaun was partial to chicken parma. When we could, we would also kick the footy around and just hang out like any other friends. Shaun even went to Port Power games, as well as inviting me to Essendon ones. At one game, in May 2010, we ended up right near the Power coaches' box.

Even my being on peritoneal dialysis and Shaun's health problems did not always stop us going to events. September 2011 will always be one of my fondest memories. This was the first time we (me, Shaun, Cameron and my dad) had attended the Royal Melbourne Show together. It was a beautiful day to head along; we spent a few hours wandering around, checking out what the show was about and what was on. At lunchtime, Cam and Dad were ordering lunch – myself and Shaun had finished already – so we briefly checked out the showbag hall. It was packed, though, so we came back out.

We decided to sit with Cam and Dad while they ate, but before too long we got bored again, so Shaun whispered to me, 'Hey, bud, should we go back in the showbag hall and try it out again?' I thought, 'Okay, but we were just in there, weren't we?'

Anyway we told the parents we'd be back soon, and we made our way back into the hall. Then Shaun suddenly dashed off, and I couldn't find him for a brief moment, till I spotted him with a small bunch of people. I just thought Shaun has spotted some of his friends, so I walked over there, to find he was talking to a couple of girls. I was so stunned and embarrassed LOL.

We walked around with them for about five minutes and Shaun and I had the biggest grin on our faces. Then they went one way and we went the other way. We both spotted the AFL showbag and decided we'd try to get the parents to buy this for us. It ends up that we couldn't or didn't, so instead we bought these two helicopter hats. We were loving life and just having some awesome fun away from hospitals, where we spent most of our lives. It was great to be outdoors and healthy.

Another great memory we had was AFL grand final week in 2011. Shaun had decided to sleep over here some of the nights. We watched parts of the *AFL Grand Final Footy Show* replay together but then we got bored, so Shaun said, 'Give me the laptop.' He showed me a store that had online collectibles, like WWE/UFC.

We checked when they closed, and it was 5 pm, so we waited till Dad got home and we made our way there.

We were so excited looking at all the WWE stuff that we'd seen on the internet. We said to the guy who owned the shop, 'Hey, mate, are they real WWE belts in the cabinet that the wrestlers wear?' He said yes and then asked us, 'Would you like to hold it?' We both looked at each other and we were stoked. I had the first hold and just said, 'OMG that's heavy.' Shaun then held it and said, 'Wow, that is heavy, but the champ is here' (as John Cena says).

It was later that night I rang Shaun and said, 'Hey, mate, what are you doing tomorrow?' He said, 'Not much planned.' So I ended up going there for the AFL grand final. Shaun and I played Xbox, right up until grand final time. It was Collingwood vs Geelong and we were all excited until the fourth quarter when Geelong just smashed Collingwood. Back then, Cameron wasn't happy as he was originally a Collingwood supporter and I guess he still had a soft spot LOL.

After the game, Shaun and I played AFL live on Xbox to continue one of our many match series. I ended up winning by three points (close game!). Now Shaun wasn't happy. So Shaun was eliminated as the winner stays on. Cameron thought he was a chance against me. Boy, was he wrong. However, at three-quarter time, the game was suddenly very close! What a game – Cameron only lost by one point. By then it was 8 pm, and I had to head home to go on dialysis for the night. I thanked Shaun and Cameron for having us for the day, and we left for home.

With my chronic renal problems and Shaun's chronic heart condition, there were many times when either one or both of us were in the hospital and sleepovers and trips to the football or wrestling had to be put on hold.

This is how much I lost when my best friend, Shaun, passed away. Since his passing, a lot of things have happened. One of the important things is that I had a second kidney transplant on 3 February 2016. I think organ donation is really important as one dearly loved heavenly angel can save up to eight other lives.

Since Shaun left this earth and grew his angel wings, I did have my toughest days, and of course my happy days. I have always and always will remember his outlook on life, and that's to smile even when it's overcast, as it can't rain all the time. Shaun taught me so much in our friendship and I am forever grateful for the times we spent together. I will always treasure the memories, and one day we will meet again. Till then I'll do what you always wanted and that's to enjoy life, live life to the fullest, and look after your day. :D

DOROTHY MILLER

Cameron had a lot of convulsions as a child and he suffered from bad asthma until he was fifteen or sixteen. He was in and out of hospitals and even a puff of wind would give him asthma. He had what we believed was the best of care we could find at the time, but it didn't seem to help. It was a real problem because you couldn't go anywhere without him getting asthma and he would land in the hospital at a drop of a hat. So those years were difficult, but we got through them.

He didn't like school at all, and I don't know whether that was because it was disjointed from the asthma or he just didn't like it. He couldn't do the things that everybody else wanted to do, and even though he looked strong, he wasn't. He couldn't compete in sports or anything like that, and he spent a lot of time watching his friends do the things he wanted to do. School camps and trips away were a complete no-no.

We had a house in Apollo Bay but even that wasn't so easy, and not just because my husband did shift work. Sometimes the minute we got there the wind would blow and that was the end of it. We'd have to rush back and put Cameron in the hospital. So he was not strong.

That was about the time he decided to leave school, which was okay by me because we had tried everything we could to help him, with tutors and the like. We even had him coached by a nun at one stage – but it just wasn't Cameron. It was funny, another lady who was coaching him gave him a chicken to look after, an unusual pet that lasted twelve years – which was incredible.

He was always interested in acting, so he did a modelling course, which was as close to enjoying schooling as he ever came. Then I was working at Preston Market and some of the people I knew were involved with the Carlton Football Club. They got him a job there which lasted four or five years. He was getting stronger now, although he still had some of the asthma. But he was finally doing things he enjoyed and it was going well and that was bringing him out of his shell a little. He'd been very withdrawn and he'd get very angry easily, which we put down to the Ventolin and asthma. We ended up with a few holes in the wall.

He started a glazing apprenticeship but didn't like that either – it was hard at times to get him out of bed to get to work. He had a pretty girlfriend named Caroline for a bit, and then there was Olivia, and that was something else.

I wouldn't have called her a girlfriend or anything – she was really a friend of a friend. In fact, it could have been a part of our life that I could have wiped right out. But anyway, it happened the way it happened. It was a very, very difficult time for us all.

I always queried whether Cameron was really the father, because she was seeing other people at the time, but when you looked at Shaun you knew he was Cameron's. Olivia and Cameron didn't even like each other that much at the start, and that only got worse. It became a very hostile environment and that made me angry too, but I coped.

Cameron was not doing too well, though. Just after he learned that there was a really good chance Shaun would die straight after he was born, he told us he didn't want to live any longer – that he'd thought about jumping off the end of the Barwon Heads pier.

Luckily he didn't, and we took him to the Austin Hospital and they said, 'This was just a cry for help. He didn't really want to – it was just that he didn't know which way to turn.' We all felt trapped, if you know what I mean, and Cameron was feeling it the worst. He really wasn't geared up to cope with stuff like this in his life.

He was trying to deal with the issues around his unborn baby and not only did he have to deal with Olivia but her family too – and it got worse after Shaun was born. Watching Olivia's behaviour was pretty tough, but our hands were tied. Cameron started to mature through the process. He had to grow stronger, didn't he? Shaun needed him to step in, and as Cameron grew he began to understand what he needed to do, although the system didn't help. When Fletch grabbed Shaun by the throat, he made it easier.

We'd watched for years the toing and froing. Olivia would say one thing and then do another. Cameron was devastated at times. He kept pushing forwards, though, and eventually was able to get what was needed, but it was never easy. During those big oper-ations, like the first heart transplant, you'd have her side of the family on one side of the bed and our family on the other, and it was pretty tense. I had a friend who was one of the head nurses, and she said she'd never seen such anger in the air.

We loved Shaun and we knew that one day Cameron would get him. It has cost us thousands of dollars but it was all worth it in the end.

Getting to that point was a very nasty situation. There were a lot of people involved and I didn't know if someone was going to get murdered – it felt as if that could happen because everybody felt threatened. We were up against it at the Children's Hospital. The social workers didn't want to know about us; they didn't believe us. Right up until the night that Cameron got Shaun, the social workers didn't agree with us, but eventually they had no choice – the evidence was there. Up until then, it was 'the mother's place to have Shaun'.

It took a while, but we eventually got Shaun away from that situation. Hopefully he felt safe and loved for those last few years.

Cameron's whole life was Shaun, so when Shaun finally passed away it could have been the end for him too. Part of his life had gone and it was definitely a worrying time for us.

It's been seven years now, and it is like Shaun is with us every day. Everybody chats away like he's here. We celebrate his birthday, and at Christmas time Cameron's always got a spare chair at the table for Shaun.

Emotionally it has affected Cameron, and those years have been another journey for us. The worst time was sending Cameron to hospital. That was very difficult – terrible, actually. I thought, 'What am I going to do?' As usual my hands were tied. He was there for about nine days, and as a family we just shut down. We closed the doors and didn't talk to anyone.

I think he is in a good place now. He's very motivated with the Shaun Miller Foundation. He would love a cure but, unfortunately as you know, there are children passing away with it every day. He just wants to help them in the way no-one was able to help him.

It has taken a long time to surface, but he has a very strong personality now and nothing will stop him. He can get up in front of thousands of people and speak. He has that sort of confidence and I don't worry so much anymore.

GARTH WOOD

I THINK IT was my mum who told me about a message on a fake Garth Wood account from a little bloke named Shaun, who had been through a bit. So I reached out to him and we got on really well. We were able to just chat and have a laugh.

Even though I was about to face the battle of my life in fighting Mundine, Shaun told me about all the operations and the like that he'd had to deal with, and it seemed to help me face what I had to go through. Mundine was an absolutely world-class fighter, and even though we'd followed a similar path he had three world championships by then. He was going to be tough.

I thought I had a lot of things to juggle, but the young bloke was always smiling and always taking the positive out of everything. Nothing phased him at all, and both him and Cameron were great supporters – they were always in my corner.

To be honest with you, I thought about not doing the fight with Mundine, and in some ways it was Shaun who helped me to get into the ring at all. I decided then that I was going to win it for him, and to keep my eye on the prize I was continually inspired by him. Because he was in Melbourne and I was in Sydney, we spoke a lot on the phone.

I take my hat off to him. He knew where he was going, but he tried to stay positive for his dad. He was very uplifting for me and he was the fuel for me to put Mundine away, to give me just a little more strength and courage.

I was a long shot in the fight, just as I was on *The Contender*, but he was always talking to me about how you should never give up. Never worry about what others are saying, just go out and do it.

During the fight I could see him. He was always yelling out and encouraging me. 'Get up,' 'You can do this,' 'Never give up.' Shaun and my girls got me through that fight.

I knew Mundine, I grew up with him, and he was spoiling the fight by hanging onto me and tying me up. It was a pretty ugly fight, but then I got some space and was able to knock him out. I was the first bloke to do that, and I did it in his prime.

After I won, Shaun was trying to get me to go for an IBO world title fight, but Mundine came back with a better offer and I took that fight and lost. Every time I started to get the body punches in, the ref would stop me.

I was pretty rattled when Shaun died. He came out of nowhere and he was so inspirational, and for him to believe in me meant so much. I was heartbroken.

Today I am still in touch with Cameron. He is pretty excited about the movie, and he said there may be a part in it for me. Regardless of that, I am happy to help out with the foundation and anything I can do to keep the positive messages from Shaun going, I will.

PHIL HANNAM, CAMERON'S OLDEST FRIEND

THERE WAS PRETTY much a group of three to five of us that always hung around together, and probably only Cameron and I are still in touch. We were pretty thick back then. We spent almost every lunchtime and after school together. Obviously we don't see each other too often now – I mean, I live in Darwin for a start – but we still have that connection whenever we're in contact.

When I first met him, I was in Grade 2 and he was in Grade 3, but our mothers were working together in the canteen and that kind of pushed us together. We were both into cricket and football and we pretty much had the same way of looking at life.

But he was in and out of school all the time with asthma. There was one stage he missed about six weeks in a row, and over the years he missed a lot of school. They actually held him back and then he was in the same grade as me. I thought we'd go to high school together but he got sent elsewhere for a year.

The asthma was such a big thing. You'd be out having fun and then you'd have to stop suddenly and get him home. It was horrible to see and must have been awful for him. Thankfully he started to grow out of it, which meant we could just hang out.

He was very mischievous, and when we were together it seemed like we were just looking for trouble. I lost count of how many times we had to sit outside the principal's office – I think we had seats named after us. It was all the usual stuff that today would be frowned on in a much bigger way, but we had a ball. We didn't go too far, though. You know, we'd throw rocks at things but never to break anything.

School wasn't his thing and you could see he wanted to get out of there as quickly as he could. He'd missed out on so much when he was young, his academic skills were just so far behind the rest of us, and he just didn't have the concentration.

Then he went through a bunch of jobs looking for something. Into the latter years of school we'd started to drift apart a little, because he was off trying to find what he wanted to do and I was trying to study. He worked at Carlton footy club – for a mad Collingwood supporter that was a bit like working for the enemy, but he did it anyway.

By the time he was with Olivia, we didn't really see each other. I was getting regular updates from my mum on him and, eventually, Shaun, and we had the odd phone call here and there. I didn't know how to help, so I stayed away for a bit, but eventually we started to catch up again and it was just like old times.

It was easy to get him involved as my best man when I married my first wife, Danielle. I don't know if she'd planned anything with Penny beforehand, since she asked Cameron to pick Penny up at the airport in Fiji before the wedding. I never thought they'd end up in a relationship, so when that happened it was just great for all of us.

I knew at times he was doing it tough with Shaun, but he was starting to get more custody and eventually got full custody. That was both hard and good for him. I think Shaun's struggles were really tough for him to deal with, but he was happy to have him around and even happier he wasn't with Olivia and was safe. That is the kind of bloke he is.

This is why I think Shaun's passing hurt so much. Because of my work in the army, we'd been taught to look for certain signs of post-traumatic stress disorder, and I could see it in Cameron. I said to everyone who both he and I knew that we had to keep in touch with him to keep an eye on him. Unfortunately, I wasn't down in Melbourne when he started to fall off the rails, so I feel really bad about that, but I tried to keep in touch.

Eventually he started to come around. I could tell when he was getting better because he'd return my calls and we could chat about things. I wanted him to contact me when he needed someone to talk to. I got stuck into him over that a few times, because I knew that the way he was going, he could mourn for ten years.

After a couple of years it was as if something had hit him – he was like a different person. He began to sort himself out and started the foundation, and ever since then he's been back to the Cameron I grew up with. Back then he cared for people and he wanted to help. Yes, he was a bit of a rogue, but he was a top bloke, and I'm so happy that he is now back with us.

MADELEINE QIEX

SHAUN'S DAD, CAMERON, and I became friends through our initial social meetings at the Debonairs Luncheon Group for the Australian Music and Entertainment Industry Notables. One of the first things I remember Cameron saying to me when we met at a Debonairs luncheon was, 'You've gotta meet my Shaun – he will just love you!' I said something like, 'You can't be serious . . . we're ages apart!'

I found it intriguing that a parent had such gusto about their child having an adult buddy, especially in today's 'stranger danger' mentality, where parents are mostly isolating children from adult acquaintances. Anyway, the time came when Cameron invited me to come to the national launch of a film he had the distribution rights for. After watching the premiere, I was feeling a little tired and went to sit down in the foyer area as far away from the madding crowd as I could. There were some rather rowdy young kids there who I'd noticed darting in and around everyone. I thought from the look of them they were about twelve to thirteen years of age – a very excitable lot.

305

I recall thinking, 'Is there another function on here? Where are their parents? Doesn't anyone control their kids at functions anymore?'

And with that very thought, one of these rambunctious kids plonked onto the private couch I'd especially chosen for its isolation from all the people at the function, kids included. As I sat guarding my space by averting my gaze, I couldn't help but overhear these happy, mischievous, spirited youngsters chirping away like a flock of finches in an aviary . . . when the young boy sitting beside me dropped a few F-bombs into his conversation with them.

'Okay, okay,' I told him, 'do your parents know it's past your bedtime? And that you swear like a trooper?' I smiled. 'Do your parents even know where you are?'

This young and very pale-skinned boy looked up at me and laughed. With a huge grin on his face, he said, 'How old do you think I am? I bet you think I'm a little kid, because I'm little, but I'm a lot older than you think I am. And, yes, my parents know where I am. He's just over there – see my dad?'

I looked into a sea of people, and for the life of me couldn't see anyone I thought looked remotely related to this cheeky young fellow. I replied, 'Nope, can't see a parent anywhere.'

By now, this kid's friends had dispersed back to the cakes and soft-drink buffet for energy replenishment. 'Look, there he is, you're looking right at my dad over there, talking with people . . . there . . .!' he said, pointing adamantly.

The boy could see me peering into the crowd quizzically, and out of frustration with my lack of recognition he stood up and called out, 'Dad!' From the crowd socialising on the other side of the foyer turned Cameron Miller, who smiled and nodded as Shaun called out. 'She's telling me I'm too young to swear and it's past my bedtime!' Cam laughed along with the boy, who I'd now realised was Shaun.

Yes, he was much older than I thought from looking at him. He was the hefty age of fifteen. Looking at me with a wry smile, he said, 'Don't worry, I get that all the time.'

I was, and still am, thankful our first meeting wasn't set up, and not having the pressure of 'liking' my friend's son. My friend-ship with Shaun as his own being was as quick and as strong a connection as Cameron had predicted it would be.

I miss Shaun. I miss our conversations, the deep and the silly ones. Most of all, I hate that we cannot shoot the breeze with our particular philosophy on Life, the Universe and Everything.

Cameron asked me to write the things Shaun and I would talk about. Everything Shaun did before he died was for his dad. Shaun made sure he coined that 'awesome ride' phrase for his father. That was the last gift he could give Cameron, though that goodbye message was meant for us all – the ones who couldn't get to the hospital room in time before he died.

My mate Shaun spent his very last few minutes sending his dad to get his favourite burger meal from Maccas to have him on an errand of love, because he didn't want his dad there as he died. Both of us had died before – Shaun during surgeries, and me after surgery; both of us having had too many surgeries. I also drowned and was revived when I was about eight years old, which was a totally different experience to dying post-surgery as an adult. The coming back into the body was a violently horrific experience in itself.

One of the major things we discussed, which upset us both, is the problem people in general have with discussing death with a person who has a short life expectancy, or terminal disease. In fact, we felt cheated of some life from that, because of their inability to confront what we were facing every time we opened our eyes to a new day. Pending death? Hmmm, now get up and get on with that life project. But that was what Shaun did, and I still do, and that's why we were great mates, just as Cameron had predicted.

Shaun would tell me how tired he was of pills and doctors and operations, and all the rest of the invasive poking and prodding to keep him alive for another year, another heart transplant, through another heart rejection; tired of the fight. Exhausted, and staying alive for Cameron. Shaun would say to me, 'Madeleine, I'm worried only about Dad, and how he'll survive my death. Promise me you won't leave my dad alone after I die? Make sure he's okay and that he stays alive after I'm gone. I'm worried when I'm gone, he'll die with me.'

I said to him, 'Shaun, Cameron needs to be prepared. I'm surprised you haven't spoken with him about all this stuff, considering he's been at the hospital with you and knows everything already.'

'Nahhh, he wouldn't handle it,' Shaun said. 'You've seen what he's like. He's the kid – you know that.'

That gave us both a laugh, because Shaun was speaking the truth. Their relationship was full-on love and intense, even if there was a role reversal in terms of being able to confront the reality of what was soon to happen. Cameron was the kid in this instance, and Shaun the old man. Anyway, I promised Shaun that I'd remain Cameron's friend, that I'd check in to see how he was, and that I'd always only be a phone call away, no matter the time, day or night.

I remember a chat with Shaun about girls and the upcoming HeartKids camp he was really looking forward to. He wouldn't say too much about girls to me, except he couldn't wait to be old enough to have a real loving relationship and experience all that was involved in that. He always said it with a twinkle in his eyes and a cheeky curl of his lips into a mischievous smile.

I remember after he returned home from that camp and I was visiting them, I asked Shaun, 'Soooooo, did "it" happen – did you get a kiss?'

And he blushed and grinned broadly as he quickly glanced at Cameron, who was chuckling. With a stern sideways look and a smile at Cameron, he said, 'Daaaaad!'

And then he beamed and blushed and said to me, 'What happens on camp, stays on camp.'

I was silently hoping he'd found more than a kiss at camp that year. I mean to say, he was the ripe old age of seventeen at that point. Yet there was still hope, as his eighteenth birthday party was beginning to be planned, and that was going to be huge.

Shaun and I spoke of the two hearts he was blessed to live with after his own had failed. Our talks were far deeper than I think I could ever give justice to here. We spoke of the spiritual connection with the living hearts inside him, and the amount of love and respect Shaun had for the sacrifice of the donors; his admiration for their supreme generosity, and how these hearts gave him more time to be with his dad. We'd talk of the hearts having 'unfinished business' and that within Shaun maybe they got to do something they still needed to do, because we considered they had individually added to his wisdom well beyond his own years.

Shaun and I were – well, we still are – great mates. I carry him in my heart and that will be the case until the day I die. I envisage that is some years off, even though I'm a Peter MacCallum Cancer Institute hospital patient and am living with diagnosed familial small intestinal polyps, along with another hereditary disease called Alpha-1 anti-trypsin deficiency.

Shaun and I had hospitals and surgeries and strangers learning all about our condition in front of us; at times during some rather invasive procedures and surgeries. And yet we'd find a way to laugh about things. We'd both go yuck to each other's suffering and we'd both say, 'I can handle what they have to do for me, but I don't think I could handle what you have to deal with.'

Shaun died . . . sooner than we thought, really. The funeral was so big, so many people making sure they walked past every television camera as I watched them from my car, still trying to decide if I could cope with going in. I felt an emotional push saying, 'Park the car, walk in and sit,' so I did when the cameras weren't looking. But I have to tell you, it was so surreal.

At the end of the service Cam stood up to the mic and said the burial was a private gathering for those closest to Shaun. I remember thinking I hadn't been told where it was, so I figured that didn't include me. There were so many people around that I couldn't get to Cameron to let him know what he meant to me, as well as Shaun.

Sitting in my car, it took a while before I could drive, and by the time I turned on the ignition, there was virtually no-one left. I didn't want to go home and I looked at my GPS and realised I was maybe forty minutes away from the grave of one of my nephews, which I hadn't been to since his funeral a couple of years earlier.

I drove in through the gates at Whittlesea Cemetery and parked as near to my nephew's grave as possible. I fell to my knees on the earth beside his tombstone and took it all in. I looked around. There was a small gathering one row over and a few graves further north. I heard music playing from there – it was the Bombers theme song. I looked over and saw balloons being released as the mourners sang, 'See the Bombers fly up, up . . .' I blinked my tears away and realised Cam was gesturing for me to come over to them.

'Shaun wanted you to be here, Madeleine,' Cameron said, 'and I thought I'd told you already – I thought you knew. Shaun got you here where you were meant to be.'

God really does work in mysterious ways, and I've had too many moments not to realise that there is something far greater than I know, something divine at work in my life, just as Shaun knew it was at work in his life too.

Shaun and I wouldn't trade our journeys in life, because even the sad parts we got through eventually ended up having 'pure gold'. I care, from my soul's heart I care, no matter what I've survived. My mate Shaun was the same. Pure gold, genuine, passionate, funny, strong, and blessed by God.

KERRY THE MEDIUM

IN THE MIDDLE of 2013, while I was trying to come to grips with my grief, in the search for some meaning I went to see a medium named Kerry Alexander. She outlined the process to me and explained what she did, and then set about a reading. At the start I wasn't sure about clairvoyants and mediums. I'd always thought of it as hocus-pocus, but after the reading from Kerry I was turned around on the matter. I went to see her a second time a few months later.

During the first reading, I started to feel Shaun's presence around me and there were things she told me that only people who were there the day that Shaun passed away knew about. After the forty-five minutes I felt a lot of pressure had been lifted off me. Looking back on it, I know I can feel Shaun hugging me from behind that day. The only way I can describe it is the absolute love I was feeling for him.

I remember on the drive home I felt like I was on top of the world and nothing could bring me down. I was singing songs on the radio out loud like Shaun and I used to do.

Here are Kerry's thoughts about the two times I saw her:

Reading 1

Shaun presented as a strong energy full of excitement at being able to communicate with his dad. The deep bond between them, their laughter and soul connection, brought tears to my eyes. Cameron felt a heaviness overshadow his body, tingly in his hands, and a sense of knowing Shaun was with us.

Shaun was clearly a highly evolved old soul – kind, caring, compassionate, funny, with an ease of communication. My mind filled with images of hospital visits, the last days of his earthbound life and his dad's bedside vigil. I was shown Cameron sleeping face down on the hospital bed, with his arms coupled around his head, reluctant to leave his son even for a moment.

Shaun's greatest concern during the reading was to make sure his father would be all right in this lifetime. He showed me the scars down the centre of his chest, drainage tubes, IV bags and his breathlessness. I sensed how he passed and that a young male energy was also with him.

Shaun gave me the colours red and black and I could see balloons, football boots and a special football guernsey. Images of a young woman filled my mind, a special friend who later Cameron explained was Maddy. Intuitively I knew he was connected heart to heart with Cameron as a protective guiding energy not yet willing to leave his father. Unconditional loving relationships cannot be broken by the veil of death.

Throughout the reading there was a sense of unfinished business, something important that needed to be manifested or completed. Shaun wanted everyone to know he was flying free of all earthly concerns and no longer in pain: 'Please don't worry about me'. The sixty minutes we shared was intense and I felt a strong bond to them both. Cameron left uplifted and smiling.

Reading 2

Three or four months later, Cameron scheduled another
appointment and I sensed something was seriously wrong. This
time he presented as a broken man, overwhelmed with grief and
depression. His soul was joyless, and his eyes were black with
pain. He had closed down. I gently asked the hard question, 'Do
you want to join Shaun?' and Cameron responded 'Yes, I do!'

I mentally gestured for Shaun to channel through me
messages of proof to reopen his dad's heart, and guide him with a
life purpose to be of service to others. Cameron then felt Shaun's
healing power envelop him in loving heat. His mood started
to lift a little as we shared communication with his son. I saw a
glimmer of light return to his dark lifeless eyes.

We both sensed Shaun's presence and felt his energy. His
playfulness lightened the mood and made us both laugh. Images
of writing a book or the completion of planned projects were
given. In a firm, directive tone Shaun suggested channelling
thoughts and ideas to his father, to help others, especially
HeartKids. 'I need you, Dad, so I can work through you,' Shaun
said. The book *An Awesome Ride* was mentioned for the first time
as a work in progress.

He often visits his dad in his dream state with happy memories
or songs where the hidden message from above is in the lyrics.
I once mentioned to Cameron that perhaps Shaun had morphed
into him somehow and was the driving force behind all the doors
that were opening. He smiled, then came a resounding 'Yes!'

Grief, love and loss elevate our consciousness to a higher level
of understanding. It is within this heartache we are given our
greatest life lessons and spiritual gifts from our departed loved
ones. Divine truth is found in that awareness.

SHAUN'S 'MY FINAL GOODBYE' VIDEO

SHAUN'S VIDEO HAD an amazing impact worldwide. It was viewed and discussed across the globe on television, radio, newspapers and the internet. Most recently, in October 2018 Shaun featured on TV on the *Dr Phil* show, which picked up its views astronomically. As I've mentioned earlier, the video has now been viewed seven million times.

Shaun is credited with saving lives, as he assists in teenage suicide prevention on a daily basis. We continually receive emails at the foundation from teenagers and parents, thanking us for his life-saving message. He is a hero to all the cardiac kids and was the only HeartKids Ambassador at the Royal Children's Hospital in 2009.

In July 2012, he was nominated for a Courage Medal in the Pride of Australia awards.

Here's a list (which is probably not complete) of the media outlets that featured Shaun's video:

Daily Mail, UK
New York Daily News

Los Angeles Daily News
Herald Sun
The Daily Telegraph
The Age
Adelaide *Advertiser*
Dr Phil, USA
AFL *Footy Show*, Channel 9
Today Tonight, Channel 7
Today Extra, Channel 9
BBC News, UK
Triple M
Fox FM
Neil Mitchell, 3AW
Kyle and Jackie O
Perez Hilton, USA
Huffington Post, USA
Google commercial

It was also uploaded online with Japanese, Spanish and Portuguese subtitles.

WHAT IS CONGENITAL HEART DISEASE (CHD)

CONGENITAL HEART DISEASE (CHD) has many ways of showing its face to the world and it is surprisingly common. CHD is a catch-all phrase for any heart or major blood vessel defect a child is born with, and sadly the list is quite long. Shaun had a combination of defects which eventually proved too much for his body, but many defects can be repaired, either in isolation or in combination.

The rate of CHD in Australia is around one in 100 births, which means up to 3000 babies are born in Australia each year with CHD. It is the leading cause of death in Australian babies, but because it is not a disease as such, there is no cure – just invasive procedures to sort out the issue at hand, if the body doesn't fix the problem or find a work-around on its own. Some simply live with the defect for the term of their lives, managing the issues with assistance from our amazing cardiac surgeons.

Some are born with issues that are not even detected until later in life, while others require immediate surgery. Shaun was

317

obviously the latter, with the first of his hundreds of medical procedures when he was about three weeks old.

Wikipedia says the real causes are unknown, but that the 'use of certain medications or drugs such as alcohol or tobacco, parents being closely related, or poor nutritional status or obesity in the mother' may play a contributing role. The defects are also graded on whether they are likely to turn the child blue or not, which depends on the amount of oxygen being pumped through the body: less oxygen equals a cyanotic heart defect. Cyanotic defects are diagnosed quickly because of the blue skin; non-cyanotic can take time to be found, if at all.

We don't know how to prevent these issues from happening, which is one of the reasons for starting the Shaun Miller Foundation, but we do know certain things help. Iodine and folic acid are important, so pregnant women should pay attention to that.

Other than that, we need to just keep learning.

Some forms of CHD

Aortic Stenosis – the aortic valve between the left ventricle and the aorta is too small, narrow or stiff.

Atrial Septal Defect (ASD) – this is what people call a 'hole in the heart'. It is an abnormal opening in the dividing wall between the atriums.

Ventricular Septal Defect (VSD) – again a hole in the heart, but this time in the ventricles.

Atrio-ventricular Septal Defect (AVSD) – yes, holes between the left and right sides of the heart, which allow blood to pass between the two ventricles and the two atriums.

Coarctation of the Aorta – a narrowing of the aorta, which means the left side of the heart has to work harder to pump blood around the body.

Cyanotic Congenital Disease – anything that turns the baby blue, meaning there is not enough oxygen pumping around the body. Generally surgery is required.

Mitral Valve Stenosis – when the mitral valve is narrower than it should be, so it doesn't allow blood to pass freely.

Patent Ductus Arteriosus (PDA) – an extra blood vessel that may or may not cause severe problems requiring surgery.

Pulmonary Atresia – when a pulmonary valve doesn't form properly, which means blood to the right ventricle may be unregulated.

Tetralogy of Fallot (TOF) – there are four defects here that change the way blood flows inside the heart. This has to be fixed via open heart surgery.

Transposition of the Great Arteries (TGA) – as logical as it sounds, the aorta is connected to the right ventricle and the pulmonary artery is connected to the left. Clearly, surgery is required here.

CAMERON'S FINAL NOTES ON CHD

DURING MY SEVENTEEN years in and out of hospital with Shaun, I learnt a lot. As a father I have slept in hospital chairs, skipped meals, cried in fear and joy and become an expert on my son's condition. I have had to make life-changing decisions for myself since Shaun's passing, and I hope my changes can make a difference now for others.

Children with congenital heart defects can do it tough. There are some who rock their scars in an attempt to attract public attention to their diagnosis, but there are many who really just have hearts with bandaids on who are living and breathing miracles . . . but also one heartbeat away from death every day.

It is a life that's not for the fainthearted. You see, CHD literally robs families of everything they have come to know and love, including extended families and friends. Unless you're living through the battle and continuously immersed in it, you cannot even begin to fathom the complexity of maintaining consistency or routine for other children within the home, and juggling medications and doctor's appointments, and still remember to care for yourself.

The stress levels in raising a child with a complex medical condition are equal to combat veterans with post-traumatic stress disorder. These families live each day with PTSD in a way that not even the best television show can reproduce. Most days parents survive on autopilot, trying to get through the day five minutes at a time.

Family dynamics are turned upside-down overnight and relationships suffer. Even the most rock-solid marriage will end up with some period of strife – some because of the financial burden, some just struggle through the stress of the pending death of their child.

For those of you who have healthy children, let me explain a little deeper. Our babies have their chests opened up, the sternum cracked open so surgeons can get access to a walnut-sized heart. A heart they stop beating for hours on end, so they can try to correct the errors present at birth, the congenital heart defects.

Every second they are in surgery, parents and family are sitting in hospital waiting rooms shedding tears and fighting emotions. Sometimes for hours. When they're finally done with the operation and our babies are returned to an ICU, they're attached to all sorts of machines with tubes everywhere. They look like something out of a science-fiction movie, and they have so many tubes they can't really move.

As a parent you're helpless as you watch them lying there, looking so pitiful. You stare at the machines, overwhelmed at everything that is going on to keep your baby alive. As they wake they moan and cry in pain and discomfort. As a parent you just want to scoop them up, but you can barely even touch them, let alone hold them. And how can you tell them everything is going to be okay when you simply don't know yourself?

In Australia, one in 100 babies born has a congenital heart defect, which means six babies a day are born here with a condition that falls into the CHD bucket. Four a week die. Globally in the western world, the figures are huge: 1.3 million a year, and in many cases the heart defect is not diagnosed until after delivery and the baby is struggling. Around twenty-five per cent of these babies will require invasive procedures and even open heart surgery in the first days of their life in order to stand a chance of surviving. Many will be lucky to survive into adulthood and more will have life-long health risks and concerns.

Even today, only 3500 heart transplants are performed around the world each year. Many recipients go on to lead a long and active life. After five years, seven out of every ten recipients have survived not just the procedure, but also the aftermath and the constant battle with rejection. The average heart transplant recipient survives between ten and twenty years. Fiona Coote is one of the most famous transplant recipients. Hers was done in 1984, which is an amazing amount of time to live with a heart transplant.

First, though, you have to find a suitable donor. In Shaun's case, the issue was finding a heart of the right size to fit in his chest cavity, which meant the death of a child (most likely from an accident) of around the same size, and with parents who would allow the heart to be used for a transplant.

The procedure itself requires the removal of the old and damaged heart with the new one replacing it. During the operation Shaun was kept alive by a heart lung machine that pumped oxygenated blood around his body while they rejoined the new one. The Australian Heart Foundation reports that up to 100 people are on the waiting list for a new heart at any given time.

Annually, approximately 182,500 children worldwide die due to complications from a congenital heart defect. This is an outstanding, crushing and disgusting number. Nearly 200,000 families each year will bury a child because research isn't catching up to the pace necessary – because we aren't putting enough money into research.

We need to change that, which was one of the reasons for starting the Shaun Miller Foundation. You can now decide whether to sit back after reading this story and do nothing, or you can help us to help families and to work towards a cure.

CHD touches everyone, including celebrities:

- Actor Arnold Schwarzenegger – Bicuspid Aortic Valve
- Actor John Ritter – Passed away in 2003 from undiagnosed CHD, aged fifty-four
- Actor Katherine Heigl – Adopted daughter with CHD
- Actor Max Page (Mini Darth Vader) – Tetralogy of Fallot
- Actor Sylvester Stallone – Daughter with Ventricular Defect
- Comedian Tom Riles – Daughter with CHD
- MMA Fighter Mark 'Fight Shark' Miller – Aortic Stenosis
- Olympic Snowboarder Shaun White – Tetralogy of Fallot
- New England Patriots Linebacker, Teddy Bruschi – Atrial Septal Defects
- Singer from Poison, Bret Michaels – Atrial Septal
- Singer Jessie J – Wolf Parkinson White Syndrome
- Singer Jimmy Osmond – Diagnosed CHD with a hole in the heart
- Singer from The Clash, Joe Strummer – Died at the age of fifty with undiagnosed CHD
- Bass guitarist with Jethro Tull, John Glascock – Passed away in 1979 from complications from CHD, aged twenty-eight
- Parent, Cameron Miller – Son with 'One with the Lot': Double Outlet Right Ventricle (DORV), Ventricle Septal Defects (VSD), an Atrial Septal Defect (ASD) and Pulmonary Stenosis

A NOTE FROM ANDREW

I MET CAMERON through a mate of mine, John Panteli, who runs a speaking agency. He was looking at booking Cameron for some talking gigs, and he thought there was a good and powerful story to be told. After we had met, we started to look a bit more at the idea of telling Cameron's story, which has morphed into this book.

Thankfully, Alison Urquhart at Penguin Random House was quickly on board. Previously I had done books on athletes whose idea of hardship was missing games of football with a hamstring that was torn off the bone, or a knee that blew out on landing a jump.

Cameron and Shaun's life was something altogether different to that. For both father and son, from the very first breaths, life was a struggle through health issues. There were no grand finals, gold medals or championships, just living.

At times the story had confronted me as a father. My biggest struggle has been dealing with screen time and a couple of hospital visits for asthma, which fortunately my daughter has outgrown and was never as bad as Cameron's, so the journey of Cameron's life astounds me. I felt his grief at times, and the pain that even today is still raw for him.

Shaun was an amazing person, very uplifting, and I am sad I didn't meet him, although I feel I know him. It took a while for Cameron to understand what he needed to do with his life, and now with the Shaun Miller Foundation he has a purpose. His plan for the 'grief houses' is amazing and born out of the journey you have read here. It will impact many lives for years to come.

I am pleased I have played a small part in that.

As ever, thank you to all those who allow me to spend time inside someone else's story – especially Byron, Gabi and Sally.

Andrew Clarke is a Melbourne-based writer. He has written more than twenty books and has contributed articles to a range of magazines and publications on topics as widespread as business and plumbing, as well as all forms of sport, especially motorsport. He has previously written autobiographies for Penguin Random House with Mark Skaife, Matthew Lloyd and Alan Jones. His spare time is consumed by two teenage children and looking for the next place to travel.

ACKNOWLEDGEMENTS

A BOOK LIKE this takes a lot of effort to become a reality. It starts with an idea that comes from the stories of my life, which was intertwined with that of my son, the most amazing person I have ever met. Many of the people I would like to thank are still here and doing amazing things in the way they always have. Sadly, many have been lost but they will always be remembered.

Let me start by thanking Professor Dr Robert Weintraub and Shaun's transplant coordinator Anne Shipp at the Royal Children's Hospital and all the people who looked after my son and me for seventeen years. You're all wonderful and you gave me an extra ten years of life with my son, and there are no words that express the value in that. Those ten years would also not have happened without parents who allow their children to be organ donors. Making a decision like that must be impossibly hard, but you are able to impact so many lives and you are all very special.

To Zane, the peace and perspective you provided Shaun, especially when it got tough, was extraordinary. Just as Shaun had an amazing heart, so do you. To Shaun's mates Maddy, Paige, Kane, Josh, Cameron, Vincent, Jade, Nick, Zav, Michael, Matthew, Kane A, Jessie, Holly and all the heart kids – you were great friends to Shaun and shared many fun times together. He will be with you wherever you go. Fellow heart kid Christian Williams was Shaun's mentor and is an inspiration to many. I know Shaun was proud to have you on his side.

To my mum and dad, you have always been pillars of strength for me and have been there when I needed to go to hospital for myself and for Shaun. Moving into the house, and doing shifts day and night with me to help look after Shaun was amazing. I couldn't have done it without you and love you with all my heart. To my sister, Susanne, words cannot express how grateful I am. You are a beautiful human being and I love you with all my heart.

Penny was amazing and she stepped up in ways that few people would at one of the times when I most needed someone. I wish I could have appreciated you more at the time.

To Sally, the love that you showed Shaun was truly amazing. You treated him like your own. Not only are you beautiful on the outside, but on the inside as well. Thank you for being part of Shaun's journey. I will love you forever. This is a promise.

Also Hollywood, Mick, Chrissy, my grandfather and grandmother Roy and Elsie Potter, Aunty Sylv, Uncle John, cousins Trevor, Geoff and Jenny, Aunty Linda, Uncle Norman, cousins Belinda and Stephen, Aunty Joyce, Uncle Robert, cousins Robert, Alan and Russell. My friends from Lalor Technical School and all the boys from Apollo Bay.

To my special two great mentors of my life, Alan Finney and actor Charles 'Bud' Tingwell, your guidance resonates and keeps me on my path. And a big thank you to everyone from the

AFL *Footy Show*, especially Sam Newman. Also, Jobe Watson and Garth Wood, who are both special to us.

Sam Pavano stepped up when I needed help setting up and learning how to run the Shaun Miller Foundation. Thank you, Sam, for believing in my vision from the start – it would not have happened without you.

In terms of the book, Graham Brosnan from AKA Publishing worked on the original book with Shaun and started this whole adventure I now find myself on. Alison Urquhart at Penguin Random House also saw something in my story, and for that I will be forever grateful.

Andrew, my co-author on this journey, helped me focus on the story and helped put it on paper in a way that has inspired people like Russell Crowe to take it seriously. Thank you.

To Shaun, you were a remarkable young man and I feel privileged to have been your dad. Your journey has given me perspective and shown me the importance of family. Not only were you my son, you were my best mate. I will love and miss you forever and cherish your memory as long as I live. Our beautiful boy – forever young.

Writing a book like this is both cleansing and painful. It has been part of my journey and development. I have cried and laughed while putting it together, but I feel it has helped me to get into the place I am in now. I hope now I am the father that Shaun wanted me to be.

Now it is up to you. The Shaun Miller Foundation is developing strongly, but is always in need of support, so please check it out at www.theshaunmillerfoundation.org. And stay tuned for the movie. That in itself will be an awesome ride.